# On Kafka
Semi-Centenary Perspectives

# On Kafka

Semi-Centenary Perspectives

Edited by Franz Kuna

BARNES & NOBLE
BOOKS
10 East 53d St. New York 10022
(a division of Harper & Row Publishers. Inc.)

Published in the U.S.A. 1976 by
HARPER & ROW PUBLISHERS, INC.,
BARNES & NOBLE IMPORT DIVISION

First Published in 1976 by Elek Books Ltd., London

Printed in Great Britain

# Contents

# Contributors

Christian Goodden
PhD candidate, Gonville and Caius College, University of Cambridge. Author of 'Two Quests for Surety. A Comparative Interpretation of Stifter's *Abdias* and Kafka's *Der Bau*', *Journal of European Studies*, Vol. V, No. 4, 1975.

Ronald Gray
University Lecturer in German, University of Cambridge, and Fellow of Emmanuel College. Author of *Goethe the Alchemist, Kafka's Castle, Brecht, Kafka. A Collection of Critical Essays* (ed.), *An Introduction to German Poetry, The German Tradition in Literature 1871–1945, Poems of Goethe. A Selection* (ed.), *Goethe. A Critical Introduction, Franz Kafka,* and *Brecht the Dramatist.*

Franz Kuna
Reader in German, School of European Studies, University of East Anglia. Author of *Komm mit! German by Television. A BBC Course* (together with John L. M. Trim), *T. S. Eliot. Die Dramen,* and *Kafka. Literature as Corrective Punishment.* Co-editor of *Journal of European Studies.*

W. G. Sebald
Lecturer in German, School of European Studies, University of East Anglia. Author of *Carl Sternheim, Kritiker oder Opfer der wilhelminischen Ära?*

Walter H. Sokel
Commonwealth Professor of German Literature, University of Virginia. Author of *The Writer in Extremis: Expressionism in Twentieth-Century German Literature, Franz Kafka, Tragik und*

*Ironie: Zur Struktur seiner Kunst, Franz Kafka* (Columbia Essays on Modern Writers), *An Anthology of German Expressionist Drama* (ed.).

Kimberly Sparks
Charles A. Dana Professor of German, Middlebury College, Vermont. Author of *German in Review, Modern German* and *Thomas Manns 'Tonio Kröger' als Weg zur Literatur.*

J. P. Stern
Professor of German, University College, London. Author of *Ernst Jünger: A Writer of Our Time, Lichtenberg: a Doctrine of Scattered Occasions, Re-Interpretations: Seven Studies in Nineteenth-Century German Literature, Thomas Mann, Idylls and Realities: Studies in Nineteenth-Century German Literature, On Realism,* and *Hitler: The Führer and the People.*

Anthony Thorlby
Professor of Comparative Literature, School of European Studies, University of Sussex. Author of *Gustave Flaubert and the Art of Realism, Penguin Companion to Literature 2: European* (ed.), *Literature and Western Civilization* (ed. with D. Daiches), and *Kafka: a Study.*

J. J. White
Lecturer in German, Westfield College, University of London. Author of *Mythology in the Modern Novel: a Study of Prefigurative Techniques,* and co-editor of *German Life and Letters.*

# Preface

In their original form, the papers in this volume were presented to the Kafka Symposium which was held at the University of East Anglia, Norwich, 7–10 July 1974, on the occasion of the fiftieth anniversary of Kafka's death. They have been revised for inclusion in this volume. Although each of them is an independent contribution, the reader will not fail to notice that in one form or another they all revolve around five major problems posed by Kafka's work: the problem of the 'Law', Kafka's central metaphor; the moral, social and political implications of his work; the wider context of the cultural and intellectual tradition within which Kafka wrote; the still highly enigmatic nature of his poetics; and, perhaps most importantly, Kafka's very status as a writer.

Even today Kafka and the aesthetic foundations of his work are as little understood as at the time when he was, in Alfred Borchardt's words, some kind of literary Snowman whose traces were visible to some but who himself could never be found. In a situation in which the very text of an author's writings continues to be an overwhelming puzzle, critics are in danger of inventing substitutes, of shifting the centre of critical attention away from the text to some cherished causes of their own—of drawing their own eyes, as Ronald Gray remarks— and criticism itself 'becomes a way of missing the point' (Anthony Thorlby). It would be presumptuous to claim that the Symposium at Norwich somehow managed to stay clear of all the traps and difficulties which lie in wait for the critic of Kafka, or to remove the veil of mystery surrounding the very texture of his writing. But as I hope the essays collected in this volume will demonstrate, it did go a long way towards dispelling some all-too-familiar misconceptions by fostering a frank discussion of the essential problems and issues. None of the contributions printed here is solely confined to its immediate topic; they all bear on problems of scholarly method and critical theory; they all reflect a concern with the wider implications of literary works of art; and they all raise, from a variety of angles, either directly or indirectly, the ever more pressing problem of the strength and limitations of Kafka's work.

The contributions may also discourage once and for all the frequently held view that it is only one type of critic who feels drawn to Kafka's work. In tone and critical temper they range from Walter Sokel's and Christian Goodden's masterpieces of philological exegesis to J. P. Stern's exemplary version of what has been termed 'an applied humanities'. John White explores a poetological problem of fundamental importance, Kimberly Sparks has contributed an eloquent essay on the space-time aspect of Kafka's stories, and the Editor is interested in the parallels between modern poetics and modern physics. Finally, a writer who on more than one occasion turned the act of writing against himself has not been spared a relentless questioning of the premises of his art and of the criticism it has inspired. The contributions of Ronald Gray and Anthony Thorlby are elegantly argued correctives to the temptations of literary hero-worship on the one hand and critical over-confidence on the other.

Perhaps we shall never pass through the doors leading to the centre of Kafka's literary universe, but in the words of one of the contributors, 'we do not go away'.

F.K.
Norwich, December 1975

# Acknowledgments

As organizer of the Kafka Symposium held at the University of East Anglia, Norwich, July 1974, I should like to record some particular obligations: to the Austrian Federal Ministry of Education and Arts; the British Academy for their most generous financial assistance; to Ministerialrat Dr Wilhelm Schlag, the then Director of the Austrian Institute in London, and Mr Robert Rauscher, his deputy, for their indispensable support and advice throughout the planning stage of the Symposium; to Dr Brigitte Lohmeyer of the German Embassy and Frau Helga Rulf of the Goethe Institute for their kind efforts in obtaining film material from German television; to Mr Colin Nears of the BBC for showing his 'Omnibus' production on *Kafka's Castle* and for contributing a stimulating talk on the problems of producing Kafka; to my colleague Dr Cedric Williams for shouldering almost all the administrative arrangements; to Mrs Edda de Souza who as Secretary of the Symposium did all the hard work with a cheerfulness matched only by her efficiency; to the University of East Anglia, its School of European Studies, and the Lord Mayor of Norwich for providing much appreciated hospitality; to the contributors for giving so freely of their time and energy, and particularly to Professor Erich Heller whose contribution has in the meantime appeared in his book—*Kafka* (Fontana Modern Masters, 1974) and for this reason is not included in the present volume; and last, but not least, to the hundred or so participants who helped to make the Symposium a memorable and challenging experience.

I am grateful to the following publishers for permission to quote extracts from their publications (see notes for full bibliographical details): Peter Smith, *Relativity* by Albert Einstein; Rowohlt Verlag GmbH, *Franz Kafka in Selbstzeugnissen* by

# Walter H. Sokel

## The Programme of K.'s Court:
## Oedipal and Existential Meanings of *The Trial*

The crucial circumstance about K.'s trial is the fact that the charge against him is never specified. The existence of a guilt—some guilt—is assumed, but its nature is left undefined and remains unknown both to the protagonist and to the reader. The conclusion is often drawn that this kind of unspecified guilt corresponds to the theological concept of original sin. However, the doctrine of original sin holds everyone guilty; this does not seem to be the case with K.'s court. The court 'arrests' only some persons, while many others are free.[1] Manager and Deputy Manager of the bank where K. works, his landlady, Fräulein Bürstner, the manufacturer in Chapter Seven, K.'s uncle and girl cousin—they all are free of the accusation which has befallen only some characters in the work. Thus the analogy between K.'s guilt and original sin does not get us very far.

What else can unspecified guilt indicate? One possibility is that it implies the accused's guilt is his whole way of life at the time of his arrest. Such guilt cannot be specified because it is total. Unlike original sin, it is a particular kind of life, the one lived by K., that is equated with guilt. It is the existence of a representative bourgeois, atypical only on account of his extreme representativeness, most of whose relationships before his arrest are based on the cash nexus or on a superficial need for diversion. The little we can learn about the other defendants does not contradict the inference that K.'s type of existence is considered guilt.

If the guilt of the accused is his whole life, his punishment can only be death. This view is expressed by K.'s uncle when he says that having such a trial amounts to having lost it, and that in turn amounts to being erased. I would call this view the Oedipal view of the trial. In his most coherent attempt at

1

an autobiography, the famous 'Letter to his Father', Kafka presented his own life in terms closely corresponding to the Freudian Oedipus conflict. A father incomparably stronger than the son aroused infinite guilt in him and burdened him with the conviction that he lived a life totally unworthy, or nearly so, when judged in the light of his father's standards and example. No matter what Franz would or would not do, he was guilty: beginning with his totally inadequate body, his whole existence, next to his father's, was guilt. In Kafka's early tale, *The Judgment*, a father condemns his son to die, in *Metamorphosis* he mortally wounds him with an apple, in *America* he brutally exiles him into a highly dangerous and uncertain fate. In *The Trial*, written two years after these works, the situation is abstracted from the family context, of which only remnants, such as K.'s uncle and mother, are left. The son has become the accused and the father has been generalized, depersonalized, and elevated into an accusing court. But the basic structure is the same as the one articulated in Kafka's 'Letter to his Father' and the earlier family tales.[2]

The Oedipal nature of the court system seems to be concentrated with special force in the law student Berthold, in the third chapter of the novel. In the service of K.'s judge, Berthold acts out the classical pattern of the paternal antagonist's behaviour in the Freudian drama of the so-called Oedipus complex. He tempts K. into aggression for the sake of the woman, the attendant's wife—whose marital status suggests not only a desirable sex object, but a mother figure as well—and then thwarts K.'s attempt to gain the woman for himself. K. has to give in to the court member's superior strength, as the male child in Freud's Oedipus complex has to learn to do without his mother's sexual love and yield her to his father. *The Trial* gives us the impression throughout of a court enjoying sexual power and liberty while denying these to the accused. This tendency is enunciated by the prison chaplain when he warns K. particularly against seeking the help of women, which, he suggests, is not 'true help'.

This Oedipal view of *The Trial* is consistent with the assumption of total guilt of the accused. For we find that the court's apparent hostility towards K.'s sexual fulfilment is only part of a general hostility towards his worldly self. The adult ego

2

of the modern bourgeois is to be broken, humbled, impoverished, made ready for death. In the very beginning, the warders frustrate K.'s desire for breakfast, take away his personal property, deny him a chair to sit on, and berate him for not showing sufficient deference to the man in authority, the Inspector. They point out to him that in the future he will not need his fine shirts. The court has the warders thrashed later on, not for the theft of K.'s shirts, but because K. complained about it. The whipping is carried out in his presence. Thereby the court makes sure that K. will suffer the disconcerting effects of his bourgeois insistence upon his property rights, and be given to understand that he has made too much of his property. He receives a similar lesson when, during the interrogation, he, so proud of his important position as a high official in a bank, is addressed as a house painter. When K. insists on his bourgeois status, laughter answers his boastful correction of the court's 'error'. K. is carried along and moved to join in this gay irreverence toward his sense of status. These instances hint at the trial's purpose as an education towards the monastic virtues of poverty, chastity, and obedience, or humility, and beyond that, towards the obliteration of the self-confident ego that distinguishes rational bourgeois man. Seen from this aspect, *The Trial* is the culmination of a pattern running through Kafka's earlier stories of family conflicts and the picture of the penal colony as given by the Officer.

Yet the fact that the court allows K. full freedom to continue his normal life seems to contradict this pattern. K. is not imprisoned. He is free to choose whether or not to heed the court's summons, since, in the completed chapters, no sanctions are mentioned for disobeying the summons.[3] This freedom in fact strikes K. as inconsistent with the idea of his being arrested. For the defendant is thereby enabled to accept or to reject his trial, and not only once, but every time he is summoned to it. The trial is the accused's own consent to it and implies his tacit acceptance of an unspecified guilt. Here a very different view of K.'s trial seems to emerge.

And indeed, the inference which lies at the bottom of the Oedipal view—that K.'s guilt is his life—is not the only possible inference to be drawn from an accusation left unspecified. An undefined guilt may also imply that the accused has to

3

discover what his guilt is. From this perspective, the arrest is the alerting of the accused, and his trial is the invitation to discover himself in his search for his guilt. 'Not to show you what is wrong with you but that something is wrong with you', so runs one of Kafka's aphorisms that seems like a commentary on this view of guilt in K.'s trial.[4] Many details point to the structure of *The Trial* as a travelogue, an aborted voyage of discovery. It is no coincidence that the first member of the court to appear to K. seems to be wearing travelling clothes, and that K., in pursuing his trial, continuously discovers unknown locales, unfamiliar districts, unsuspected circumstances, etc. According to this inference, the trial should be considered a process of exploration and questioning. The double meaning of the German title, *Der Prozess*, meaning both trial and process, would lend support to the view that the trial is, or should be, the process of the discovery of K.'s guilt.[5]

At one point, K. himself seems to approximate to this view of his trial, when he thinks of dismissing his lawyer and starting work on a plea by himself. His plea would recall and examine every one of his actions and experiences and try to illuminate it from all angles. This total self-examination he feels is necessary 'because of his ignorance of the charge' (P 154).[6] He would have to devote nights and Sundays and every available free moment to this labour. Here K. comes closer than anywhere else in the novel to the realization that his trial should be a process of self-confrontation. He also realizes that it would be endless. However, K. fails to understand that the reason for this unending nature of the process is not the amount of work required but the essence of self-confrontation itself. An unspecified accusation concerning an unknown guilt cannot be related to a particular fact or facts to be discovered by detective work. The unknown guilt in K.'s trial is identical with his being, not in the sense of original sin, but as a consequence of the silence of the court as to what constitutes guilt. Whatever the accused might discover would still come up against this silence. In the face of it, any act or omission in one's entire existence might be guilt. If the defendant adjudges a particular act innocent, even if in good faith (which K. incidentally lacks), it might yet—who knows—contain aspects that the self-examining mind has overlooked or seen in an inadequate or incorrect light, and that might make his act guilty. Worse still, in the absence of any standard and definition of guilt and non-guilt, what might appear most innocent to the examiner might be precisely the root of his guilt if viewed from another perspective. It is not a matter of the impossibility of a good outcome for this process of self-examination, as has been maintained,[7] but rather of the impossibility of any outcome. The reason for this is not only the silence of the court. Even if a dialogue with the court were conceivable, there would still be no possible end to the process. For the self that is to be examined is living and continuous and constantly adds new acts and aspects to itself during the very process of self-evaluation. Only death can put an end to the process that is the trial.

K. furthermore overlooks the additional impossibility of self-discovery by merely cognitive and reflective self-examination. 'Truth', said Kafka, 'is indivisible, and therefore cannot know itself; he who desires to know it, must be a lie.'[8] The same reservations Kafka harboured against the necessarily deceptive and fraudulent character of self-observation would apply to K.'s idea of a plea based upon a scrutinizing examination of his past acts.[9]

There is, however, built into K.'s trial a different route of self-discovery, namely self-revelation through action based upon choice. In a 'procedure'[10] that leaves the accused freedom to heed the summons or not to heed them, he chooses his self, in the Kierkegaardian sense, as one who either accepts or rejects the accountability which his own hand has called for. (We remember that it is K. who, ringing his bell for his breakfast, has made the warder Franz appear before him. Literally and unconsciously, he calls for his own arrest.) That his trial is a true choice by K. becomes clear at the beginning of the present Chapter Two (which should actually be Chapter Three). K. receives a phone call at his office, telling him to appear at the court for his interrogation the following Sunday. But for that Sunday he also has an enticing invitation from the Deputy Manager of his bank, to spend the day on his yacht. When K. prefers the court's summons to the Deputy Manager's invitation, he clearly makes a choice that can be called existential. He deliberately puts his trial above his pleasure and social advantage, thereby establishing a pattern which he will follow henceforth. By this choice K. defines his true self.

The obvious policy of the court is to allow K. to reveal himself by this freedom to choose. This existential policy differs markedly from the Oedipal strategy of breaking the self and its will. It tends to make K. the free arbiter of his fate. There is, within the court system itself, a conflict between the two views of the trial. This conflict is explicitly stated by the law student Berthold who severely criticizes the examining judge for allowing K. 'to run around so free'. He calls it a 'mistake', about which he had complained to the judge. 'Between the interrogations at least, [K.] should have been held captive in his room' (P 74). The student's view of K.'s trial conforms to the Oedipal pattern of Kafka's earlier story, *Metamorphosis*, in which Gregor's family keeps him prisoner in his room. The student would make confinement the policy towards the arrested. He would not seek K.'s free commitment, but his captivity, the repression of his ego, the reduction of his vital capacities, a harsh and severe education towards inwardness, and ultimately a preparation for the grave. The student's policy would conform to the treatment accorded to the prisoners in *In the Penal Colony*, in that golden age of the Old Commander's rule which the Officer so nostalgically evokes. The plot of *In the Penal Colony* shows the decline and breakdown of this older system. Begun shortly before and continued after *In the Penal Colony*, *The Trial* presents the older system, as desired by the student, countermanded and superseded by the judge's new policy of physical freedom for the accused, which changes the whole concept of the trial from an Oedipal to an existential intent. For the student, the new policy, as represented by the judge, is 'incomprehensible'.

We are dealing, in *The Trial*, with two contrasting layers of intention, which explains a good deal of the particular obscurity and ambiguity of this novel, which is extreme even for Kafka's opus. This duality conforms to Kafka's development, which makes *The Trial*, like *In the Penal Colony*, a work of transition and evolution from the harsh Oedipal law of the family tales of 1912 to the ironic existentialism of his late phase, as represented by *The Castle*, *A Hunger-Artist* and *Investigations of a Dog*. The

*Trial* shows a primitive layer, expressed by the lower court organs—the warders and the student—advocating physical coercion, being contravened by the higher and official law of the court, enunciated and practised by the Inspector and the Examining Judge, which insists on the accused's freedom to commit himself to his trial. In composing *The Trial* Kafka made the Oedipal law of *Metamorphosis* and the penal machine be literally superseded by the new law of *The Trial* as a series of existential decisions. The structure of self-alienation is very similar to that of *Metamorphosis*, but the difference is even more significant. In *Metamorphosis* Gregor is physically forced into his alienation before the action starts. Extremely limited options remain to him. But in *The Trial*, the Inspector expressly states that the arrest only serves the function of 'informing' Josef K. of his condition and seeing 'how he has received it' (P 24), leaving him the freedom to continue his previous life, and to neglect his trial or to concentrate on it, as he chooses. This difference in intent makes for a difference in form between the two works. The fatalistic realism of *Metamorphosis* in which the initial event inexorably determines the outcome, in a tight plot, gives way, in *The Trial*, to a loose sequence of scenes reminiscent of old morality plays. In these the protagonist has to choose between several options. *The Trial* is not, like Gregor Samsa's metamorphosis, a determining condition from the start. It is a series of challenges. The protagonist's reactions to or evasions of them determine the structure. This structure corresponds to the existential policy of the court.

The Inspector tells K. that his sole task was to inform him that he is arrested and to see how he has taken it. In this statement two factors can be distinguished. 1. The arresting power merely brings K.'s condition to his consciousness. 2. It observes his reaction to this new awareness. The court functions as K.'s observer, and one meaning of his trial is his being challenged to reveal himself to an audience as well as to himself. This audience is the court, and we the readers are an extension of K.'s court—a point which we shall take up later. This meaning of the trial makes for the theatrical and dramatic structure of the novel. It is not for nothing that the two executioners remind K. of actors. K. literally stands on a stage, on the raised platform of the present second chapter, holding forth for an audience, which, as he finds out later, is the court, with a demagogic speech full of rhetorical flourishes. Even where an actual stage is absent, K. moves about on an invisible stage because his interplay with the other characters is so structured that it constantly exhibits him but not the other 'players'. The function of all the other characters is very pointedly that of prompters. The 'interrogation' to which the court summons him looks as if designed to give K. the chance to react and act and to show by his behaviour who he is. We are reminded of the *theatrum mundi* structure: the court is in the role of God, i.e. spectator and judge in one; K., or everyman, is the actor, and the various locales of K.'s city are the stage that represents human existence. As in *Everyman* there is a single real actor with all other figures fulfilling subordinate functions in *his* plot. The use of the initial in place of a real name points up the abstract aspect of his character.

Yet K. is far from being an abstract Everyman, 'a man without qualities'. He is a very definite type of person with definite qualities which we come to recognize through his confrontations with the court organs and related characters. For instance, when the warders deny K. his breakfast (which they eat themselves) and then offer to fetch him 'a more modest one' from the cafe across the street, K. ignores the offer because he does not want to owe anything to them and because the apple he eats in defiance is surely better than anything they could get from 'that filthy cafe' (P 17). His reaction and thinking reveal his aggressive defiance and his snobbish-bourgeois contempt of the cheap and low-class place. His general arrogance, in both thought and behaviour, towards the warders, the lowly bank clerks, the court itself, and many other figures encountered, consistently repeats and reinforces this initial impression throughout the novel.

However, even though we are able to infer from K.'s mental, emotional, and behavioural reactions a certain type of character with definite qualities, these are not the issue, as they would be in a psychological novel in which exposé of character is the main purpose, or in a social-realistic novel in which exposure of a social type is the *raison d'être* of the work. K.'s qualities are merely instrumental in revealing him by his reactions to situations presented by his trial. Each of these situations could call forth several possible reactions. The action (or more frequently inaction) chosen by K. in preference to alternatives is what matters.

A good example is his initial reaction to the arrest itself. It occurs to K. that he might attempt to walk out of the door against his warders' 'advice'—significantly they only 'advise' and do not command him—and that such a resolute action might perhaps be the simplest solution to his predicament. But he decides against risking it, because he is afraid that in that event the warders might perhaps grab him, after all, and knock him down, in which case he would lose 'all the superiority which now he was still able to keep' vis-à-vis them (P 16). Thus he decides to return to his room and let the natural course of events take care of things. The function of the door points, of course, to the close parallelism between K. and the man from the country in the prison chaplain's parable to which we shall soon turn. What strikes the reader in this and many other instances, is the function of the trial as a series of challenges compelling K. to adopt one or the other course of behaviour and thus to show himself, or rather to show how he chooses the self he is.

This presupposes that he is being presented with situations that seem to show him something, although the meaning that is shown is never explained. The subordinate court members first supply him with hints, advice, warnings, bits of information. By summoning him to the slums, the court shows K. a type of setting which had been unknown to his bourgeois middle-class existence. By failing to issue a further summons to him, and by being absent when K. comes the second time, after he had announced he would never come to the court again, he is being notified that his words are taken seriously. The whipping of the warders in a junk room of his bank gives him the same message. Because K. had complained about their thieving and blackmailing, the warders are being punished. The court puts on a grim show for him which drives home the seriousness and effectiveness of all words, attitudes, and 'principles'. K. claims he had not intended the warders' punishment, since he was only concerned with 'a principle'. The court teaches him a lesson in consistency between opinion and action which can only be called a lesson in the essence of morality. It teaches him responsibility. For by his charges against them, K. has assumed a responsibility for the warders, a responsibility which is expressed in drastic and physical terms. K. is made to witness and to feel the sufferings which he, or rather his 'principles', have caused, and he is made to feel that his 'principles' cannot be separated from his self. At the same time, he is literally being called upon to act, and by the very same persons who had responded to his own unconscious call in the first place. By the kind of action he will now take in answer to his fellow men's desperate appeals, he must show himself, disclose his being.

The two aspects of the arrest, as defined by the Inspector, unite in this twofold show. A performance staged for K. shows him the consequences of words and opinions. At the same time, his victims, beseeching him to liberate them from the plight that he has caused, make him the chief player in his own show. Their torment is the cue that K. has to take one way or another. He simply cannot help but reveal himself to the court, to the reader, and above all to himself, a revelation, to be sure, which his consciousness does not pick up.

That the existential emphasis on personal responsibility is consistent court policy is also shown by K.'s lawyer, Huld. Huld informs K. that the court does not recognize counsel for the defendant, and bars lawyers from all official proceedings. The judges' hilariously contemptuous treatment of lawyers reflects this complete lack of official standing and function. In K.'s kind of trial, the defendant must face his court in radical aloneness. In advanced stages of a trial, K. is told, the defendant even vanishes from sight.[11]

However, while admitting that lawyers have no official standing whatsoever in the court, Huld argues strongly for their crucial importance to the defendant. This contradiction is much more than self-serving double-talk; it is part of the fundamental contradiction between two opposed views of the nature and purpose of the trial. If the trial is interpreted as the challenge of arriving at one's self-determination, counsel is irrelevant and even vitiating. But if the trial is seen as a defensive struggle against an external foe, counsel is essential, and to do without it would, as Huld warns K., entail the gravest peril to the defendant.

Titorelli reveals, with even greater clarity, this juxtaposition of the existential and the Oedipal view of the trial. Titorelli makes it clear to K. that real acquittal can never be obtained through helpers, but must be based solely upon the defendant's innocence. Innocence is an inner certainty which is not in need of external confirmation. Where innocence is involved, acquittal flows naturally from it, and judges cannot be influenced. But real acquittals lie outside experience. They are rumoured from ancient legends and no proof exists of their attainability. In fact, holding out for real acquittal is an enormous risk precisely because of the Oedipal nature of the lower court, which is the only one accessible to empirical experience. For Titorelli the actual court—in contrast to the unknown and unknowable Highest Court, which alone has the power to acquit—has the appearance of a merciless Oedipal power of horrifyingly wrathful divinity. Like the penal colony under the Old Commander, the known court takes guilt for granted in any accused. Never can it be dissuaded from its conviction of guilt. 'If I paint all the judges in a row here on a canvas', says Titorelli to K., 'and you'll defend yourself before this canvas, you will be more successful than if you stand before the real court' (P 180). Faced with such a court, the dream of gaining real acquittal can only be a wish for suicide or else an overwhelmingly strong and venturesome faith of the self in itself. Like the entrance into the law, in the legend of the priest, it can only be the kind of faith that would bear out Kafka's dictum, 'Believing means: to liberate the indestructible in oneself, or better: to liberate oneself, or still better: to be indestructible, or better: to be'.[12] K.'s way of going about his trial, therefore, appears ironic from Titorelli's perspective, because K. says he is innocent and yet searches for helpers in his trial.

Titorelli's comments on the court show the same contradiction in its programme as is revealed by the lawyer's intimations. Titorelli admits the possibility of a defendant's innocence and complete acquittal. This possibility conflicts flagrantly with the guilty verdict for every accused which Titorelli assumes with certainty on the basis of his own and all known experience with the court. However, if the trial is interpreted as a choice between one's faith regardless of

11

consequences, and precautions for one's survival, the contradiction falls away. For then the defendant is free to commit himself or not to commit himself to his faith in himself.[13] In these terms innocence appears as a resolve. It is a choice of being—of being innocent. Such a choice of the self precludes, of course, the usefulness of any helpers.

When K. considers dismissing his lawyer and making his plea by himself, he seems to be veering towards such a course. He decides never to admit guilt under any circumstances. Yet this is only an apparent convergence between K.'s plan and the court's programme. For his refusal to admit guilt would not be at all the same as the innocence of which Titorelli speaks. Refusal to admit guilt would be a device, a strategy in a struggle with the court; unlike innocence it would not be a commitment to be.

However, according to Titorelli, innocence and real acquittal are legendary exceptions to the rule of human reality. For the real, i.e., the regular case, Titorelli recommends two other courses—ostensible acquittal and indefinite procrastination. The assumptions on which these two possibilities rest are diametrically opposed to the assumptions of innocence. For them guilt or innocence is not the issue. In relation to these options, the trial is conceived as an attack upon the accused against which he has to protect himself for his survival. Therefore, helpers, compromises, and subterfuges are necessary as a matter of course.

Thus there issue from Titorelli two mutually contradictory concepts of the trial—the trial as self-choosing and the trial as self-defence. One is concerned with being, the other with surviving. The former is the existential, the latter the Oedipal view.

While the existential interpretation always pertains to official and explicit court policy, ascribed to the unseen high court, the Oedipal view is based upon the weaknesses and limitations of the lower judges. According to Titorelli's advice, the existential possibility, real acquittal, can issue only from the highest court, while the subterfuges of ostensible acquittal and procrastination exist by virtue of the corruptibility of the lower court members. In all instances, the existential meaning of the trial relates to the genuine and pure essence of the court whereas deviations and corruptions on the lower levels support the pattern of an Oedipal struggle.

This by no means invalidates the reality and seriousness of the Oedipal aspect of the trial. The trial operates on two levels at once, and both are necessary to an understanding of it. The existential aspect of court policy as described by the lawyer can, for instance, easily be interpreted as an extreme of Oedipal intimidation. The defendant is to be isolated and deprived of all human fellowship and comfort in order to be more quickly destroyed. The text certainly allows for such a reading.

This co-existence of two opposed levels of meaning, however, intensifies the protagonist's necessity to choose between different interpretations of his situation. Interpretation must precede choice as choice must precede action. Interpretation is a careful weighing of the various meanings implied in a situation. One of these the protagonist has to choose in order to act. Thus his reading of his situation must be the antecedent of his acting on it. K.'s whole trial, from the moment of his awakening, is a single challenge to him to read, and interpret, and then to act. K.'s arresting warder, Willem, reads a book when K. first sees him. This sign seems to tell K. that he is asked to read. Both warders and the Inspector explicitly admonish K. to listen more and to talk less. They ask him to concentrate and to reflect, they advise him not to jump to hasty conclusions, and warn him that great efforts are in store for him. All that points to the fact that he will be asked to find the meaning of his trial by himself. It is in the same vein when we hear Frau Grubach refer to K.'s arrest as 'something scholarly . . . which does not have to be understood' (P 30), i.e., for which there does not seem to exist a meaning prepared for the accused. Huld by implication, and Titorelli explicitly, make clear to K. that it is he who has to choose what meaning he will give to his trial by choosing a course of action from the several possibilities outlined to him. Basically the choice boils down to one of two interpretations—the existential and the Oedipal—the choice of treating his trial as a commitment to self-exploration or as a struggle in self-defence. Both are possible and both are applicable according to Titorelli. The main point is the choice itself. Its urgency cannot be overlooked in Titorelli's insistent admoni-

tions to K. to make his choice soon. Regardless of what it will
be, the choice itself must not be deferred.

This necessity to choose culminates in the necessity to
interpret with which the prison chaplain confronts K. It is no
accident that the trial culminates in a parable to which the
listener, K., seems to be called upon to supply the key and make
the application to his own case. The legend of the doorkeeper
who stands before the law abstracts the challenge which the
trial itself represents.

The priest tells K. the legend of the doorkeeper as an illustration of K.'s delusion in regard to the court. This delusion is
explicitly stated in the text of the parable. At the end of his
life, the man from the country asks why no one else has come
to ask for the entrance, although everyone strives to enter the
law. The doorkeeper answers that this entrance was destined
for this man alone. The man's delusion consisted in the belief
that the entrance into the law is something universal.

This delusion is implicit in the parable from the beginning.
It is so strong that it easily escapes the reader because it is built
into the man's perspective, which the reader, like K., tends to
share. The delusion is implied in the man's initial reaction to
finding the doorkeeper blocking his way. The text says the man
has 'not expected such difficulties', for he assumes 'that the
law is supposed to be accessible at any time' (P 256). The man,
in other words, has come with the expectation that entrance
into the law is an automatic right available to everyone and
at all times. To be sure, he does ask for permission to enter, but
assumes that the permission will be a formality.

The doorkeeper says that he cannot allow the man to enter
'now'. The word is crucial because it is intimately tied to the
man's expectation that the law would be open at any time.
The doorkeeper's 'not now' proves this expectation is the man's
primary illusion. The implication in his answer is this: At the
moment of his asking for permission the man is not allowed to
enter. Left open is the possibility that he might be able to enter
if and when he does not ask for permission. This implication
becomes explicit almost immediately. The doorkeeper suddenly
steps aside and laughingly invites the man to go in despite his
prohibition. Now 'the door', the text tells us, 'stands open as
always'. That is, no physical force whatsoever prevents the man

14

from going in. The doorkeeper underlines the man's freedom by his jocular invitation. To be sure, in the same breath, he warns him of the frightening appearance of further doorkeepers inside.

Now there is nothing in the man's way except his fear. It is not the doorkeeper, but the man's fear that keeps him from entering. His desire for the law is great, but his fear is greater. To enter would involve a grave risk. The man decides not to take this risk. Intimidated by the doorkeeper's words and looks, he prefers to wait for permission. And this permission never comes.

The timing is a decisive key to the understanding of the parable. Entrance into the law is possible only at a definite, unique moment, which the man allows to pass by unused. The unique moment is linked to the unique individual for whom alone this entrance is destined. Uniqueness of moment and uniqueness of person are united in the free decision that is necessary to enter the law. No one else can make the man's entrance possible since it is *his* alone, and the one single moment for it must be seized by him who is to enter. If the doorkeeper were to grant the entrance, it would not be the man's entrance. It would be a gift bestowed on him by another or it would be a general right belonging to anyone and everyone. Further-more, the entrance can truly belong to the man alone only if it results from his own free decision. Given the absolutely indi-vidual nature of the entrance, the man must lose it from the moment he fails to choose it. We are reminded of Kierkegaard's *Fear and Trembling* in which the individual's relation to the Absolute—in terms of Kafka's parable 'the law', i.e., that which everyone strives for—can only be individual, i.e., completely and utterly unique.

The function of the doorkeeper as a figure of denial is neces-sary for the existential meaning of the parable. The obstacle is essential to the quest. Significantly the text does not begin with the man, but with the doorkeeper standing in front of the entrance.[14] If there were no doorkeeper, the entrance would be a simple wish fulfilment. Only by overcoming difficult resistances can the entrance become the man's entrance. For that, the nay-saying authority is necessary. This explains the priest's later remark that one does not have to accept everything the doorkeeper says as true, but only as necessary. Whether there really are such horrible doorkeepers inside the law, i.e., the truth, is impossible to ascertain. However, the fear aroused by them is necessary to make the entrance a true decision.

With his challenge to the man to try the entrance in the face of possibly terrifying odds, the doorkeeper imposes the existential meaning on the parable.[15] For he burdens the man with the necessity of making a decision which will determine his further existence. His choice will reveal what he is. Like Heidegger's *Dasein*, Sartre's *réalité humaine*, and Kierkegaard's eternal self, the man before the law creates himself by his choice. He is free to put his passion for the law above his life, which he would risk if the inner doorkeepers were really what the doorkeeper says they are. But at the same time, he is also free to place his life above the law and wait. In fact, he would even be free to leave his quest altogether and go home. Thus the doorkeeper makes the man choose himself before our very eyes. And the man, carefully deliberating, does make his choice. Among his three possible existences he chooses himself as one who rejects his freedom and waits for the permission of another. He has chosen himself for all his life as a dependent and supplicant and thereby literally cheated himself of his true existence, his authentic life.

The man from the country is K.'s mirror image. K. too has decided to seek his law, i.e., his trial, by choosing the court over the yacht. But, like the man from the country, he then refuses to accept the paradox of the self-determined entrance. He wants the court, *his* doorkeeper, to relieve him of his own self-discovery and hand him his acquittal, or else take the blame for murdering him. Listening to the parable, K. mistakes the Kierkegaardian paradox of a law of freedom for an authority figure's dirty trick. He takes an Oedipal view of the doorkeeper, as he does of his trial. The doorkeeper appears to him as an oppressive deceiver, withholding and denying the man's right to enter. K. completely ignores the intent of the law, the uniquely personal nature of the entrance into this law, even though the parable itself had explained it to him.

Thus the doorkeeper legend illustrates K.'s delusion in regard to the court. K. views his trial as an unjust attack by illegitimate power figures. He misunderstands the fact that the trial is his own choice, in which acquittal cannot come from another, even as the doorkeeper cannot give the man an entrance that belongs to the man alone. K. experiences his trial as a fight inflicted upon him by a vicious antagonist, and therefore he looks for aid. Although he does not go as far as Block or the man from the country in enslaving himself to helpers, he cannot see his way without them, either. The parable 'Before the Law', like the degrading spectacle staged by K.'s lawyer and Merchant Block, illustrates the priest's warning to him, 'You are looking too hard for the help of others . . . Don't you realize that it is not the true help?' (P 253). But K. fails to connect the priest's clear warning with the 'legend' that illustrates it. Otherwise he would be able to see that it is not the doorkeeper's malice, but the man's fearful dependence that cheats him of his entrance into the law.

It is K.'s Oedipal perspective that blocks his understanding of both the parable and his own trial. He sees the court as a gang of corrupt lechers who, if a woman is shown to them, 'would overrun the bench and the defendant to get there in time' (P 253). The image drastically conveys the Oedipal sense of the trial in which a feeble defendant is literally victimized by the sex drive of his judges. This view seems to appal the priest, as though it were not only blasphemous, but a most dangerous misapprehension. He shouts at K., 'Can't you see two steps ahead?' (P 254). Yet, even though the priest seems to consider it a fatal blindness, K.'s experiences in the novel do not contradict his Oedipal view. The priest himself contributes to the Oedipal atmosphere of *The Trial* when he singles out the help of women as a particularly illusory form of help. Here we come up once more against the two meanings of the trial as, on the one hand, an Oedipal assault upon the defendant's male adulthood and ego, and on the other, an existential challenge to choose and define oneself. K. himself has to find his own interpretation as the man has to find his own entrance into the law.

Hermeneutics, or the art of choosing the appropriate understanding of a text, and the trial, or the process of choosing the appropriate reaction to one's condition, are forms of one another. This explains the crucial importance of the priest's observation on hermeneutics in his discussion with K., 'I only show you the current opinions', he says to K. 'You must not pay too much attention to opinions. The text is unchangeable and its interpretations are often only expressions of despair over that fact' (P 260). In the context of the parable, this remark is not an absolute discouragement of the hermeneutic attempt, as it is usually interpreted, but the opposite, a forceful suggestion of the necessity to find one's own interpretation. In his discussion of the legend, the priest behaves like a careful New Critic, restraining a hasty student from identifying the text's meaning with the protagonist's point of view. He always seeks to bring K. back to the text and points out the need to be faithful to the literal wording. Furthermore, although he shows all sorts of interpretations, he never offers his own, or any definitive one. K. himself has to find *his* interpretation, just as the man from the country has to find *his* entrance into the law. Text and doorkeeper parallel each other. The unchangeable text stubbornly retains its ambiguities and withholds its meaning, functioning like the doorkeeper who withholds permission.

As we have seen, interpretation is the necessary first step in the process of deciding on a course of action. The parable tells of a man who has to interpret the doorkeeper's words and gestures. He has to weigh one meaning—the invitation to go in—against another which contradicts it. To which should he give preference? He has to choose his interpretation before he can decide his action. He has to choose between his own desire for entrance and his fear of the possible consequences. In fact, there is no way for the man to discover the true meaning of the doorkeeper prior to his own action. Only by attempting the entrance can the man find out the truth or falsehood of the doorkeeper's statements and the truth about the law. Before he can understand doorkeeper and law, the man must reveal himself by his choice of action.

As K. is the reader of the legend, the court is the reader of K. As we have seen, K.'s arrest, so the Inspector informs him, amounts only to his being made aware of the condition of being arrested and to show the court how he will take it. Kafka wrote K.'s story from the vantage point of the court. He made himself the reader of the situation in which his character, on whom he bestowed his own initial, finds himself. The first member of the court who comes to 'arrest' K. bears

Kafka's own first name, Franz.[16] Franz, or the court, is Kafka's writing and recording self, arresting, inspecting, and seeking to read Kafka's other—his living—self, K., truncated and reduced to the ignominious condition of life, which forces us to choose between equally essential but mutually contradictory courses of action. In his letters to his fiancée, Felice Bauer, which shortly preceded *The Trial*, Kafka had constantly shown his awareness of the overwhelming need for decision and his inability to arrive at any.[17] Now, in writing about K.'s trial, he arrests himself for close inspection of the possibilities given to him. It is significant, in this context, that the man who presides over K.'s arrest carries the title of 'Inspector' or 'Supervisor', '*Aufseher*', in the original German. In the designation of his function, the word 'to see' is built in. It attests to the universality of Kafka's metaphoric language, and therefore its subliminal power, that the metaphoric meaning, which carries the action, applies even to the translation.

*The Trial* is a self-confrontation not only on account of Kafka's recorded self-identification with K.[18] Kafka himself shared the Oedipal perspective, which finds its most cogent formulation in his famous 'Letter' to his father. In it he traces his all-pervasive guilt feelings and the wretchedness of his whole life directly back to his father's disastrous influence upon him. Given his own sensitive and vulnerable character, next to and under the overpowering and uncomprehending vitality of his father, the former had to become deformed, short of being totally crushed. To be sure, Kafka absolves his father of all intentional guilt and malice, but instead invokes an inexorable necessity, a tragic fate, condemning both himself and his father to interminable sufferings from and through each other. Until the 'correction' at the end of the letter, which Kafka puts into his father's mouth, his letter appears to be the document of a strict determinist. It could have come from the pen of a refined writer of the naturalist school. The tormented relationship between father and son depicted in it resembles a marriage portrayed by Strindberg in his naturalistic phase. It reflects the mental climate of late nineteenth-century positivism in which Freud also had his intellectual roots. The determinism of the letter shows itself linguistically in such phrases as 'you *had to have* such effects on me', '*I could not* according to my nature . . .', 'my feeling *stems from your* influence'.[19] In this very important document, Kafka blames heredity (his being a mixture of the paternal Kafka and the maternal Löwy line) and early environment for his predicaments, and raises circumstance to the level of fate. There is hardly any room here for free self-determination through choice and act, only a modicum of resigned peace to be gained from insight into one's situation. In terms of existential thought, Kafka's letter to his father is a prime example of what Sartre calls 'bad faith', with which we deny our freedom by making nature, fate, situation, circumstances, and The Other, bear the responsibility for our being. At the end of *The Trial*, it is Josef K. who echoes Kafka's own determinism, as expressed not only in his letter to his father, but in a more subtle and less systematic form throughout his diaries and the letters to Felice. K., having recognized that it would be his inner duty to seize the knife and kill himself, finds that he lacks the strength for the act. For his lack of strength he blames someone else.

> He could not completely prove himself adequate to his task; he could not relieve the authorities of all their work; the responsibility for this ultimate failure bore he who had denied him the remnant of strength needed for that. (P 271.)

This leaves it unclear who is to bear responsibility for K.'s failure to live up to his own expectations—whether the Supreme Judge, or his father and progenitor, or God who created him. But in any case, it is not he himself who bears responsibility. He claims by implication that he could not have acted in any other way than he did. Here Josef K. adumbrates the same deterministic view which his author exhibits five years later in his autobiographical document.

Subsequently K. is slaughtered 'like a dog' rather than allowed to die like a man, and it looks as if the shame of this will survive him. There are several meanings contained in this ending.[20] But one of them surely refers to the fact that K. is condemned to such a degrading inhuman death by his own evasion of the self-determined end which he has shirked against his own explicit understanding. Seen together with Kafka's letter to his father, *The Trial* represents a confrontation between

Kafka's own deterministic perspective, assumed by him from time to time, and the possibility of a faith transcending the conditioning of human existence, which he also envisaged. But that this confrontation was also a judgment of the Oedipal by the existential perspective is shown by this aphorism written three years after *The Trial*: 'There was a time when I did not understand why I received no answer to my question; today I do not understand how I could ever have believed that I could ask. But, of course, I did not believe, I only asked'.[21]

Beyond K., and beyond his creator, the court reaches out to the parable's reader—ourselves. Like the man before the door, the reader assumes that a definitive entrance into the law, or into the text, is to be offered by the proper authority, and he assumes that this entrance is general and relatively easy to obtain—one and the same door for every seeker, one and the same meaning for every reader. But the text resists the attempt at unambiguous understanding. The events depicted and the statements perceived remain contradictory. K.'s preliminary interrogation takes place in Fräulein Bürstner's room. Is the meaning of this to punish K. for his desire for the girl? Or is it the opposite, a signal drawing him to a more personal form of eros, which his weekly visits to Elsa have drowned in routine? There is no answer given, only the unchangeably ambiguous text. But the open question challenges us, as it challenges K. There does not seem a way to meaning except by a choice entailing the risk of error. K.'s guilt remains impenetrable because the only access to it is interpretation, which is risk, instead of revelation, which gives certainty.

# J. P. Stern

## The Law of *The Trial*

The deep distrust and distaste we have for our social institutions are reflected in our literary criticism. Great writers, especially the great writers of the twentieth century, we feel, cannot be seriously concerned with man in any of his public functions. The recent spate of Kafka criticism is a case in point. In their eagerness to distil his metaphysical meanings, however destructive the results may turn out to be, the critics consistently ignore the realistic aspects of his fiction, turning to those higher meanings not at the end of their interpretive undertaking but instantly, at its inception. 'When he says . . ., what does he *really* mean?' is the kind of impatient question that ignores the circumstantiality of his fiction and regards it as an impediment to his message. The fiftieth anniversary of Kafka's death is a good occasion to remind ourselves that in some of his most remarkable writings—and especially in the two novels of his maturity, *The Trial* (written 1914, published 1925), and *The Castle* (written 1922, published 1926)—he explores the *données* of the institutions he has chosen to place in the centre of his narrative, transcending their limits only rarely, and always with a set metaphysical purpose. Earlier critics[1] were not just literal-minded pedants when they took seriously the physical settings and social dimensions which Kafka reconstructed with great accuracy and imaginative care, and when they matched the metaphysical implications with social and political ones. And Kafka's stories would speak less directly to our experience (however different it may be from the experience of their creator) if they were really the 'hermetically sealed artifacts' or the 'self-contained worlds' of the esoteric interpreters, or if they were really about the ordeal of writing stories which are hermetically sealed artifacts about the ordeal of writing . . .

My purpose in this essay is not to deny the metaphysical

or religious dimension of the world of Kafka's stories, but on
the contrary to suggest that all interpretations which move
towards it must remain arbitrary and chimeric unless they are
founded in an understanding and just evaluation of the realistic
dimension, which includes its historicity, its being the fictional
world of a certain era; to do this one need do no more than
follow Kafka's own hint: 'I have intensely absorbed the
negative aspect of my time—a time which is very close to me
and which I have not the right to challenge, but only as it
were to represent'.[2] In a novel at all events it is quite impossible
to show a man's existential predicament *in vacuo*: the presentation of his sociability is the necessary precondition—is the foil
of concrete circumstance—against which alone the effects of
his existential exposure can be demonstrated. (Just as, in
literature, we are all on this side of death and cannot show it
except by pointing to all that we shall soon be leaving, so also
we cannot present alienation without showing what it is a man
is alienated from.)

Seeing that Kafka himself was a fully qualified lawyer and
spent a good many years practising as such, patiently and with
immense conscientiousness, in a large assurance company
concerned with compensation for industrial accidents, it is
surely not surprising that he should have been not just 'interested'
in the exercise of justice but deeply concerned to show it at
work in the world of his fiction. What most critics imply, by
way of an unexamined premise, is that somehow or other it is
unworthy of the high seriousness of Kafka's art to see it concern
itself 'merely' with bureaucracy or the law. After all (they
argue) you don't have to be interested in entomology in order
to understand something of the parabolic meaning of *Metamorphosis*. Yet the analogy is obviously grotesque: a giant
cockroach, a singing mouse, or a performing ape occupy a
radically different place in our experience from a court or a
hierarchy of officials. A place in our experience: the Kafka
world may be on the dark side of the moon, but we have been
there, too. Wittgenstein speaks of the illusory expectation of
those who think they 'could have pure beauty unadulterated by
anything that is beautiful'[3]: just so many critics proceed in the
expectation that you can have a vision of pure desolateness

without having to consider the very particular form under which that desolateness is presented. And the form this takes in a large number of Kafka's stories is the dysfunction of an institution.

In saying this I am extending an argument central to Erich Heller's first Kafka essay of 1952, in which he speaks of the dispute between Luther and Zwingli about the ontological status of the Sacrament, which for Zwingli is merely an allegory, a representation of that which in itself it is not: 'From then onwards', Heller writes, 'the word "merely" has been attaching itself ever more firmly to the word "symbol", soon gaining sufficient strength to bring about a complete alienation between the two spheres'[4]—the worldly and the spiritual. Similarly, the word 'merely' now attaches itself to the social institutions, which Kafka presents as though they were pieces of rare and exquisite lace; they are brushed aside as 'mere symbols' or outward trappings, and his meanings are sought not in them but behind, *beyond* them. My purpose is certainly not to deny that his stories point to a 'beyond', but to show that what gives his metaphysical venture its seriousness is its being rooted in the historicity and institutional patterns of the world he builds up and then demolishes: this is the condition of his negative ontology. The split between the two spheres to which Heller points is, I would suggest, part of our intimate experience. But we are also aware that the two spheres—the spiritual and the worldly; or again, the metaphysical and the empirical—join, as it were on the dark side of the moon, in negativity. For our most ready access to the spiritual seems to be through evil. To put it another way: if in our own day we have no very clear idea of absolute goodness, we seem to have an idea of what constitutes something like absolute evil. Discreetly, quietly, with only a few dramatic touches, Kafka's art intimates just that. And that, too, is its historicity. When Nietzsche wrote that we would be living in an age when 'all is possible and all is permitted', he still meant *all*, the good and the bad; we take it for granted that he could only have meant the bad.

Other writers before Kafka and since have given fictional accounts of evil. He does it in the idiom of a time which is still ours. This idiom is determined by the fact that ours is an age of unprecedented institutionalization. At the beginning of this century it seems that only Kafka and Max Weber were fully and creatively aware of this fact. And Kafka's negative ontology ('I have intensely absorbed the negative side of my time') is an anticipation of evils which are different from the evil of other ages in as much as their appearance in our world is inseparable from their non-private, institutional character. It is this that makes all Freudian and 'individual' psychological analyses of Kafka's work *and* of our world equally inadequate.

In 1927, three years after Franz Kafka's death, there appeared the first and (up to the present) only volume of Martin Heidegger's *Sein und Zeit*. On its first two pages we read:

> Have we an answer today to the question: What do we really mean by the word 'Being'? No, we have not. And so it is our task *to ask anew the question concerning the meaning of Being* . . . Today this question has fallen into oblivion . . .

Heidegger then sets out to repair the omission of all Western philosophy since the days of the pre-Socratic thinkers. He proposes to 'return' to the original, to the only authentic philosophical question there is, the question concerning the relationship between pure Being and the being of Man. For behind and beyond all our doing and functioning, all our getting and forfeiting, beyond all opinion and patter ('Meinen und Gerede'), there is (Heidegger tells us) the silent ground of Being, which must be 'un-covered' if philosophy is to move away from the merely trivial and ephemeral to the perennially valid. Neither Heidegger's cavalier treatment of more than two thousand years of Western philosophy, nor his claim that this 'question concerning the meaning of Being' is the one philosophical question that matters, need concern us here beyond saying that the absolutism of both assertions is characteristic of his time and place. But this absolutism is relevant to my argument. Heidegger's pure Being turns out to be a good deal less esoteric than it seems at first sight, and the 'ontic' question he asks receives a very concrete answer in his time and place. In the circumstances of lawlessness which prevailed in the 1920s and 30s, a negative ontology comes into being and dominates all social life. It is the doctrine according to which certain people are classified and grouped, judged and condemned and eventually done to death, not because of what they do or the way they function in society, nor because of what they say or think or believe—in all of which respects it is virtually impossible to distinguish them from the rest of society—but simply because of what, indisputably and unalterably, they are. Fascism of one kind or another comes nearer to the *praxis* of that 'pure ontology' than any other ideology to be found in our age.

Realistically speaking there is nothing particularly 'ontic' about this situation. What it comes to, in sociological terms, is that fascist propaganda favours *ascribed* social status over *acquired*, and disguises the fact by talking about 'natural states of Being'. What it comes to, in concrete terms, is that we cannot ever tell what a person *is* except as an aggregate of what he does, of what he is *in relation to* . . . But the same, after all, is true of Heidegger's grand project for the 'un-covering of Being': not even he can 'have pure Being unadulterated by anything that *is*'. He cannot disguise the fact that the only Being he can talk about is 'Seiendes', i.e., 'being-in-the-world', which is always a doing and a being-in-relation-to . . . Fascism's use of the language of authenticity and philosophical absolutism is one of the reasons (though not the only one) for its immense popularity among Heidegger's intellectual contemporaries. If we ask how national socialist propaganda and party ideology found it possible to square the circle in accusing the Jews of diametrically opposite and (one would have thought) self-cancelling crimes—of being both Marxists and international capitalists—the answer is that these obviously acquired designations were represented as 'natural', i.e., ascribed, and proclaimed to be mere foreground manifestations of an unalterably (because 'naturally') depraved state of being which lies behind and beyond all doing, all inessential 'patter and opinion'.

This is the situation Kafka anticipates in a number of his stories, most directly in those which are concerned with juridical matters. (His preoccupation is not confined to those stories which show it in their titles: *The Trial, The Verdict, In the Penal Colony, The New Attorney, Before the Law, The Question of the Laws*.) An important aim of his remarkable prose patterns is to establish an all but unbreakable spider-web of insinuations which connects the guilt his 'heroes' are involved in with the feeling of guilt they experience. Their punishment never fits the crime. The feeling of guilt is always greater than the guilt entailed by the action they are responsible for—a gap which the insinuatory prose is intended to bridge. However, the gap remains. The ultimate justification for the verdict passed on his 'heroes', which is always a verdict of 'guilty', is that they are what they are (which means, realistically speaking, that they are guilty because guilt is ascribed to them, by others and by the other in them, i.e., by the self alienated from itself). They have 'done' as little as is necessary to show that 'they are what they are', that the presentation of their 'being' should retain a bare modicum of meaning. And the least that one can say about such a judgment, which resembles the judgments of German justice under national socialism, is that Kafka does very little to dissociate himself from it. He is a writer who has 'intensely absorbed the negative aspect' of his time. He does not feel he has the right to challenge it.

'Someone must have falsely denounced Josef K., for without having done anything wrong he was arrested one morning',[5] runs the famous first sentence of *The Trial*; and from this opening to Josef K.'s execution at the end, neither he nor anyone else in the novel ever asks a single question about what this very ordinary bachelor of thirty is supposed to be guilty of. Similarly, the jurisdiction, composition, and indeed the legality of the court that is supposed to be trying him remain indeterminate. The reason for Josef K.'s peculiar arrest and apparently inescapable involvement in the protracted trial is never formulated; what is significant is that guilt is ascribed to him the moment he acknowledges the jurisdiction of the court, and that 'the trial' quickly becomes justified in the eyes of others simply by becoming '*his* trial'.

The implication is that Josef K. has been denounced (and is thus guilty) because of what he is rather than because of anything he has done. (Trying to answer what he has done, we must turn to the realistic interpretation; trying to answer what he is, we must turn to the metaphysical one; both will

27

remain incomplete.) In this sense, as concerning not an *offence by* his person but the total *existence of* his person, the sentence eventually passed on Josef K. will be absolute, as from a divinity: it will be sentence of death. But this will not give it a correspondingly objective validity—not in Kafka's view or (to put it more accurately) in the view he seeks to elicit in his reader. To use the tantalizingly cryptic paradox with the aid of which the chaplain 'plays' Josef K. as Kafka 'plays' his reader: the verdict of the court will not be 'true' but 'necessary'. Nevertheless the effect of the trial is total. Involvement in its proceedings stamps Josef K. as with a blemish or disease ('You have a trial, don't you!', people whisper sympathetically); many acquaintances whom he meets once the trial is under way won't shake hands with him, and his alienated self soon comes to share their revulsion: 'If you want to keep your boarding-house clean', he tells his landlady, 'I'm the first person you ought to give notice to'. Other members of his family come to be involved in the malignant, sinister affair from which, it soon transpires, no complete discharge is ever possible. Certainly, as Josef K. eventually asserts, 'My innocence doesn't simplify the case', for he remains the man that he is: not God in the burning bush but a fearful, wary and unfree man, under an inscrutable but acknowledged indictment. When Kafka has Josef K. remonstrate, in the cathedral scene, 'But how can a man be guilty at all? Surely we are all men here, one like another!', to which the chaplain replies, 'That's right, but that is what the guilty usually say', he is presenting the situation, common enough in fascist societies, where the outlaw's appeal to be considered a member of that society—a German Jew's avowal that he is a German—is deemed a criminal act. Again, when Josef K. exclaims, 'Ah, but I've only got my experience to go by!', to which the chaplain no longer replies because he could only repeat what he said before, no more than a slight fictional exaggeration separates us from national socialist legislation and its law courts after 1936, where the admission of being one kind of person (having one kind of 'experience to go by') rather than another was tantamount to an admission of guilt under the law. Suspended throughout almost the entire structure of Kafka's story is that peculiar narrative spider-web I have mentioned, used now to connect, not merely guilt with feeling of guilt, but arrest with examination, examination with trial, trial with verdict and verdict with sentence—a continuity summed up in the words, 'The verdict does not come all at once, the proceedings gradually merge with the verdict'. But this in turn describes, accurately and with hardly any departure from the known facts, the reversal of the ordinary functions of the judiciary and the police: a reversal characteristic of every totalitarian régime, where the courts are no more than the formal means of making it 'legal' for the police to pass and execute its sentence upon the prisoner. And when one of Josef K.'s relations observes, 'Looking at you, one might almost believe the saying "To be involved in a trial like this is the same as having already been convicted" ', we are once again in that area of total, 'ontic' condemnation which, in the practice of national socialist law, equated 'being'—that is, status ascribed by society—with guilt. 'Why, do you think we would summons anybody unless they have committed some crime?' is not a quotation from *The Trial*, but the remark of a Gestapo official to a Gentile husband who wants to know what his Jewish wife has done that she should be deported to her death.[6]

That guilt is a state of being, a negative ontology which no expiation or punishment can reverse; that mere arraignment in a court of law is tantamount to conviction from which no absolute acquittal is ever likely, perhaps even possible—these are the notorious terms on which Josef K. enters the jurisdiction of the courts. And these, too, are the terms outlined by the chief public prosecutor of the People's Courts in a letter to the Reich Minister of Justice dated 29 July 1940:

> Unless otherwise instructed, I shall in future proceed as follows: in all cases of acquittal or when sentence has expired during the period of imprisonment awaiting trial, I shall, as a matter of principle and in agreement with the President of the People's Court, hand the persons concerned to the Gestapo. Whenever acquittal is consequent upon proof of innocence, I shall inform the Gestapo before disposal takes place, and I shall enquire whether this procedure is to be dispensed with. If however the Gestapo considers protective custody appropriate, I shall arrange for disposal to take place forthwith.[7]

Three years later, after the assassination of Reinhard Heydrich, the chief of the Reich Security Office informed its officials that legal proceedings, as opposed to summary 'trials', were to take place only 'if it has been ascertained through previous enquiry that the court will pronounce sentence of death'.[8]

This, then, is the burden of my argument: that in its structure, its overall theoretical conception and many of its details, Kafka's *The Trial* is a prophetic—or rather an anticipatory—fictional account of both the concepts underlying national socialist legislation and the practice of its law courts.

National socialist law is not, as the law is in Dickens, 'an ass': that is, extravagant, purblind, a mechanical legalistic pomposity remote from the true interests of the litigants and the community at large. On the contrary, it is an attempt—in theory but also in practice—to de-legalize the judicial process, to personalize it, to draw it away from impersonal and generally valid formulations and make it subservient to a natural or instinctive feeling for what is right, to 'the healthy sentiment of the Nation'. Some time before the assumption of power by Hitler in February 1933, German academic lawyers proclaimed that this legal maxim alone enabled them to solve 'the paramount task of our profession, which is to overcome the dilemma, all too common today, between justice and morality',[9] to achieve what Lord Justice Devlin has called 'the crimation of sin'. This *Volksempfinden* is represented in the will of one man. That the Führer's will is law is confirmed by a decree of 26 April 1942, which also specifically mentions that he is 'not bound by existing legal regulations'.[10] But what is his attitude towards the law? It is clearly stated in a number of passages in the *Table Talk*:[11]

[The Chief said:] Dietrich Eckart, himself having studied jurisprudence for a few terms, always had an exceptionally clear opinion about everything to do with the law. According to his own statements he, Eckart, had broken off his studies 'in order not to become a total idiot . . .'

Therefore, he ['the Chief'] declared today clearly and unambiguously that in his view anyone who is a lawyer must be either mentally defective by nature or else is bound to become so in time . . .

Hitler said he would therefore do everything to make the study of law, that is the study of these [humanitarian] interpretations of the law, as contemptible as possible. Besides, to spend a life-time defending malefactors could really not be described as a decent occupation . . .

But then, the lawyers are every bit as international as the criminals, only not so clever . . . and also as regards their international connections there is no difference between them.

The personality-type whose views of the law are reflected in statements such as these is described by Kafka twenty-five years earlier with the utmost exactitude in the 'Letter to his Father':

You had worked your way up alone by your own efforts, therefore you had unbounded confidence in your opinion. From your armchair you ruled the world. *Your* opinion was right, every other opinion was crazy, unbalanced, 'meschugge', not normal. And with all this your self confidence was so immense that you had no need to be consistent at all and yet never ceased to be in the right. Sometimes it happened that you had no opinion at all about something—therefore all possible opinions on that matter were bound to be wrong, without exception. You could, for instance, run down the Czechs, and then the Germans, and then the Jews—not just selectively but wholesale, until at last no-one was left but yourself. You assumed for me that mysteriousness which belongs to all tyrants, whose right is founded not in thought, but in their persons.[12]

The biographical and historical actualities shine through this strange document on the borderline between fact and fiction with an unmistakable light, illuminating a picture of the things to come.

Now, such an interpretation is based on the hypothesis, which is hardly very daring, that when Kafka speaks of 'das Gesetz' he does not mean Divine Grace, or Fate, or the father-figure conceptualized, but he means, first and foremost, the Law or a law; when he says 'the law' he means, not some *obiter dictum*, but what we all mean by that word, an institutional concept framed so as to apply, necessarily, to a category of persons; and when he calls his father a tyrant, he is not just exorcizing his own father-complex but describing one who, instead of founding his right over others in the necessities of reason, bases it upon arbitrariness and the caprice of his person.

Others have written about the law's delays and the insolence of office. In Dickens, whom Kafka admired and envied, the law is abused and corrupted and twisted to suit the convenience of litigants and, more especially, their lawyers. These are traditional themes. In national socialist law the situation is rather different. There an arbitrary maxim, such as 'the healthy sentiment of the Nation', is given objective, universal and unassailable validity through its spokesman and interpreter, Hitler as the supreme judiciary of the Reich. And a similar sort of maxim, elevating a subjective dictum to the apparent objectivity of a law, seems to lie behind the proceedings of the court in Kafka's novel. Seems to lie: for we don't really know; the law is never stated, all we have to go by is Josef K.'s experience. This 'existential' situation, which is not one of casual injustice, is unprecedented, as far as I can see, if not in history, then certainly in literature. Moreover, it is hardly resisted in Kafka's novel, and only marginally in the historical reality. There is only one sentence of unambiguous protest in the whole work, which Josef K. utters before his last hour: 'The lie is made the order of the world'; but he hardly expects his protest to make any difference.

The world of *The Trial* and national socialist Germany, then, are governed not by casual injustice but by a certain personal 'order of the world'. Behind this order we must assume a hypothetical legislator who has the all-encompassing mental characteristics of 'the Father' in Kafka's letter and of Hitler, 'the Chief' of the *Table Talk*. Both are intent on a condemnation of the whole world, 'the Czechs, the Germans, the Jews, until nobody was left but yourself'. And this legislator's law, again both in the anticipatory fiction and in the historical reality, is the law 'founded in [the tyrant's] person'. It amounts to the elevation of the subjective maxim to objective status—a procedure more obvious in its effects than in its principle.

In the historical situation after 1933 this absolute arbitrariness was felt to be a liberation, an immense simplification and personalization of abstruse legal technicalities, a 'return to natural justice'. Legislation took on the shape of a nightmare, yet it also had a fairy-tale quality. Overnight and quite literally, the Queen of Hearts' 'Off with their heads!' became law. The most remarkable piece of this new legislation, and the one that has a direct bearing on *The Trial*, was a law 'against Communist acts of violence', passed on the day following the Reichstag fire of 27 February 1933, whereby seven articles of the Constitution were suspended and a number of crimes, including arson, previously punishable by life sentence, were declared capital crimes; as though this were not enough, on 29 March a further law, known as *lex van der Lubbe*, was formulated in such a way as to antedate the validity of the law of 28 February in order to 'legalize' the execution of the young Dutch communist convicted of the crime.

The *lex van der Lubbe* is a paradigm of national socialist legislation as it is the paradigm of the law that determines Josef K.'s fate. The point about this law (and a whole host of others, including most of the laws relating to juvenile delinquents) is that it is as it were tailor-made, designed to fit exactly the case of the offender.

Every man's existence within a code of justice involves him in a peculiar paradox. The law to which he owes obedience is of its nature a generalization designed to cover a variety of cases, all of them related but each slightly different from the rest. The national socialists sought to solve this paradox by creating a procedure called 'Willensstrafrecht', that is, criminal law which takes into consideration 'the will' or intention behind the act. In this way the areas of legitimate enquiry and admissible evidence of motivation were widened until they included the whole of a man's life, all his circumstances, and above all his intentions: once again we are back at the 'existential' indictment of Kafka's story, where a man's entire being is on trial. And the notion of 'Willensstrafrecht' in turn contributed to the impression of the law that fitted the crime by being designed for the punishment of one man. The perfect law, Kafka writes, is 'attracted' by the offence.

This extraordinary conjunction of a total subjectivity and a spurious objectivity—a categorical imperative designed for a single practitioner—is illustrated in the most telling manner in the complexly ambiguous tale-within-the-tale which is told to Josef K. by the chaplain in the cathedral chapter of *The Trial*, the parable of 'Before the Law'. After waiting for a whole lifetime at the outermost gates which are guarded by one of the law's lowliest custodians, 'the Man from the Country' is allowed his one question: 'All men strive after the law', says the man, 'how is it that in all these years nobody but me has ever asked to be admitted?'

Let me emphasize once more what in any context less heady than Kafka criticism would be obvious: that even in the convention of a parable, Kafka is talking about the law as we understand the word. This is not to deny that he may also be talking about 'the Law' in a larger, religious sense. Nor do I think that what is often, after Dante, called the 'literal' interpretation is separate and sharply to be distinguished from others. But it must be the critic's first task to make out the first and most obvious meaning, and Kafka encourages him to do so, for instance by saying, 'All men strive after the law'; and again (as though this were not clear enough) by confirming that it is in the nature of every law as the courts, including our courts, transact it that it should be freely available to all men: 'The law', the man from the country is thinking to himself, 'should surely be accessible at all times and to every man!' The critical point here is one which arises with other authors too, but rarely in such a radical way. It is of course true (as critics have often emphasized) that Kafka creates verbal contexts in which very ordinary words assume unusual meanings, or at least connotations. Yet it is equally important to remember that these new connotations are not free-floating and arbitrary, but derive from the contrast and tension he has built up between the old, accustomed meaning and the use of the word in its new, unexpected context. (No prose text, however esoteric, can proceed differently.) It is only when we have recalled the perfectly ordinary meaning of the word 'Gesetz' that we can fully understand the peculiar use to which it is being put in this story. For only after the man from the country has pointed to its very ordinary meaning and the expectation he, an ordinary man, derives from *that* ('All men strive after the law . . .')—only then does he point to its peculiarity by saying, 'How is it that in all these years nobody but me has ever asked to be admitted?'

The rest of the story is quickly told. The keeper realizes that the man is at the point of death and, so as to reach the man while he can still hear, he shouts at him: 'Here no-one else could gain admission, for this door was meant only for you. I shall now go and shut it.' This is the consummation of national socialist justice, the elevation of caprice and of the special plea to the status of a law, the *lex van der Lubbe*. The law here is not merely attracted but created by the offence, by the guilty being, the negative ontology; it fits only the one man whose life it will take, whom it is specially and exclusively designed to destroy, 'like a dog'.

Yet even this is not the full story of the topical parallels between the fiction and subsequent history. The most problematic implications of Kafka's novel arise with our awareness that his evaluation of this law and of its courts and their procedures is far from clear and unambiguous. The prisoners, we read, are distinguished by a very special beauty, the signs of a positive election of some kind. Josef K. is told that he is free to leave the jurisdiction of the court, and doesn't. He speaks more than once as though he were proud of the complexity of 'his' trial, and correspondingly impatient of other men's attempts to get him off. Finally, it seems as if only under the impact of that invisible prosecution was Josef K.'s dim life given some meaning, a meaning it had lacked before: as if his 'arrest' amounted to some strange validation. The victim behaves as if what held him captive were something other, something more, than the tormentor's might masquerading as right. True, Josef K. utters that sentence of protest, 'The lie has become the order of the world'. But by the time this is said, he has missed his chance (it is not the only one he is given) of stepping out of the jurisdiction of the court. For the rest he is all too eager to comply with what he thinks is expected of him. Why is his attitude at the prospect of his execution so unresisting? Why is he so ready to help 'the authorities' in their hideous preparations? True, he could not help them all the way: 'He could not completely prove his worth, nor could he take all the work of the authorities upon himself: the responsibility for that last failure lay with whoever had denied him the remnant of the strength necessary for the deed'. No passage in Samuel Beckett intimates a more radical alienation of the self from its sustaining will to live, or of words from their ordinary meanings, than this sentence, where 'his worth' and 'the necessary strength' refer to Josef K.'s readiness to act as his own executioner, where 'work' is murder, where 'failure' is the failure to anticipate execution by suicide. Why is he so eager to see the scene of his own death through the eyes of 'the authorities'? Why should he, too, connive at the substitution of might for right? Does he, in the hour of his death, agree that he has no right, no right to live? ' "Like a dog!" *he* said, and it was as if the shame of it should survive him': the shame, it seems ultimately, not of being in the wrong, but of being alone and weak, or rather of being in the wrong because he is alone and weak.

The objections against extending the parallel to cover this, the most terrible aspect of the novel, seem obvious; they have been voiced in a recent study:

'The most inappropriate feature of the story from a realistic point of view is the way the hero is left so largely free in public life, able outwardly at least to go about his ordinary business . . . *The Trial* cannot be read as even a symbolic account of totalitarian prosecution, simply because the whole of the uncanny train of events narrated here are responded to by the hero in a manner that makes no political sense.'[13]

Let it be said straight away that in respect of the court's declaration that 'it receives you when you come and it dismisses you when you go', there is of course no direct parallel in the totalitarian practice of the law. But does this declaration amount to a real offer of freedom? It occurs at the end of an exchange of ambiguities between Josef K. and the chaplain, the ultimate meaning of which is perfectly clear. We may abbreviate the exchange as follows:

'Do you want to leave already?' [asks the clergyman]
'Certainly, I must go now. I'm an assistant manager in the bank . . .'

'Well then . . . go . . .' The clergyman had only moved away a few steps, but K. called very loudly: 'Wait a minute, please!'
'I'm waiting', said the clergyman.
'Is there anything else you want from me?' K. asked.
'No', said the clergyman . . . 'You said you had to go' . . .
'Why, yes—surely you must see that!' . . .

In other words: so powerful is the hold the court has over Josef K., so complete is his bondage to its authority, that the clergyman who has just admitted that he is the court's representative may tell Josef K. to go away in the sure knowledge that he will stay. Just so, each half of *Waiting for Godot* ends with the same words:

Vladimir/Estragon: 'Well, shall we go?'
Estragon/Vladimir: 'Yes, let's go.'
*They do not move.*

It is the bondage to the law—whether that law be just or not, whether it fulfils the true function of all laws, which is to protect those who come under it, or whether it grotesquely subverts that function—it is the bondage to the court and its law that is the novel's central issue. And this spiritual bondage, subtly joined with the physical, provides the true parallel to the situation of the 1930s.

Of course, Josef K.'s behaviour in response to the mounting pressure of the court 'makes no political sense'—nor did the behaviour of the liberal middle classes, Jewish or Gentile, in the early thirties. Those critics who offer a Freudian analysis of that situation—according to which the law 'is really' the Father, justice 'is really' a repressed feeling of guilt, the trial 'is really' a state of deep neurosis, and the whole scenario 'happens really' inside Josef K.'s or Franz Kafka's mind—misrepresent the novel by robbing it of its historicity, and thus reduce it to its least distinct element. (If Freudianism can contribute anything to our understanding of that world, this is because it was itself one of the minor factors in hastening the end of it.)

What Kafka expresses through the idea of an unjust 'objective' law is not a neurosis but a profound religious doubt—a doubt assailing if not the idea of divine justice and thus of divinity itself, then our ability to recognize divine justice in such a guise as it here assumes. The law and its implications for Josef K. are the objective correlative of that religious doubt.

But all expressions of doubt, whether in real life or in fiction, must include an intimation of its positive resolution; all images of suffering and evil make sense only by virtue of their opposite; and 'the law' of *The Trial* would be no law at all were it not also shown to contain the possibility of a positive purpose. It is this glimpse of a validation that makes the parable of 'Before the Law' so tantalizing.

While waiting before the gate, the man from the country has grown old, weak in body and mind, and almost blind. He no longer knows 'whether it is really growing dark around him or whether it is only his eyes that are deceiving him. But now he recognizes in the darkness a radiance which streams forth, inextinguishably, from the door of the law.' For once the reality of what is reported remains unquestioned either by the narrator or by the characters in the story. Nor can we for our part doubt that this inextinguishable light is anything other than an intimation of a divine principle: a radiance from beyond.

And yet, what is it that is being conveyed in this scene? Is it, as numerous critics have so readily claimed, a positive religious message, a hope of delivery? And is it really true to say (as Max Brod proclaims) that 'Because they are wrested from a radical scepticism and put to the ultimate test, the rudiments of faith [presented in Franz Kafka's work] are infinitely valuable and strong in their truthfulness'?[14] Almost the opposite is the case: the truthfulness is there, but not the faith. The man from the country (we read in the next sentence) 'has not much longer to live'. The light he 'recognized' is not mentioned again, except at the end of the long, Talmud-like exegesis to which the priest subjects the parable. In such a context, what else can that glimpse of a radiance from beyond mean except a last turn of the screw, a tantalus-like torment comparable to that radiance of the blessed, the vision of which is said to highlight the torments of the damned? Max Brod's sentence characterizes the religiosity of an age. It reveals, not the nature of Kafka's faith, but the reason why so many of Kafka's readers were (and perhaps still are) so eager to accept a religious message from him: because he offers it on the only terms readily acceptable to them: at the issue of the gravest doubt, beyond—though only just beyond—the last possibility of realization, on the dark side of the moon.

The realism of *The Trial*, as perhaps of all of Kafka's stories, is precarious, one element in a complex structure.[15] And since realism is always bound up with its own day and age (an age which, in this respect at all events, is still ours), its realistic element is to be sought in the distance, the unattainability, the tantalizing 'beyond' of that radiance which streams forth from the Law. Or—to put it as Kafka would—so it seems. After all, 'we have only our experiences to go by'.

But what enables Kafka to draw the parallels, to anticipate the terrors of the thirties? He is not a prophet: he is too be-mused, too much the novelist fascinated by material and method, to raise his voice in warning. The age to which he belongs in Germany culminates in the rule of national socialism. Hindsight enables us to see this rule and the circumstances that made it possible as continuous with the inhumanities of the age in which he lived. (In this respect at all events *The Trial* may be compared with *1984*.) What needs stressing in Kafka's biography as the source of his anticipations is not so much his Jewishness as a religious phenomenon (in some ways it is a Jewishness not of faith but of the anti-Semite), but rather its socially representative nature; his status as a Jew is symbolic of the powerlessness and conformism of humane and liberal beliefs everywhere, as well as of the heightened capacity for insight that goes with such powerlessness. He is able to anticipate the future because he is not very much at home in the present.

The period just before the First World War (when *The Trial* was written) was the peak period of Jewish German assimilation, and of the attempts of the Prague Jews to find their place in a German culture. It was then that the Jews expected to be treated as members of one cultural community, one Germany of the mind, and they were all made equal before the law. ('But I am innocent', Josef K. protests, 'it is a mistake. Surely we're all human beings here . . .'). But there was one great difference: the Jews were without power. This did not matter much as long as there was a law and they were allowed to devote themselves to it; and was not interpreting the law *like* having power? (We can see that Kafka's choice of the things that go into his fiction, apart from being autobiographically motivated, is also historically significant.) The position of the Jews was not, after all, different from that of the middle classes generally: and if the Central European Jews of Kafka's generation were largely unaccustomed to fighting for justice and liberty, so were their Gentile neighbours. It is obvious what a vital place the law had, or should have had, in their lives. By making the law ambiguous and problematic, Kafka is challenging that which, after the desuetude of their ancient faith, remained the central support of their lives. But in this, again, what is at issue is not their Jewishness as such, but the fact that it was representative of the weakness of middle-class culture generally. The life of the Jews among the Germans started as a noble and highminded experiment in assimilation and enlightened tolerance; and they all, Jews and Gentiles alike, were proud of no longer reaching for the sky, proud of having 'only their experiences to go by'. The more successful the experiment, the more terrible was their eventual destruction. At the end of their life among the Germans, no other values and no other patterns of behaviour were available to the German Jews than those of their erstwhile fellow-citizens, later enemies. Here too Kafka, uttering no warning, is representative. He is not a prophet but remains the infinitely perceptive novelist of some of Europe's darkest days.

But is he still a *novelist*, after the interpretation that has been offered here? My insistence on the historical dimension is not intended to undermine the integrity of the work as fiction, but to restore the critical balance. Kafka's writings are among those which challenge the problematic assumption—which surely has now had its day— that there is a 'literary' way of looking at a work of art which excludes the historical and the philosophical.

The realistic and political interpretation of the novel as an anticipation of the totalitarian state has been rejected because (it is said) the novel is 'written from the standpoint of the victim, not of the persecutor'. This is both true and false. For while it is true that the narrator's point of view is closely associated with that of the 'hero', Josef K., it is equally important to realize that this 'hero' who is really a victim, a man full of apprehensions and fears, has little by way of an independent point of view, and tends to look at the world through the eyes of any man or woman whom he happens to meet and think useful or powerful, including, once or twice, through the eyes of his persecutors. And the narrator's evaluation of the law—the standpoint from which it and the courts are presented—does not resolve this ambivalence, for it is notoriously unstable and ambiguous. The suggestion, indeed the insinuation, that the exterminators and the law they enact are not wholly in the wrong, that there *is* a foothold for their authority in the victim's soul, as though their hold were somehow a matter not merely of might but also of right—that insinuation, too, is part of Kafka's anticipation.

# W. G. Sebald

## The Law of Ignominy: Authority, Messianism and Exile in *The Castle*

In Kafka's work—and in *The Castle* in particular—ugliness and deformity appear to be occasioned by the presence of an irrational power which cannot in any way be vindicated. Nowhere does the novel extend to us conclusive information about the actual goings-on inside the Castle, about the origin and purpose of this untouchable organization; yet nowhere is it maintained that the Castle is inscrutable—the domain of supernatural beings. Conjectures along those lines remain mere fragments of our interpretation. We are, however, repeatedly and quite unmistakably told that the Castle is powerful, this being the cruel lesson which K., in spite of all his initial defiance, will have to learn. Thus, at the beginning of the novel, the humble landlord informs K. that even Schwarzer's father, although only 'Unterkastellan' and one of the lowest at that, is in a position of power; as for K. himself, however (towards whom the landlord affects after all a kind of awe, if not reverence), he is not considered as being in the least bit powerful. K. points out that even if his mission were doomed, he would still feel the satisfaction 'frei vor einem Mächtigen gesprochen zu haben' ('of having spoken freely to a great and powerful man').[1] And the fable-like simile of the eagle and the blindworm, through which K.—at one of the turning points of the novel—visually comprehends the relationship between Klamm and himself, also implies the distinction between power and impotence. Soon after, K. compares the formal, barely tangible power which Klamm exercises in his assumed function as a land-surveyor with the concrete power through which Klamm appears to make himself felt even in K.'s bedroom. Pursuing reflections of this kind, K. begins to abandon himself to the acknowledgment of a power that relentlessly obtrudes upon him until he finally admits 'that the difference in strength between the authorities and himself was so enormous that all the guile of which he was capable would hardly have served appreciably to reduce the difference in his favour.' (p. 158) K. has now perceived his own impotence. He recognizes in it the hub of his forlorn predicament, the part allocated to him by the powers that be.

It is, I think, generally accepted that the only possible rationalization of power is to seize upon it in order to exploit it for a creative purpose. Accordingly the claims of great works of art to dominate and subjugate the individual imagination are counterbalanced, and thereby made acceptable, by their critical achievements. The power of the Castle authorities, however, is anything but creative; it is completely sterile and its sole aim seems pointless self-perpetuation. The condition of its continued survival is the identification of those who are powerless with the principles of their repression. The Castle's lasting power is therefore less an absolute quality than the product of a symbiosis through which its subjects are fused with it once the experience of impotence has become second nature to them. It is for this reason that Kafka's inexorable portrayal of power defines it, in the first instance, as parasitic rather than powerful. And it is precisely the parasitic features that provide an explanation for the strangely listless, hypersensitive and noisome nature of the officials. Resembling each other to an uncanny degree and with few individual traits, they appear to have regressed to an earlier stage of evolution. Not unlike insects, they are of a limited mobility and their unplanned industry seems, as K. at one point remarks, no more than the ludicrous confusion of primitive organisms. In their helplessness they depend on the habitual assistance of less degenerate beings. Thus Barnabas's father, while still serving with the fire-brigade, had to carry the obese Galater from the Herrenhof, although the alleged risk of a fire was largely a figment of the official's over-apprehensive mind. Similarly the vampiric lasciviousness with which the functionaries of the Castle are wont to demand virginal sacrifice and public prostitution appears in its true light only if seen in the context of their parasitic condition.

In the train of such hypotheses one begins to appreciate the significance of the observations which Pepi, in the course of the final chapter, intimates to K., observations concerning the Brückenhof's official guests: that they leave their rooms in such a state 'that not even the Flood could wash them clean' and that 'one had to make a great effort to overcome one's disgust so as to be able to clean up after them.' (p. 275) It seems that only the most oppressed inhabitants of the village, the maids, deprived as they are of almost all rights and destined to dwell in subterranean haunts, have some inkling of the true degradation of those in power; but as the maids are, at the same time, furthest removed from them, they do not constitute any immediate threat. They only know the excrement of power, not power itself.

This is Kafka's critical insight into the perfected machinery of the societal system. It anticipates in a number of respects the fragmentary 'Theorie des Unrats' which Christian Enzensberger has provided in his *Grösserer Versuch über den Schmutz*. In this treatise we are reminded:

> that power and filth invariably go together . . . Faced with power one bows one's head, one shrinks, one goes on one's knees, grovels in the dust, turns into a wriggling worm, into a mere nothing; throughout one's being one is subject to contractions, even in a physiological sense, including excessive perspiration and humiliating defecation. In the presence of power a person will withdraw into himself, feel incapable of preserving his unity and the principles of his structural organization are turned upside down.[2]

Furthermore Enzensberger points to such phenomena as the juxtaposition of scatological tendencies and the craving for power as exemplified in the works of de Sade, to the functional relationship, in other words, that exists between order and ordure: 'The more rigid a system of order, the greater is the amount of filth it generates . . . some systems turn man himself into waste and filth.'[3] And later:

> Those in power banish to the confines of their systems as many forms of behaviour as possible, even though they may have been hitherto quite acceptable, declaring them to be marginal infringements and thus mere filth. The point is that

such prohibitive orders increase the terror which they wish
to see engendered. Even the most willing of subjects cannot,
in the end, comply with all the demands made on him, is
overtaken by guilt and henceforth in need of exoneration.
The more violent power is claimed, the greater, as a rule,
the clamour for order and propriety. That this generates
even more filth is a fact which those in power are at pains
to conceal. In reality their one wish is for a universal pig-sty;
their true desire is not to increase hygiene but to cleanse
themselves. The exercising of power, according to all that
has gone before, is thus a dirty business in the real sense
of the word.[4]

These sentences furnish an abstract analogy to Kafka's novel
and hardly require further interpretation. The filth and debris
which parasitic power entails are allotted to the people who
live under its sway as their fateful inheritance. Although power,
in the last resort, is seen as the source of depravity, this depravity
is associated less with the fact of oppression than with the lives
of the oppressed. In this state of affairs we recognize the
objective correlative of ugliness and deformity in Kafka's
works, an ugliness and deformity which paradoxically grow
more cruel in proportion to the distance between the victims
and the centre of power. One would not go far wrong if one
were to interpret this insight as Kafka's knowledge of the
temptations of beauty—illustrated in *Das Schweigen der Sirenen*
(*The Silence of the Sirens*)—and conversely as his hopeful con-
jecture that in ugliness we behold our inborn relation to an
abstract, powerless deity, to a deliberately constructed counterpart of power and dominion.

To revolutionize a system in which power and impotence
almost purposefully complement each other is a logical impossibility. This problem, which ever since Kleist and Büchner
has had its place in the more radical works of German literature, was repeatedly considered by Kafka, most perceptively
perhaps in the parable of the rusty old toy-guns nobody is
prepared to pick up.[5] Kafka's way of representing the dilemma
seems to imply that a revolution is nevertheless necessary and
that it is all the more imperative, the more impossible it becomes
to translate its idea into practice. This reflection marks the

median point between societal reality and utopia. Given these circumstances which show power and impotence to be invariable, ahistorical, mythical categories, dialectical reasoning at length begins to toy with ways of transcending this hopeless situation. One of the most complex examples of such abstract designs can be recognized in messianism, the aspirations and weakness of which form a central issue of the Castle novel.

Jewish messianism, of which christology represents but a variant, is a diffuse and immensely variable phenomenon which I cannot hope to describe here even in outline. Suffice it to say that its implications are political as well as metaphysical and that in cases of messianic movements it is usually difficult to distinguish between sedition and surrender. Messianism knows no dogma and indeed has never developed a theology except when it felt historically discredited as, for instance, by the apostasy of Sabbatai Zwi. Apart from such examples, however, messianism remained a tradition in the authentic sense of the word, that is to say unsystematic, contradictory and unstable. Consequently the image of the messiah can hardly be ascertained. It oscillates between that of the king and that of the beggar, between the Zaddik, the epitome of justness, and the criminal, between the representative and the outsider. The contradictions cannot be resolved, not even under the aspect of ethics. Revelation and confidence trick, merit and guilt, submission and violence—such distinctions are of little relevance where messianic striving is the dominant factor. The only invariable and decisive feature is the concept of hope as the guiding principle in a maze of illusions.

*The Castle* comprises a number of visual and reflective reminiscences of the messianic tradition and frequently the parallels are so pronounced as to suggest that the author may quite consciously have attempted to represent and analyse the messianic idea. Even K.'s arrival in the village reminds one of characteristic features of messianic lore. Like K., about whose looks and origin we never learn anything conclusive, the messiah is of uncertain provenance and his physiognomy is indistinct. In hassidic tales which gave the messianic figure perhaps its most vivid expression one encounters the unknown wanderer—his insignia the knapsack and the walking stick—traversing the country or sitting in wayside inns uttering truth

upon truth.[6] He turns up unexpectedly, as a guest perhaps for
the *seder*, in the uniform of one pressed into life-long military
service in the czarist army, and disappears without a trace as
soon as the community has recognized him. The archetypal
experience of the exile informs his elusive persona; the image
of one who has come far from his native land, of a God, fallen
from grace, as portrayed by Döblin, with all the defects of
desperation, in his *Babylonische Wandrung*, (Babylonian
Travels).

Without much difficulty, one can discern in K. an incarna-
tion of this kind of figure. A variant of the opening of the novel
(which Kafka rejected) tells us that the 'Fürstenzimmer' of the
Brückenhof has been prepared for K., who is not so much
announced as always expected; it is this irrational expectation
of the stranger which, if we can take K.'s irritation at its face
value, penetrates his incognito and endangers his mission.
Although far from unambiguous the scene betrays too much
of K.'s possible identity—which may be why Kafka chose a less
explicit opening. The beginning of the novel as we now know
it offers rather more sparse hints, so that it is almost exclusively
the term 'land-surveyor' itself which gives rise to speculations.
The Hebrew word for land-surveyor, *moshoakh*, is but one
unwritten vowel removed from *moshiakh*, the Hebrew word for
messiah. Kafka employed ciphers such as this one in order to
conceal a meaning which direct presentation would have
deprived of its resonance. The secret code which turns Kafka's
texts into palimpsests was based on his belated exercises in
Hebrew and his love of Grimm's Dictionary, a synthesis of
poles so disparate that one can infer from it the tension which
Kafka attempted to live out.

The urgency of K.'s mission is evident from those numerous
instances where the text of the novel refers to the protagonist's
determination and to his readiness to fight. Right at the
beginning we are informed that K. has not ventured into the
Castle world by chance; he had *expected* efficient arrangements,
even if the existence of a telephone somewhat surprises him.
K. mentions to Olga that he thinks he had a fairly clear notion
of the place even before his arrival. And now he is in the village
to risk a duel which, he believes, is agreed to by the Castle with
no more than a smile. Nor does the crucial letter omit to

mention 'the fact that if it should come to a struggle K. had had the hardihood to make the first advances.' (p. 30) How much K. is conscious of this strained situation is shown by a passage where he reflects on the risk he is running and finally reminds himself that he had not, after all, come to the village simply 'to lead an honoured and comfortable life'. (p. 146) And later on he affirms once again: 'I came here of my own accord, and of my own accord I have settled here.' (p. 187) However unfavourable the actual conditions may have proved to be, they cannot alter K.'s determination to force the Castle into a confrontation—an aim which had crystallized even before his arrival. 'I have come to fight', he explains in a variant of the beginning; about the nature of this confrontation, however, the text remains largely silent.

At best we know that it is not K.'s immediate objective to assist those oppressed by the Castle; he has come 'to fight for himself'. If one takes into consideration the novel as a whole, the 'for himself' is likely to refer to the principles which K. represents rather than to his person. According to the teleology of Jewish messianism this principle could perhaps be defined as the liberation not of an individual or of a particular group but of the entire community of the oppressed.

This could also explain why K. cannot redeem any of the hopes invested in him. There are the peasants 'mit ihren förmlich gequälten Gesichtern' ('with their literally tortured faces'), which appear to have been formed 'im Schmerz des Geschlagenwerdens' ('in the pain of beating'). K. initially believes that their exaggerated interest in him is designed to hamper his freedom of movement, but then asks himself whether they might not have hoped to find in him an advocate of their inarticulate desires. When K. evades what thus approaches him, he seems to become guilty of ignoring the urgent demands of a specific group of people, a striking parallel to the dilemma of the revolutionary who in the interest of the general cause cannot afford to show his compassion towards any particular case. Thus Frieda and Pepi too must inevitably be disappointed by their liberator and the Barnabas family, who for so long had been waiting for somebody to reverse developments in the village, equally begin to fear that K. will not be capable of taking upon himself this crucial task. For Olga the glimpse of light which K.'s arrival has brought into the world of the Castle is already a fading memory:

> A Land-Surveyor had come and I didn't even know what a Land-Surveyor was. But next evening Barnabas . . . came home earlier than usual . . . drew me out into the street, laid his head on my shoulder, and cried for several minutes. He was again the little boy he used to be. Something had happened to him, and he could not bear the joy and the anxieties of all this newness. It was as if a whole new world had suddenly opened to him. (p. 214)

The subjunctive 'as if a whole new world had suddenly opened to him' is a token of the desperate disparity between the messianic promise and its actual achievement. The insufferable tension between the deprivations of this world and the longed-for *Parousia* propels those who believe that the renewal is imminent into self-negation. Characteristic of this is a passage which Kafka rejected in which Olga implores K., "Take away my fear and you possess me utterly." "What kind of fear", asked K. "The fear of losing you." ' Olga's life consists entirely of the apprehension that her hope might be ill-founded. Through the eyes of this utterly reduced creature we finally recognize that K., in his failure to fulfil any of their dreams, is ultimately identical with the downtrodden and the powerless.

This, however, holds true only if we overlook the dialectical insight of the young boy Hans who has a better, more differentiated judgment of K. Though Hans seeks to emulate K., he certainly knows of K.'s present abjectness; but he has also had occasion to note how other people in search of help seem to have been attracted by K. 'because nobody in the old environment had been able to help.' These contradictions had engendered in him the belief that though for the moment K. was wretched and looked down on, yet in an almost unimaginable and distant future he would excel everybody. Accordingly, Hans looks on K. 'as on a younger brother whose future would reach further than his own, the future of a very little boy.' (p. 144) This paradox is meaningful only if one sees K. not as a person but as the embodiment of a principle exempt from the passage of time. K., 'the eternal Land-

Surveyor', as the text at one point tells us, is a cipher for a future that perpetually retreats ahead of a disheartening reality, a cipher of hope, deeply engrained in privation and never redeemed. Even if this principle is forlorn in its own unreality there remains the desire for its realization, the moral dimension, which is anathema to empire and oppression.

That K. represents a threat to the Castle is suggested several times in the text. Although Kafka refrained from unambiguous hints in the novel itself, it is perhaps significant here that an embryonic sketch contained in the diaries describes the wanderer who drifts into the village as possessing a revolver.[7] And when K., in the last chapter, is about to disappear it is said of him that he is either a fool or a child or a very wicked person. Similarly, when K.'s intention to address himself directly to Klamm is mentioned, the landlady attempts to dissuade him. K.'s retort ('you don't fear for Klamm, do you?') exposes the apprehension concealed in this request. Can we not infer that the Castle authorities, for reasons of self-preservation, seek to avoid a direct confrontation with the intruder K.? The landlord of the Herrenhof is convinced that the officials are unable and unprepared to endure the sight of a stranger. In one of the variants, K. learns from an official that Klamm was forced to postpone his departure for two hours as he could not bear to confront K., whereupon K. examines the face of the secretary 'as though trying to discover the law to which one's features had to conform if Klamm was to be able to endure them.' K.'s tactics, to attempt to *force* his way into the centre of power, thus appear justified, particularly if one considers Momus's remark about 'Klamm's extreme sensitivity'. And is it not the case with power in general that the more exalted it is, the more vulnerable it becomes? Only after due preparations and adequate warning are the powerful in a position to face the challenge of the powerless. (cf. p. 267) The litigant's chance is therefore to come 'unannounced in the middle of the night', like a thief. 'Every lock', a hassidic story tells us, 'has its own key . . . but there are strong thieves who know how to open without keys: they break the lock.'[8] This exactly describes K.'s intention. Were he to succeed in confronting the powers that be, in presenting them with his message, they might dissolve before his eyes and *ten* words, as K. indicates in the memorandum he entrusts to Barnabas, would suffice to usher in a new law.

Parallel with such possibilities, however, a final and perplexing irony is being developed: K. is not in a fit state to seize the opportunity when at last it offers itself. Even in the first chapter we read that K. feels, 'at the wrong time', 'really tired', 'the consequences of his exertion making themselves felt.' (p. 17) Furthermore he is well aware of the pressure of a discouraging environment, of his growing resignation to disappointment 'the pressure of the imperceptible influences of every moment.' (p. 30) The difficulties facing K. are in fact a paradigm of those encountered in the process of Jewish assimilation. And it is unlikely that K. will succeed in resisting its insidious influence—so much so that we may speculate whether the ruling power was not in a position to anticipate his final capitulation all along. Weariness and adaptation, the traditional sins of exile, infringe upon K.'s determination and, at the decisive moment, outweigh his willpower and banish the threat he represents to the system. The image of K. overcome by the temptations of sleep in Bürgel's room illustrates this turn of events; it is a preliminary sketch for the novel's conclusion when K. is visited by the mysteriously old-fashioned figure of the landlady, an allegory of death.[9] Kafka's imagination quite explicitly conceived of this sombre female as the reppresentation of powerlessness. One of Kafka's notebooks contains the following passage:

> Yesterday I was visited by a swoon. She lives in the house next door. I have quite often seen her disappearing in through the low gate-way, bent down, in the evenings. A tall lady in a long flowing dress and a broad-rimmed hat with feathers on it. Very hastily, with rustling skirt, she came through my door, like a doctor who is afraid he has come too late to a patient whose life is flickering out.[10]

Just as K. submits to a sudden attack of fatigue, so too the narrator of this passage is the victim of a strange kind of *Ohnmacht* (swoon) which prefigures an imminent death. Messianism has only a short step left to take. And yet one is surprised by the daring, extravagant and uninhibited confession

51

in which Bürgel discloses the crucial secret. It is almost as if power desired its own annihilation, as if power too stood in need of redemption.

That messianism is doomed to miss the fulfilment of its hopes by a hair's breadth appears to be the mark of its calamitous origin. If K. embodies messianism then the family of Barnabas represents the state of exile, the *Galut* which prompted the revival of messianic hope and zeal. It is hardly necessary to recall the deprivations this ostracized family has to endure; nor do we have to quote here the numerous instances where Kafka, exposing the irrationality of the whole business, provides us with some of the most profound literary marginalia on the psychology of anti-semitism. The fate of the Barnabas family is a synoptic sociology of the Jewish people. In its most radical consequences their subsidiary drama demonstrates the attempt of an oppressed minority to rationalize their situation by trying to see themselves from the point of view of their oppressors, i.e., in the language of the Castle. Thus the charges levelled against them are internalized and become part of the minority's own view of themselves.

K. recognizes, at least subliminally, his own predicament in the Barnabas family and its twofold disaster. It is as if this recognition preoccupies his subconscious, as if he only just fails to articulate it. Right at the outset he believes that the Barnabas family will have to accept him without reservations, and we further read: 'He had no feeling of shame where they were concerned.' (p. 37) A secret unexposed identification characterizes their relationship and seems to be the cause of their mutual attraction and of the intimate rapport K. and Olga enjoy in their extended conversations. This correspondence strikes one as simple and yet complex, for one can see in K. the representation of a dream, 'the dream', in Jakob Wassermann's words, 'of a secret emperor which exiles sometimes nurture out of a perverse love of their own misfortune.'[11]

Wassermann's phrase intimates the emergence of hope out of despair, a process which we see embodied in the Barnabas family's attitude towards K. And as K. begins to realize the secret of his own origin in the despairing hopes of this family, it dawns on him that what impedes his progress is a constitutional, inbred weakness. The origins of messianism in despair are the inherent cause of its unavoidable failure and incongruity. 'The Messiah', one of Kafka's notebooks relates, 'will come only when he is no longer needed, he will come only one day after his arrival, he will not come on the last day, but on the last day of all.' Philosophically this well-nigh absurd answer implies that the questions messianism raises will always turn back on themselves; historically it means that each messianic figure actually implicated in the scenario of human affairs—be it Bar Kochba, Sabbatai Zwi or Jakob Frank—necessarily bears the stigma of an imposter. Small wonder therefore if K.'s messianic identity seems—as Richard Sheppard has recently pointed out[12]—fictive and merely assumed. This would be the decisive argument against the spirit of messianism in general and against Kafka's novel in particular, were it not for the fact that the fundamental weaknesses have in both cases been consciously acknowledged and weighed in the balance. These weaknesses are deemed to be the irrefutable proof of a truth otherwise stifled and obscured by an oppressive reality. Seen in this light even the false messiah with all his failures acquires the positive function which Buber describes in one of his hassidic tales:

When God saw that the soul of Israel was sick he clothed it in the searing shroud of exile in order that it might endure. He laid the sleep of numbness upon it. Lest this sleep should destroy it, he wakens it at times with false hopes of the messiah and lulls it back to sleep till the night is over and the true Messiah appears.[13]

Conceivably the true messiah mentioned towards the end of this passage will also turn out to be a charlatan. But this is beside the point. What is important in messianic thought is solely the viability of what Ernst Bloch called *das Prinzip Hoffnung*, 'the Hope Principle', a principle which to Franz Rosenzweig appeared to be *der Stern der Erlösung*, 'the Star of Salvation'.

A further purposeful element in Kafka's delineation of messianism seems to be the peculiar intensity that governs K.'s relationship with Amalia and Barnabas. As has variously been mooted, Amalia's presence provides the only positive counterpart to the land-surveyor K. We are told of her pride, of her craving for solitude and her strange elevated manner. Kafka was painstakingly explicit in describing Amalia's attitude and yet its significance remains uncertain. We know that Amalia undermines K.'s confidence and determination; one of the rejected passages goes so far as to call her 'an evil obstacle'. If K. fails to win her over he will remain 'in the dark', trying to build a house without foundations. It is difficult to ascertain precisely what these hints suggest, but it seems feasible to argue that Amalia stands for the decisive obstacle which messianism has to overcome in trying to fulfil its own yearning. One is almost tempted to say that Amalia embodies the static counterpart of the dynamic principle represented in K. Kafka discussed a similar relationship in a note of 18 January 1922 dealing with the alternatives of courage and fearlessness: 'Fear means unhappiness but it does not follow from this that courage means happiness; . . . not courage then, but fearlessness with its calm, open eye and stoical resolution.'[14] These sentences have their bearing on Amalia and K. as well as on a conflict which has always played an important role in determining Jewish self-esteem. Ultimately they imply the question of whether a hostile reality ought to be opposed actively or passively. Amalia's attitude is passive, the attitude of traditional Jewish exclusiveness.

To begin with, Amalia may have been horrified at the expression of sexual greed in Sortini's persistent gaze, she may have recognized the ratified power of men over women and perhaps too the violent and base determination with which those in power approach their victims. In turning away from all this, Amalia becomes the object of persecution and it is through this transformation that she gains an insight into the pitiless fate of those who do not belong to the community. Her happiness can only be ephemeral, that of a temporary respite, but it is also untinged by any compromise with power. In a slim book published in Paris in 1947 under the title *Kafka ou le mystère juif*, André Nemeth summed up this kind of experience in a brief formula. 'Persécutés, ils se savent déjà élus. Voilà le paradoxe de leur condition.' (p. 20)

The destiny of the outsider, mediated by the idea of vocation, takes on the quality of exclusiveness, a kind of self-assertion that can be traced back to the books of the prophets and to Isaiah in particular. Combined with the historical reality of exile this makes for an image of Judaism of which Amalia, an outcast of high estate, is a reflection. In an essay entitled *Galut* which appeared in Berlin as late as 1936, Jizchak Fritz Baer outlined the traditional meaning of life in the diaspora. 'The unobtrusive influence of the Jewish can be likened to the mystery of the seed-grain which must seemingly disintegrate and perish in order to assimilate and translate the surrounding matter.' (p. 26) It almost seems too much of a coincidence that Kafka, according to Gustav Janouch, should have considered this problem in almost identical terms:

> The Jewish people is scattered, as a seed is scattered. As a seed of corn absorbs matter from its surroundings, stores it up, and achieves further growth, so the destiny of the Jews is to absorb the potentialities of mankind, purify them, and give them a higher development. Moses is still a reality. As Abiram and Dathan opposed Moses with the words '*Lo naale!* We will not go up!' so the world opposes him with the cry of anti-semitism.[15]

It is of little importance whether Kafka actually spoke sentences to this effect or whether they are merely—as the sceptical would surely maintain—Janouch's invention; what matters is rather that in Amalia we possess the image of a traditional moralistic attitude which vindicates and justifies a whole way of life, a way of life so completely opposed to the idea of political dominion that it failed to create an earthly domicile for itself.

Compared with Amalia's moral determination, with her almost tragic composure, K.'s political restlessness seems a token of the pathological origin of messianism. Where exile can no longer be endured, messianism emerges as the vision of its annihilation. Not prepared to acknowledge the positive function of the *Galut*, messianism sees in it but a grievous stage preceding redemption. Whereas Amalia in a situation of utter despair still exemplifies human dignity and offers the guilty community around her a chance to come to know the idea of justice, K. for his part intends to break out of this confinement by transcending her merely static confrontation with the powers that be. Pressing for a solution, the messianic figure is the agent of the unceasing endeavour of man to revolutionize his situation.

One of the most carefully planned features in Kafka's novel is the way K. comes face to face, in the Barnabas family, not only with his origin and a critical alternative to his own pursuits but also with the image of his futile exertions. The passages which describe K.'s encounters with Barnabas all but reveal the closely guarded emotions of the author, for the simple reason perhaps that in Barnabas K. recognizes a brother who—like himself—attempts to instigate a new departure in a case that for too long has remained unresolved. K., of course, is not aware of this when he first meets Barnabas. But Kafka with unparalleled artistic discretion induces in us the gradual realization that Barnabas appears to K. as an epiphany, as the longed-for companion of one who feels himself to be on his own. The aura surrounding Barnabas is that of an angel, epitomized in his smile whose radiance cannot be dimmed; this impression is reinforced in his answer to K.'s enquiry: ' "Who are you"—"My name is Barnabas. I am a messenger." ' The illusion in which K. is here allowed to place his trust for a brief moment encourages the hope that there may be a connection between the sordid real world and his better vision. It is in the proximity of such hopeful radiance that theology is inclined to dwell as a foil to the 'ausdrucksbildende Kraft der Finsternis'[16] ('expressive power of darkness') which Martin Walser noticed in Kafka's works.

K.'s intention parallels that of theology: the dispersing of darkness. It is therefore quite consistent that he should entertain precise, if inarticulate notions concerning the messengers of light. I have in mind here the strange passage where K. tutors that poor girl Pepi. The position in the taproom, he tells her, 'is a job like any other, but for you it is heaven, consequently you set about everything . . . with exaggerated eagerness, trick yourself out as in your opinion the angels are tricked out—but in reality they are different.' (p. 291) This negative piece of information about the angels makes us wonder if they might not be figures like Barnabas, creating a feeling of humaneness in a hostile environment. In any case, there is here no definite indication, merely a mirage of supernatural forces. Kafka's image of the angel has nothing to do with metaphysics and pertains rather—not unlike the teaching of Plato, Philo or Aquinas—to the ontological realm. It is therefore of great visual consequence that the hopeful manifestation at the beginning of the novel dissolves as Barnabas strips off his messenger's garb. This does not, however, impair the validity of his first appearance representing man as an incomplete angel; an idea which Paul Klee once described in sentences that could well have been Kafka's own. 'This creature', Klee wrote in January 1905, 'born in contrast to divine beings with only one wing, makes ceaseless attempts to fly. Thereby his limbs are broken and yet he remains true to his idea.'[17] Klee's figure *Der Held mit dem Flügel*, the Winged Hero, embodies, in his ruinous state, precisely the distinction between vision and reality which Kafka's novel critically implies by making K. and Barnabas dependent upon one another. The rest is resignation to a pointless striving which neither of them can abandon because they are identical with it. Beckett's *Molloy* contains a similar constellation of 'agent' and 'messenger', of the narrator of the story and a certain Gaber whose memory is as rudimentary as that of Barnabas is phenomenal. The analogy, significant in many respects, cannot be pursued further here. Let me end therefore with a quotation in which the agent, the figure corresponding to K., ponders with characteristic scepticism the fate he shares with the messenger:

That we thought of ourselves as members of a vast organisation was doubtless also due to the all too human feeling that trouble shared, or is it sorrow, is trouble something, I forget the word. But to me at least, who knew how to listen to the falsetto of reason, it was obvious that we were perhaps alone in what we did. Yes, in my moments of lucidity I thought it possible. And, to keep nothing from you, this lucidity was so acute at times that I came even to doubt the existence of Gaber himself. And if I had not hastily sunk back into my darkness I might have gone to the extreme of conjuring away the chief too and regarding myself as solely responsible for my wretched existence. For I knew I was wretched, at six pounds ten a week plus bonuses and expenses. And having made away with Gaber and the chief (one Youdi), could I have denied myself the pleasure of—you know. But I was not made for the great light that devours, a dim lamp was all I had been given, and patience without end, to shine it on the empty shadows.[18]

# Anthony Thorlby

## Anti-Mimesis: Kafka and Wittgenstein

The more years one spends reading Kafka, the more one begins to suspect that Kafka himself foresaw what one's reading would be like, and described the whole process—describing it, of course, more wittily, beautifully, movingly (and very much more succinctly) than any critical reader can ever hope to—in his parable 'Before the Law'. Permission to enter is never granted, yet we do not go away; if we see a radiance shining out from within the text, then we can be fairly sure we are approaching the end—our end. Yet we have not been deceived, for the door our reading opened on the text was indeed a door, and intended just for us. Or as Kafka wrote with reference to the meaning of another story: 'If it didn't express some inner truth (which can never be universally established, but has to be accepted or denied every time by each reader or listener in turn), it would be nothing.'

If one happens also to be a teacher, one may consider oneself to be in the position less of the man from the country than of Josef K. who hears the parable, and can argue about its meaning. But their situations are ultimately the same, except that Josef K.'s may be worse, because he is deceived into thinking he can understand how the man from the country has been deceived. And our dilemma too is similar, but worse if we think we understand Josef K.'s situation. The more intelligently we think about the situation, the less we experience its essential reality. Criticism becomes a way of missing the point. This proposition is sometimes made of all critical approaches to literature, but it is true with regard to Kafka in a quite radical sense. For the point that is missed is a matter not just of aesthetic appreciation, but of metaphysical realization.

In general, critics explain texts in terms they derive from

some aspect of the world: the life of the author, perhaps, or his social environment, or the intellectual and spiritual tradition to which he belongs, or the artistic conventions he uses. The presumption is that if these terms make sense, then the text makes sense. The sense in the text may be richer, more concentrated than any instance of it we can point to in the world; but it is assumed nevertheless to derive from the world by a process of imitation. And it can therefore be referred back to the world; otherwise we should not recognize it as sense. The sense of Kafka's stories does not, however, depend primarily on any other reality than their own.

Now it is not, in fact, very difficult to refer Kafka's texts to the world; Kafka criticism has offered various possible ways of reading them. But even after we have read a story in this or that way, even after inventing a new reading (and perhaps— *miserere nobis*—teaching it), we are likely to be left with a distinct feeling that there is something still there which we have by no means accounted for. This feeling is, I believe, different from the wonder we feel at the ultimately always unaccountable quality of beauty in great writing—in a passage from Shakespeare, for example. The basis of this difference can be described, at least, by saying that Shakespeare's poetry assumes a realistic (or conventionally recognizable) context in the world, whereas Kafka's prose quite explicitly does not. The wonder aroused in us by Shakespeare feels like a wonderment at life, whereas Kafka engenders a wonderment—if even that is the right word—which is not recognizably *at* anything other than what we are reading. We may admittedly be able to visualize what is going on and understand what is being said, but we are constantly reminded by Kafka that the context is mysterious beyond all comprehension, and quite inconceivable as an imitation of life. When ordinary things and thoughts are introduced into this strange medium Kafka gives them almost no conventional literary colouring, in the form of metaphor or characterization or other artistic device. Kafka's imagination does not set out to mirror, mingle with, and embellish the world. Anything it has ever taken over from reality it has appropriated entirely; only relics of the real are preserved, as bare and ghastly as bones, in the no-man's land of his inward vision. We can, if we like, try to think what they might represent, or have represented, in life; but to do so is to overlook the state in which we find them.

Kafka criticism has consequently been pulled in two opposite directions, and I believe most readers of Kafka must feel this two-way tug within themselves. Sooner or later comes the urge to regard Kafka's writing as symbolic, and to explain it by reference to something in the world: Kafka's father, Kafka's tuberculosis, Kafka's Jewishness, or more generally: bureaucracy, fascism, cultural pessimism, spiritual alienation, and the like. In my own experience, most students immediately look for some such explanation, and are satisfied only when they find one they consider profound. Occasionally, however, a student will argue that he is being made to contrive a meaning for Kafka's fiction because of the expectations and pressures of the educational system, and that what Kafka's text offers him is a kind of liberation from these expectations and pressures which there appear as manifestly inappropriate and unnecessary. This brings me to consider what other kind of reading and understanding—to avoid the question-begging word 'criticism'—is available to us.

There is, of course, a great deal of non-symbolic literature in existence, beginning with fairy stories and myths and ending with the most commonplace fiction. The latter often seems not to need any interpretation, simply because it looks like an account of events that either did, or easily could, happen. As regards what could happen, the imagination is quite credulous. It almost never hears about events it is familiar with from its own backyard, and seems even to prefer experiences it has never actually had in life. Whenever we read a book we stretch our mind to encompass aspects of the world we did not know before, and our accommodating attitude has merely to go a bit further when we hear about Hercules, harpies and hobbits, centaurs and Winnie-the-Pooh. It is probable that myths were originally conceived and received in this unquestioning fashion; and then that later, more sophisticated minds sought for a meaning, wanting to interpret myths as allegories. Interpretation, at first unnecessary, begins at the point where a story is felt to mean something other than what it says. The story as it is first said, the story in itself—that is, a number of events arranged in sequence—already does mean something to the imagination.

We do not puzzle over the relationship of such stories to the real world, even though they contain much we have never seen, simply because we accept them as a sort of reality in their own right. The reference to reality is not a critical problem because at this level all stories are equally real; meaning is identical with the tale.

Kafka's fiction can doubtless partly be read at this level, but not entirely so, for the simple reason that the question of meaning is itself raised in so many of his stories. His dog, ape, hunger-artist, penal officer, not to speak of K., are all trying to understand and explain their own stories. Kafka's fiction draws attention to the critical point of separation between story and meaning. He both treats his tale as entirely self-evident (no matter how implausible it is), and yet dwells on the meaning of what is happening—but in such a way as never adequately to explain it; indeed, the explanations become as mysterious as the events. Many readers have been struck by the fact that in the novels K. at least seems to keep his head above water and to differ, like a hero, from the other characters by virtue of his struggle; he does not accept inadequate explanations of the incomprehensible. But sooner or later every reader surely finds that the same kind of division does after all open up between himself and K., who does not grasp the incomprehensibility of his situation as fully as the reader does. This need not lead us to the conclusion that the whole text is simply engulfed in an unrelieved night of senselessness. On the contrary, the reader of Kafka is in an unusually good position to understand the character of meaning, through all its shades, from the clear solidarity of a physical event, down through all the darkening shades of reflection upon it.

Kafka himself, then, has set up a tension in his writing between what is enacted in his stories and what they mean. Shades of meaning are perceptible in relationship to one another and in relationship to the almost pedantic clarity of the narrative. No matter that they shade off finally into impenetrable darkness; darkness is as good a foil as light for the purpose of throwing into relief the experience of understanding. In fact, it may be seen to be a better foil than light, once we assume that Kafka's purpose could have been to illumine the character of meaning rather than to illumine the character of the world.

Conventional literature generally illumines the world, by narrating something that simulates real situations and people. Even fantastic tales represent a possible shape that real-life experience could take. Then, as soon as anyone begins to ponder the fact that real experience is not as shapely as art, some interpretation naturally begins in an effort to bridge the gap between them. To say how art relates to life is the most natural way of saying what art means, and the relationship is assumed to be a positive one: each illumines the other; art's concentrated form and life's vast potential do correspond. The reason for not seeking this kind of correspondence in Kafka's case (apart from suspicion that no particular correspondence works well) is the possibility that it is the relationship itself, the problem of meaning and interpretation, that his work 'represents'. This is a problem that cannot be defined as lying on either side of the relationship, either in explicit, concentrated, or symbolic form in his text, or in recognizable, directly experienceable form in life. It lies precisely in the relationship, in the *use* of language; not in what words say, but in what they are. This problem is not what the novels, descriptively or even symbolically speaking, are 'about'; it rather *comes about*, comes into being, through the process of writing. As Kafka himself sensed and sometimes feared, the problem might not exist, were he not to write.

Kafka's writing, then, relates to itself in an unusually absolute sense. He sets up both terms of a correspondence, as it were, within his text, both a kind of 'world' and a kind of commentary on that world—ranging from actual comments and explanations (usually inscrutable) to a peculiarly pedantic, studied style of statement that never lets us look at and believe in the narrated material alone, but always calls attention to the writing, the language. The terms relate to one another negatively, the correspondence between them is interrupted, the flow of illumination is halted. The connection—what we might expect to be the meaning—remains frozen. But for this very reason it becomes exceptionally visible, in a way that does not happen where meaning passes smoothly to and fro between words and things. In this, the conventional, case we do not notice what meaning itself is, as distinct from meaning em-

ANTHONY THORLBY

bodied in words (as beauty) and meaning embodied in things (as truth).

Possibly it is a delusion to suppose that meaning can be disembodied at all and held up for inspection as a problem in itself. Kafka is far from alone, however, in taking up the problem of meaning—the meaning of meaning—in so radical a manner. A glance at some other, well known instances of this problem may help to clarify what he was doing, even though Kafka's way of treating the problem strikes me as unique (I am not arguing for any influences or parallels in what follows). Meanwhile, the much more difficult question of why Kafka's fiction, if it is as entirely self-relating as I have suggested, should *nevertheless* be so suggestive of symbolic meanings, may be left for consideration at the end. I admit that, far from appearing to be about nothing in the world, it has struck innumerable critics and readers as being about practically every aspect of it they could possibly name. But at this stage I wish to keep these lines of interpretation, of meaningful connection with the processes of living (as distinct from the process of writing), as much suspended, broken off, frozen as is Kafka's actual text. Had Kafka wished for any one symbolic interpretation of his work in the normal sense, he would surely have provided some more obvious point of reference to reality. As it is, his texts remain curiously inviolable, as uncompromisingly withdrawn from real life as Kafka felt himself to be in his nocturnal hours of writing. What he could then see, undistracted by any thought of actual circumstances in the world, was an image of the literary imagination itself, of language suspended in a void, the meaning itself of all other localized, particularized, connective meanings.

We are confronted here, I believe, by a logical problem of unusual interest and importance, not only because Kafka's writing constitutes a formulation of it, but also because it has exercised the minds of the greatest contemporary thinkers; expressed in different ways we find it in the work of Russell and Wittgenstein, of Sartre and of Popper. If Kafka ever thought about the problem abstractly at all, it could possibly have been as a result of his knowledge of Kierkegaard and perhaps also of Nietzsche. As an abstract idea, however, the problem tends to lose its interest and even to become a rather banal cliché. The cliché version is perhaps worth stating, if

64

only for convenience; it runs like this: the structure of language does not correspond to the structure of reality. Critics and teachers may be forgiven for resorting to this kind of convenient formulation of the problem, which doubtless lies at the bottom of many complexities and absurdities in modern literature and philosophy. But, alas, the formula gets noted down; instead of being a crude description of a question, it becomes a falsely defined answer, an interpretation, an eagerly accepted 'meaning'. The whole point of the problem must be that it engulfs all efforts at writing; it must apply to itself; it raises Russell's celebrated paradox that if the statement is true it must be false.* In the context of Kafka criticism this paradox might possibly explain how all interpretations can ultimately be false even though they may also be true. To draw this parallel suggests, of course, that we are thinking of Kafka's text as in some sense a 'structure of reality' (to which the structure of the critics' language does not correspond). But before any critic could discover this paradox, Kafka must surely have discovered it in his own use of language. And, as I have been arguing, he could have remained true to the paradox only if he showed that it lies already in the structure itself of language. Thus, there is no conceivable 'structure of reality' in or behind his texts that can be thought of separately from the structure of their utterance. If we think that Kafka saw the paradox as one that language can point to in the world, as though its mysterious structure lay there (for critics to

---

* If any general proposition regarding the falsity of language is an instance of itself, it is clearly self-refuting at once. If it is not an instance of itself, then it falls victim to Russell's heterological paradox at a later stage. We place the proposition in the class of propositions that are not instances of themselves. And we then ask: Is the class of propositions that are not instances of themselves an instance of itself? We then get Russell's famous absurdity: if it is it isn't, and if it isn't it is; i.e., (i) The class x (of propositions that are not instances of themselves) is an instance of the class x, means that x is an instance of what it is not an instance of. Or conversely, (ii) the class x is not an instance of x means that x is not an instance of what it is an instance of.

Russell, of course, did not leave the problem there. The reason for describing it here is to show what kind of complexities it contains. Russell's further work on different orders of statement (as distinct from mere classes) might be compared with Kafka's use of narratives within narrative and his play with such questions as what is true of K.'s case and what is not.

unearth) and language merely recorded the mystery, we imply that Kafka was himself deceived by the paradox, that he was its victim rather than its master. Whereas the burden of so much of his remarkable self-understanding regarding his life as writer is that he was at once master and victim of an utterly ambiguous instrument.

The only reason for introducing logical considerations of this kind into a discussion of Kafka's manner of writing is to illustrate just how complicated any 'answers' become once we question the relationship of language to the world. Kafka certainly grasped, in imaginative terms that have the subtlety of logic and much else besides, the depth and difficulty of the problem posed by language, writing, and literature. He is never in any danger of becoming imaginatively simple-minded in the manner, say, of Sartre who wrote—and we should stress this verb: he *wrote*—an altogether conventional, realistic novel about the total breakdown of a man's confidence in language. Into the bargain, the novel is supposedly written by the man whose confidence in words, and consequently in all social and moral conventions that depend on words, has collapsed. This led Sartre to imply a conclusion that only partly makes sense: namely, that writing a novel somehow escapes the dilemma that language cannot represent reality. When Sartre wrote his autobiography twenty-five years later he commented wittily on the fraudulent aspect of *La nausée,* and he exposed its self-deception by admitting that he had pretended he was reporting objectively on himself, when he was in fact play-acting and enjoying his own performance as well—the performance, that is, of desperate existential anxiety about words. Of course, we may not entirely believe his autobiography either, which is called *Words* and pretends to be an objective report on how Sartre came to lend such exaggerated importance to the problem of language. We fortunately do not have to become entangled here in Sartre's efforts to extricate himself from the first great, perhaps the only great, fascination of his intellectual life, which he has continuously felt he should use in the service of his social conscience (or else reject). Suffice it to say that Sartre has continued to hold a realist view of language, and aimed to expose, with realistic examples on stage or in real terms taken from history, incorrect interpretations of the world.

He presupposes the possibility of a correct interpretation when he denounces all the others, and he turned to dialectical materialism to guide him towards that goal of correctness.

Is it possible, however, to conceive of a language for the correct use of which we do not depend on the world to supply the true and necessary conditions? That was the question we raised with regard to Kafka, and neither Russell's dismissive paradoxes, nor Sartre's Hegelian rationalism will bring us much nearer to an answer. The philosopher who has proposed a radically different conception of language in our time—and at least proximately in Kafka's cultural ambiance—is Wittgenstein. He began by advancing a scientific philosophy based upon a realist view of language, but in his later work he abandoned and often severely criticized it. The event that appears to have changed his outlook so profoundly was a lecture he attended (ironically, with great reluctance) by L. E. J. Brouwer in Vienna on the 'language' of mathematics. Brouwer argued that mathematics, science, and more generally language, should be understood as human activities; they tell us not about the world, but about the way man lives as a conscious being in the world. Recent scholarship has shown that Brouwer was influenced in his thinking by Schopenhauer, though Wittgenstein is hardly likely to have cared about this, and such distant philosophical ancestry is scarcely perceptible in any of his own work. But the fact is worth mentioning for two reasons. First, Schopenhauer's metaphysics could be adduced as a kind of theoretical explanation of Kafka's work without much stretching on either side—though I certainly do not want to suggest that Kafka is in fact writing about the world as will and idea. Secondly, there is a flicker of something like 'family resemblance' in the tone and style in which both Kafka and Wittgenstein report hypothetical cases, clarify instances, reflect upon small and apparently insignificant details, define the seemingly obvious with pedantic exactitude. Even less do I wish to suggest here that Kafka anticipated Wittgenstein's philosophical investigations. Kafka is quite obviously not 'doing philosophy' in Wittgenstein's sense; the immediate effect of his writing is not at all to remove our puzzlement at spurious problems—if anything Kafka strikes us as a *mystificateur* who invests ordinary language with an air

67

of inscrutable mystery. The reassuring outcome that Wittgenstein hoped for if we would simply look and see what the grammar of human speech was trying to tell us, is manifestly lacking in Kafka's use of language. Despite these differences, however, Wittgenstein's focus of attention upon the phenomenon of language, in the belief that it contains the clue to everything we think, understand, and attempt in the world, allows one to wonder whether the focus of Kafka's attention may not have been the same. Kafka's way of writing fiction, we might say, stands in about the same relation to conventional fiction as Wittgenstein's way of doing philosophy stands to most earlier philosophical systems.

If we assume that Kafka's writing is primarily about writing, then we shall at least have solved our paradox: namely, how his work can appear at one and the same time to bear some profound relationship to reality and yet never to gain anything like a sufficient or necessary meaning from interpretation in terms of one set of referents. Moreover, this is precisely the character of language in Wittgenstein's analysis of it, and philosophical problems (he believed) arise from our confusing different possible uses of words and syntactical conventions. Would this not also be a good description of how critical problems have arisen as regards *the* meaning of Kafka's text? Let us at least expand this hypothesis a little to see what it looks like. I am suggesting that Kafka's writing is mimetic in a quite special sense that forces us to think just what we usually mean when we say that art is mimesis.

We tend to mean, I suppose, that the work of art looks like life, either superficially or symbolically. What we overlook in that case is that some*thing* is there—something is being done or made—to which this lifelike appearance is given. To concentrate on the picture or mirror quality of art as the only (or even primary) source of its significance, so that we expect art to be a spiritual map of the world, is to be insensitive to the most obvious aspect of any experience of any art: namely, that it is *not* like any other experience in life at all. With pleasurable exaltation we watch the most terrible deeds taking place upon the stage, largely because we know that they are not really taking place. The thing itself, there before us as we watch, is not the real thing; it is an altogether different kind of activity, which has been made to resemble life, and not resemble it very closely at that.

If we follow this hypothesis, then, we see that the mimetic aspect of a work of art is superficial, like décor or make-up. It may be realistic, or it may be symbolic (as when masks are worn in the theatre and actors speak in poetic form); in either event, the acceptance of these signs as signifying life is based upon a convention. As with most conventions to which we become accustomed, this one gets overlooked too easily; we do not distinguish between the thing itself and its appearance, indeed we forget how inconceivable the thing itself (or literature) is, because we have grown so used to conceiving of it as identical with its lifelike appearance. The same problem arises, of course, with the thing that language is, which is where this problem really starts. Our mind responds so quickly to what language says, that we mistake its life-denoting message for its substance. Since we think by means of language, we have no place outside language where we can think about what language is, independently of what it says. It may, however, be possible to imagine such a place, and to invent a technique for nullifying the illusion that language actually grasps the world and that the world is truly represented in language. From such a place language would appear to be no more than one human activity among others, a phenomenon arising concomitantly with the process of human consciousness. And from this standpoint, the question of the truth of language (or of art) no longer arises. Language superficially and conventionally *applies* to the world, but the thing itself cannot be said to correspond to anything or constitute anything that could meaningfully be called truth. (It makes no sense to ask whether a piece of carpentry or a game of chess is true.) Kafka, it seems to me, was able to imagine such a standpoint; in a famous aphorism he called it the 'Archimedean point' and observed that he could only imagine it if he turned it against himself. In a rather similar way Wittgenstein also proposed a new way of doing philosophy by 'looking and seeing', as it were from the outside, at what language already says; and this new technique he certainly turned against his own earlier work.

It may be that men have always looked, or tried to look, beyond the purely mimetic aspect of art, ever since Plato first introduced the term mimesis—to describe (we may recall) an aspect of art which he wished to disparage. To the extent that art merely resembled life, it was for him at a still further remove from truth than the reality it portrayed. Plato, and Aristotle after him, knew perfectly well that something quite distinct from mere imitation took place in poetic and dramatic literature. Plato saw this other thing in the emotions of the poet, his divine frenzy of inspiration; Aristotle saw it in the emotions of the audience, their catharsis through pity and fear. Neither of them, however, says much about this other aspect of art, which must exist as indubitably as the other side of the moon, but which it may be impossible to see independently of the face that shines towards us. Impossible, that is, unless we were to learn to see through the bodily, imitated surface of art and become aware of the otherwise invisible substance of the thing itself.

If this expression is not very clear, let me turn again to the example of Wittgenstein when he decided to treat the phenomenon of language itself, in the forms in which it actually exists and is practised, as the subject of his philosophy. Instead of endeavouring to found language on some logical basis and to define what could then truthfully be said with it (which chiefly meant defining what could not be said), Wittgenstein's eyes were suddenly opened to the great body of actual usage; he saw words not as corresponding to the world but as part of actual situations. Language is manifestly not confined to the limited uses of logic; instead of seeing merely how far language permits of logical thinking, why not look at the immense wealth of thinking already taking place within language as it is ordinarily used?

Now, the result of coming to know the linguistic process in this way was not to reinstate philosophy, but rather the reverse. Wittgenstein simply found that in ordinary usage the meanings of words fluctuate, whereas all philosophy consists in the attempt to fix their meaning. What philosophy can establish, by comparison with its own standards of fixity and relationship, is the fact and extent of fluctuation in language. It can also arrive at some conception of the rules that conventionally govern this fluctuating usage, though it cannot justify or explain these conventions themselves; it can merely describe them. The point of connection here with Kafka's work is evident enough. He also strove to describe what cannot ultimately be either explained or justified. He shared with Wittgenstein the belief in some kind of ultimate liberation if only language could be made entirely perspicuous to itself; for both of them, entanglement with language was the disease which language had to cure. 'Doing philosophy' in Wittgenstein's sense was supposed to show that philosophical problems are false problems; he repeatedly speaks of the unease, the discomfort, the bruises the mind inflicts upon itself by its failure to understand what language is.

Opinions differ as to the state of mind that Wittgenstein hoped to achieve by turning philosophy into a self-defeating game; was it to be sanity and serenity at last after the exhilarating accomplishment of putting an end to all philosophy's false pretensions? Opinions similarly differ about the degree of anguish communicated by Kafka's stories, particularly those he published himself; for in them, but also in much of the unpublished and unfinished writing, the style is so beautifully poised upon the edge of humour, so continuously sustained by wit and intelligence, that a solemn interpretation of the story as a symbolic picture of man's spiritual tragedy seems quite out of place. It is as if one were falling back into an error that Kafka's writing had overcome—'thinking that the facts *must* conform to certain pictures embedded in our language', to quote a saying of Wittgenstein's.

The hypothesis I am advancing—namely, that Kafka's primary interest was in language and in language in the form of writing—must lead us to put on one side thoughts about the symbolic representativeness of his works: that is, their much remarked significance as spiritual mirrors of the age. (I am arguing still that we should put these thoughts on one side, not dismiss them entirely; I hope to conclude by showing how we may after all return to them.) Hypothetically, we should be prepared to see whatever dilemmas and paradoxes confront us in Kafka's writing, as dilemmas and paradoxes arising out of this contorted activity of trying, through writing, to lay hands on the process and procedures of writing itself. It follows, then, that the mimetic aspect of language is of merely secondary importance for Kafka, and it is therefore misleading to push

71

ANTHONY THORLBY

into the foreground meanings in terms of the world, even if these are symbolic ones. Kafka's interest in the medium of his art, rather than in its conventional objects or themes, should startle us no more than a similar tendency observable among many modern artists; painters, musicians, and poets, besides novelists, have become self-consciously preoccupied with the medium itself of their arts. If Kafka does nevertheless startle us, this is chiefly because he followed this tendency more rigorously than they and perhaps understood more profoundly where it led. It can be argued that the tendency itself 'represents' alienation of some kind; and this distraction of interest from what man should be interested in, or his obsession with what he should not, can then be described in Marxist, or psychological, or humanist, or religious terms. One glance at a page of Kafka is enough to remind us, however, that it certainly does not 'represent' any such thing.

The next step to be taken in following our hypothesis is a difficult one. We must beware of saying, for instance, that what Kafka's stories *do* represent is the experience of writing. To say this is merely to add one more symbolic reading to the already long list of interpretations which (as I have just argued) distract attention from the unique reality of the actual text. As I have in the past myself made some misleading suggestions along these lines, may I say, in self defence and warning, just how tempting this kind of interpretation is. Once you begin to read Kafka's stories as symbolic descriptions of himself sitting alone in his room at night, exploring the deep divisions within himself, between his daytime world and his inner life, between his mind and his body, between what he writes and what he is, between what he wants and what he can achieve—the dialectical possibilities are endless—then everything he ever wrote seems to refer to this situation alone. Who can, in fact, read the story of the animal who has withdrawn from life to its burrow, built so painstakingly out of a need for security, only to find all its defences useless against the approach of the last enemy, without being overwhelmed by the pathos of this patently autobiographical allegory? And similarly, when we read of the trapeze artist who succeeds in living permanently up on his trapeze (only, one day, to realize he wants a second trapeze); or of the feminine little body who is attracted to the narrator out of pure malevolence, inescapable as love that is not reciprocated; or of the hunger-artist, whose art nobody now understands, and whose renunciation of food turns into a conviction that the world contains no food that he would ever have wanted . . . What else *can* these stories be about than Kafka and his art? This kind of reading enables one to assign quite specific meanings to details in the stories: the horses from the unnoticed pigsty of the country doctor must surely be substitute Pegasus figures; father and fiancée figures spring up all over the place—and they are precisely psychological rather than real figures, who inhabit the fantasy world of Kafka's mind rather than the real world. Words, too, take on double meanings as they pass from one world of meaning to represent something quite different in another.

Despite the plausibility of this manner of interpreting Kafka, however, I still want to resist it. One reason for resistance is that it makes the great variety of Kafka's inventions all mean one thing. A more weighty reason for doing so is that it undoes the very process of disguise and transformation that Kafka has engaged in. According to our hypothesis, he wants to show us what the substance and reality of language actually is, while we want, as it were, to brush aside his examples to see what they say, and to insist that they must have a mimetic significance. What happens if we keep our nerve and acknowledge the obvious fact about Kafka's texts: namely, that they contain a totally mysterious, incomprehensible element—not just here and there, but in every sentence—and that Kafka has obviously immersed bits and pieces of his own limited experience in this weird element, in the hope presumably that the reader will not immediately recognize them and that no critic will foolishly retrieve them. If, to borrow a well-known image from his own writing, we could see at once that we were watching a tubercular artist going through an endlessly repetitive, pointless routine we should not want the performance to go on. So Kafka draws us into accepting as real a performance which we know can be nothing of the sort; he makes us accept a kind of world that is totally different from anything we have ever known in life. And where he is successful (which may chiefly be in places where criticism is least successful), he makes us aware of that equally strange reality, that is equally unlike anything we can ever know in actual life, which is what art *is* —as opposed (and it is totally opposed for Kafka) to what it says. For an art that uses the medium of words is bound still to say something, bound still to preserve something of the mimetic illusion of language. But the point of such imitation lies entirely in the act of imitating itself, rather than in any likeness or symbolic relationship to the real thing we may descry there. Kafka often seems to illustrate this important difference between the imitation and the real thing: in the simulated human behaviour of the ape who reports to the academy, for instance, or the simulated singing of Josephine, or the simulated deafness of Odysseus (he pretends he cannot hear what is in fact silence). I say that Kafka seems to illustrate the point I am making about his non-mimetic use of language, but of course I ought not to say this, or I fall into paradox. I cannot quietly say that Kafka's stories illustrate the dreadful problem that language *is* something altogether different from what it says, because if they do then they don't. It is a case of Russell's paradox again.

Let me turn, as I did before, to Wittgenstein in the hope of finding a conceptual path around this dilemma. Let us assume, consistently with everything we have so far said about his non-realist view of language, that Kafka is playing a kind of language-game. A language-game may be played by fixing, in some arbitrary way, the rules for the use of certain words. This rigidity then reveals the fluctuating behaviour of ordinary language by contrast. The words to which Kafka assigns special, fixed meanings are obvious enough: castle, trial, arrest, official, beetle, stoker, hunger-artist, and so on. The whole point of these words is that we should not be able to establish in any other way than that laid down, what these words mean—mean, that is, in the conventional sense of 'correspond' to in the world. If a critic comes along and tells us that really they stand for this or that, then he has wrecked the game (assuming we believe him). Now, the words that Kafka has fixed in this inscrutable way are the foundation stones of his story, though we may not at once realize this. Perhaps Kafka himself did not immediately realize what he was doing, to judge from *The Judgment*, the story in which he seems first to have discovered his own method. There the meaning of the words 'father' and 'friend', for instance, are gradually revealed in a totally impenetrable light (an impenetrably *bright* light, I should say, rather than the murky, shadowy kind of half-light in which psychoanalysis descries hidden relationships with the real). Georg Bendemann begins by addressing himself to both friend and father as though he understands what he is doing, namely, relating to the people we conventionally assume we reach and can deal with when we use these names. He turns out to be mistaken, however; he is not dealing with people whom it is possible to recognize or reach at all. They have a reality, they are something, that is not encompassed or influenced by any words he can use towards them or about them, or that he hears from them or about them. They represent what is known, in the language of mad militancy, as a non-negotiable position. There is therefore, as Kafka remarked in his diary, a solidarity between friend and father so powerful that it destroys Georg (just as the solidarity aspired to by the exponents of non-negotiable positions would—if they could achieve this non-human status —destroy us all. But I must resist the temptation to use Kafka's stories as parables: militancy was certainly not what he was writing about in *The Judgment*).

If, as I am suggesting, we are not intended even to under-stand the basic concepts on which Kafka founds his fiction, what, you may ask, is the point of it? The question is not unanswerable. We gain, in the first place, an extraordinarily vivid and lucid view of something we cannot ordinarily see: namely, the play of ordinary language, ordinary feeling, imagi-nation, and thought, around and about a basically incompre-hensible reality. (The temptation should be resisted to say: ah! that is just the situation we find ourselves in in life.) Though this reality cannot be further illumined, but only obscured, by telling ourselves what it stands for, we can nevertheless say something about what the experience of incomprehensible reality is 'like'—not by pointing to things extraneous to the novels and stories, but by pointing to their own essential substance. It is sudden, a little comic, a little more obscene, yet not without its solemnity and seriousness, inducing a whole range of emotions from ecstasy to tedium, stimulating the mind to unwonted exertions of protest, pleading and prevarication . . . and so on, and so on. But all, of course, in vain. Just this vanity, however, or what we called, despite this long string of nameable attributes, the incomprehensible reality of Kafka's writing, throws still more light on the vain efforts of language to grasp it. We may see few recognizable people or places in Kafka's fiction, but we definitely do see a mass of brilliantly rendered forms of speech and thought: factual observation, reasoned argument, moral judgment, psychological speculation, philosophical aphorism . . . and so on, and so on. But all, of course, in vain.

There is, we may tentatively conclude, a kind of negative agreement between the language and the reality of Kafka's fiction. Further, this negative basis of agreement is altogether unlike the positive correspondence between words and the world which a realist view of language (or a mimetic view of art) leads us to expect. As a result, Kafka avoids the paradox we have been warily treading round in our discussion of the modern philosophical dilemma. In Russell's jargon, Kafka's fictional vocabulary is homological, that is, it *is* an instance of the incomprehensibility it represents, and thereby escapes the nonsense of the heterological paradox. Put less technically, we may say that Kafka does enable us to see that words refer to nothing beyond themselves; they are entirely embedded in a reality which they themselves sustain and perpetrate. Or in Wittgenstein's terminology: language is seen to be entirely a function of the circumstances in which it is used and lived.

Coming back, then, to our discussion of the assumed mimetic character of art, which makes us overlook what art *is* because of what it appears to be saying about the world, we may say that Kafka has succeeded in making us see what we ordinarily cannot see. For (stated negatively now) what we ordinarily cannot see is that we cannot see something. And what we cannot see is that our language already is embedded in reality, is inseparable from that reality, may in fact be called the only intelligible reality we have, and consequently, does not correspond to anything. There is no mystery to be solved outside language (and thus, as I have said, there is no need to look for an interpretation outside Kafka's text); it already *is* a totally impenetrable mystery in itself. And this linguistic mystery, the mysterious one-ness of our world and of our language, which makes it impossible for language ever to get to know itself or the world as two beings might who were separate and could come to know one another, *this* Kafka has succeeded in representing. He can only represent it negatively, by annihilating the difference between them, and plunging both world and language into a common nothingness and vanity. We no longer have, as a result, any impression of a text (or experience in words, in the mind) that relates to a supposed reality that is different from words and outside the mind. The normal condition of life, in which what I think and feel is (as I know 'from' experience) at best a fleeting approximation to the truth, appears to be suspended. Kafka has looked beyond the familiar dualism to a condition of wondrous one-ness.

This condition of one-ness, which is unlike life as we know it, has (I have argued) always been implied by art, and might serve as the basis for an alternative view of art to the mimetic one. Much art anyway has no mimetic character—music, for instance. The condition of one-ness is in that case not especially remarkable, since no experience is implied distinct from the artifact itself. It is much more remarkable if a literary work produces such a musical impression, because words seem to point to things in the world and do not normally have a single identity as artistic artifacts. If words are made to tend towards the condition of music, the usual result (as modern literary experiments in this direction have shown) is for them to lose much of their normal signification. Coherent art is then achieved at the cost of a rather incoherent or nebulous 'picture' of experience. Kafka's picture, however, remains vividly concrete; his words appear still to signify some very real and very painful experience—at the same time that he has gone as far as any modern writer in concentration on the medium alone of his art, identifying experience and expression, words and things with such extraordinary absoluteness that his text will no longer relate satisfactorily to any other known order of things.

In order to give some sort of name to Kafka's unified vision, a religious vocabulary may be appropriate. I do not suggest we should look for the contents of any particular religion in Kafka's work, for then I should be interpreting allegorically what Kafka's words are supposed to point to or say. Sticking, however, to my aim of defining rather what his words *are*, I believe we could classify them as belonging to the *kind* that a god might use, albeit a demonic or demented god. The language of the 'Archimedean point' (to use Kafka's image again), language conceived from a point outside the world altogether, might be just this: a binding together, a fusion, of what on earth is forever separate—spiritual and material reality, self and other, intention and action, desire and truth. In the mind of God, what I think and what I am, what words say and what life is, the world of human consciousness and the world as it is, may conceivably be imagined as one. No matter, for the moment, whether God is here a convenient fiction, or a Hegelian consummation, or any other modern hypothesis— including the hypothesis that the very duality we seek to resolve is a mental misunderstanding and therefore 'ought' to be made to go away by some other means—the *possibility* of a reality not ultimately divided against itself in the way it appears to be, is at least a thinkable one. Kafka gives a demonstration of what such thinking is like, of what such a possible unity of language and being could be. In doing so he achieves a kind of religious vision, but it is distinctly negative in character. He goes further than a conventionally religious mind, which halts before the belief that only God knows how spirit and matter can be one; (there may be sacred symbols and rites that em- body the spirit, but these are intelligible mainly as forms of action and all but inscrutable as forms of knowledge).

Kafka uses language with religious absoluteness—there is nothing else meant, or implied, or hidden than what he has said (consequently no critic can find it)—and conjures into being a state of human existence which is totally identical with this verbal consciousness of it, where there is nothing else for words to mean than what they say. Kafka thus disabuses me perhaps of a primary illusion: that life means something more than can ever actually be said, that language can find or create meanings beyond actual usage. His fiction may seem to be about alienation, perhaps, or some other state of false or unhappy consciousness. But inasmuch as his writing realizes this state completely, without referring to anything beyond itself in the world which might be either its cause or its end, Kafka dispels its illusion more radically. The whole fiction of hopes and despairs, struggle and failure, impossible vindication and incomprehensible guilt is grasped for what it is; a verbal

fabrication. We are released from bondage to it by an awareness of its negative identity, a higher nothingness into which
both body and spirit have been cancelled. 'Nothingness' was
a word Kafka more than once used in connection with his
work; he felt it indeed to be his basic 'element'.

In reaching this point I reach at last a conclusion, and one
which (as I anticipated) raises again the question of interpretation. If I say that Kafka demonstrates the character of
an ideal towards which other minds too have striven, and
striven in other, non-literary ways, then I am in effect admitting
that his writing can after all be related beyond itself to things
in the world. And it would, of course, be silly to go on denying
this in the face of overwhelming evidence of how relevant to
actual experience, and particularly modern experience, so
many readers have found Kafka to be. The puzzle is that he
can appear relevant while at the same time giving no distinct
clues, so that quite different interpretations have proved
equally possible. One logical implication is especially puzzling:
if different areas of modern experience can be related to Kafka,
they can also be related to one another. They become linked
by what might be called the 'Kafkaesque' which they have in
common. We should therefore conclude by trying to define,
in terms that do not refer only to language, what this Kafkaesque element is that can be discovered evidently in such a
variety of places in the modern world.

The point I have reached suggests, first, that this element is
metaphysical in character. That is to say, it does not inhere
in specific details of this or that modern activity, but in the
overall shape, the basic presuppositions, of all modern activities
—assuming it to be possible to stand 'totally' outside all of
these (including language) and say what, as a whole and apart
from their actual features, any one of them is. Now Kafka
himself often tried to say what he was trying to achieve when
he wrote—not what he was trying to express in particular
books, but in and through writing itself (though I believe that
the problem of writing is also symbolized in the actual content
of his books). This ultimate element of his literary aspiration
he characterized repeatedly as negative, as nothingness.
Furthermore, the problem posed by Kafka criticism has led
one to the conclusion that there is an unusual degree of

identity in his writing between words and things, the structure of the writing and the structure of the world as there presented. This identity is latent doubtless in all art, but most literature distracts attention from it in order to point deliberately to as much of reality outside itself as it can (the opposite of what Kafka does). We find, then, that the condition in which identity of language with reality is achieved or approached, is a negative one.

If we interpret this basic fact of Kafka's experience as a writer, we may see that it typifies a universal aspiration in a particularly modern form. Towards such an identity all knowledge must aspire: to get as 'near' as possible to the truth. If old-fashioned religious conditions and prescriptions are no longer attached to this ideal (such as love, grace, divine transcendence, and so on), then a simple dialectic emerges in which the human spirit and the world are the two sole terms and a progressive interaction, approximation, and final identity between them becomes conceivable. The dialectical process sees man progressively shedding misconceptions of himself and modifying the real character of the world at the same time. False consciousness, alienation, material misery and helplessness are alike overcome and eliminated, as any dialectician will tell us. What Kafka seems rather disturbingly to tell us, however, is that such absolute aspiration will inevitably lead to a negative achievement, a negative elimination of all significant difference between consciousness and existence. Kafka criticism often begins by noticing the motif of striving or spiritual quest, which is undeniably there; still more undeniable however, is the utterly secular, earthily unspiritual, not to say bestial and futile material in which Kafka has embedded his struggles and quests. These conventionally opposing terms—let us call them 'matter' and 'form'—turn out in the end to be indistinguishable. Their unity, which is just what idealizers of art have pointed to and praised as the fullest consummation of man's spiritual aspirations, has a quite empty ideality. We find we have been reaching not towards any higher reconciliation or resolution, but towards a fearful realization of their essential sameness, and equal negativeness, from the start.

I may now risk saying why I think that Kafka's writing does, after all, illumine so many aspects of modern thought and experience: because he encountered in writing, in his dealings with language, a parent problem in metaphysics that reveals a family resemblance among a mass of otherwise distinct individuals. The sociology of bureaucratic societies, the theory and practice of totalitarian politics, Freudian psychology and so-called negative theology, Judaic traditions and Jewish mentalities, existentialist philosophy and structuralism, even scientific research itself and at the opposite extreme innumerable varieties of subjective experience: all of these things can be brought into relationship with Kafka's writing only by reference to the parent problem. Similarities pursued sideways, as it were, between superficial resemblances, as though Kafka were writing directly about any of these things, will lead at best to partial, at worst to overstretched, implausible interpretation. The parent problem concerns the point of contact between language (in all its forms, in all conscious activity), and the world, or what consciousness is conscious of. Are they the same, are they different? How can we know one apart from the other? How well does language reach, grasp, express what is there? We cannot have a look at the thing itself and our expression of it in order to find out—a logical impossibility that explains why it is futile to judge how well Kafka's fiction explains (or is explained by) this or that phenomenon in life. For Kafka did not forget that his metaphysical doubts and questions could not be answered by writing about instances of them in the world (even if his critics forget this). His writing has itself to be an instance of the truth he wished to instance.

This truth concerns, then, the condition of consciousness in the world, where consciousness exists entirely for the world, the world for human consciousness, and the relationship between them is dialectical. Writing exemplifies this condition, perhaps in its primary form, and all knowledge is entangled in it, whether it reflects selfconsciously on itself or not. The very existence of consciousness as distinct from the world turns out to be highly problematical in this dialectical context. Consciousness can neither accept itself as it is, for it cannot be sure that it is anything independently of the other thing—'its' world—from which it is nevertheless excluded, as though guilty of some breach with it; nor can it realize its one-ness with the world (though what in the world else can it be?). In the absence of any positive reason why the mind is excluded from the promised land, the dialectic between them becomes unendurable and its resolution a destructive one that abolishes any grounds for difference between the partners. Doubtless the desire to resolve the dialectic is in itself a 'spiritual' one that the merely negative difference between the partners does not justify or explain. Hence Kafka's doubt whether he should write at all, and his sense that writing has a perversely religious significance in the modern godless situation. (Yet how starkly this situation throws into relief the apparently ineradicable urge to write, and to resolve even negatively the elements of man's divided condition.)

For Kafka saw the 'spiritual' mystery of language in at best demonic terms. He is in the position of the man who knows what parables are. That is to say, he knows that their seemingly objective way of talking about the spirit, as having somewhere to go beyond its own world, better than language can express, is only mystification, escapism, a substitution of metaphor for reality. He understands well enough that if one did believe in metaphor, one's whole life would become metaphorical. But the very understanding of this makes it impossible. In a simple dialectic of consciousness and world, the partners are brought together by the fact that both lose. Consciousness reclaims all meaning back from the world, only to discover that its meanings are now as empty of real substance as the world is empty of spiritual meaning. This spiritually empty character of man's modern grasp of his own condition is the problem that haunts all his sciences, all his acts of self understanding; and it is what Kafka's writing exemplifies.

# Franz Kuna

## Rage for Verification: Kafka and Einstein

There is little agreement among critics, to say nothing of
scientists, as to the wisdom of bringing literature and science
together in an attempt to illuminate one in terms of the other.
At one end of the spectrum there are those who, with George
Steiner, consider it 'arrogant, if not irresponsible' to discuss
scientific matters if one cannot do so in the language appropriate to them, i.e., in mathematical language: 'When a critic
seeks to apply the indeterminacy principle to his discussion of
action painting or of the use of improvisation in certain
contemporary music, he is not relating two spheres of experience; he is merely talking nonsense.' And if one recalls the
kind of external analogies which have been made between the
arts and the sciences, between 'indeterminacy' and aleatory
principles in the arts, between non-Euclidean geometry and
non-metrical verse, between 'relativity' and 'point of view' in
fiction, etc., then one is persuaded to agree with him. But
the problem does not appear to be as simple as that, and
George Steiner himself added a telling footnote to the above
words ('I am no longer certain that this is so') when he reprinted them in his collection of essays on *Language and Silence*.[1]

At the other end of the spectrum there are those who, with
Martin Green, argue for a brave attack on the demarcation
lines between the arts and the sciences, believing, for example,
that 'a very interesting book could be written about Einstein's
work on the General Theory of Relativity, comparing it with
D. H. Lawrence's contemporary work on *Women in Love*.'[2] As
a study in dissimilarity such a comparison might have its own
peculiar appeal but the general attitude behind this proposal
is, to my mind, no less extreme than its opposite: 'There is no
need for any striking moral—either of likenesses or differences
between the two—to emerge from the comparison . . . to make

an interesting book all that is needed is that each [the 'General Theory' and *Women in Love*] should be fully presented in its historical setting as an achievement of the Western intellectual tradition.'[3]

If a happy mean is called for anywhere, then it is surely here. In the following I shall adopt an approach which I hope will do justice to both the historical and the symbolical importance of 'relativistic' thinking and its 'influence' on what appears to be a highly developed 'experimental'[4] interest on the part of Kafka. I am aware of the risks involved in making comparisons between basic assumptions held by theoretical scientists and what novelists are trying to say about experience and reality. But I am also aware of the need for interdisciplinary approaches in literary criticism where certain fundamental principles affecting the whole of a writer's poetics are concerned.

I believe that Kafka's work constitutes among other things a critique of certain metaphysical doctrines which received expression in nineteenth-century literature. More often than not this critique is implicit in the structure and texture of the work rather than explicitly stated. It reveals itself indirectly, through Kafka's 'experimental' method, the way he submits familiar assumptions about experience and reality to rigorous tests. In this respect Kafka's critique has an impressive parallel in the logical positivist (in the widest sense of the term) critique of traditional metaphysical concepts, particularly as far as their occurrence in physics is concerned. It will be readily seen that a full account of the problem would involve a thorough discussion of the very complex situation which characterizes the interrelationship of philosophy, theoretical science and modernist poetics at the beginning of this century. As long as the critical biographies of the crucial figures remain unwritten, and intellectual historians and historians of science continue to pursue different paths,[5] attempts to illuminate literature and science in terms of each other will necessarily be of a sketchy nature and, more embarrassingly, depend heavily on arguments of an ahistorical and merely 'illustrative' kind. It is hardly possible today, for example, to offer causal explanations of the suspected lively interrelationship between twentieth-century literature, science and philosophy. Very often, all one can do is to establish 'a certain ideological and psychological paralelism' (Kuznetsov). It is possible that in my own contribution the basic point about Kafka could equally well have been made by choosing certain figures other than Einstein for comparative purposes; say, Wittgenstein or similarly influential philosophers or scientists of the period. However, by opting for Einstein I hope to have put the emphasis squarely on the point where, in Kafka's case, the overlaps between the verification principle of meaning and the 'experimentalist' nature of literary Modernism are particularly obvious. Moreover, Einstein's explicit and rigorous critique of the concept of 'simultaneity' and Kafka's implicit but no less rigorous critique of the idea of harmony are particularly striking and illuminating examples of analogous thinking.

The actual points of contact between Kafka and Einstein are both interesting and disappointing. Though Einstein was Professor of Theoretical Physics at the German university in Prague (1911/12) and was soon after his arrival introduced to the Brod circle, where he 'met Franz Kafka, and became particularly friendly with Hugo Bergmann and Max Brod',[6] not even Einstein's name is mentioned in Kafka's writing. Max Brod however tells us in one of his autobiographical works how the Fanta circle debated with Einstein, and later with Einstein's successor, Philipp Frank, problems of philosophy and modern physics. The Theory of Relativity was frequently discussed at these meetings, despite the fact that their main purpose was the joint reading of Kant's two Critiques, a task which was taken very seriously indeed: 'The reading of these two works occupied our Tuesday evenings for two whole years. It was followed by a year of Fichte's *Theory of Science* and by a further year's study of Hegel's *Phenomenology of Mind*, though by then in a more superficial way.'[7]

What Max Brod has to say about these giants of German idealism in his rather defensive autobiography makes one think that he had not learnt all that much from Einstein. But he was impressed by him and used him as a model for the character of Kepler in his novel *Tycho Brahes Weg zu Gott* (1916). Unfortunately, Einstein does not appear to have returned the compliment and, only a few years after his departure from Prague, seems to have had difficulty in remembering Brod. In

1916, when he returned a book by Max Brod to Hedwig Born, he wrote to her: 'I believe that I met him in Prague. I think he belongs to a small circle there of philosophical and Zionist enthusiasts, which was loosely grouped around the university philosophers, a medieval-like band of unworldly people whom you got to know by reading the book.'[8] And upon returning a Kafka novel to Thomas Mann, Einstein is reported to have remarked: 'I couldn't read it for its perversity. The human mind isn't complicated enough.'[9] These are not very encouraging starting points for anybody who rightly or wrongly has convinced himself that there is nevertheless a story to be told involving the names of Kafka and Einstein.

The fact that Kafka himself does not appear to have mentioned Einstein's name in his writings, or in conversations with others, comes as less of a surprise if one thinks of all the other names which one may justifiably expect to have meant something to Kafka, but which are either conspicuously absent in the letters and diaries or mentioned only in passing: Nietzsche, Brentano, Ehrenfels, Mach, Freud, Sacher-Masoch; certain Romantic writers; most of the writers and thinkers who were intensively discussed in the 'Louvrezirkel' or in Berta Fanta's house; and a whole host of major and minor turn-of-the-century sociologists, cultural historians and authors of anarchist and socialist literature whose influence can be detected in his work. Just as he refrains from the discussion of public issues, is suspicious of great systems and ideologies, and hates great debates, so too he shows little inclination to discuss in detail the work of those who influenced him. This does not mean, however, that Kafka shut himself off from the important issues of the day. Far from it. In the face of Max Brod's curious attempt to create and uphold an antiseptic image of Kafka, we need to remind ourselves of what Klaus Wagenbach said some time ago, an assessment which has since been substantiated by many Kafka scholars and by the kind of 'witnesses' Max Brod likes to treat so scathingly in his autobiographical writings:

In the years before the First World War Kafka therefore not only met the most important, though as yet almost unknown Czech avant-garde writers . . . but he also acquainted himself to some extent with the theoretical foundations of socialism.

In addition, during this same period he paid regular visits to the talks and evening gatherings which were arranged by the indefatigable Berta Fanta, wife of a chemist, and to which she invited the leading intellectuals of Prague: the mathematician Kowalewski, the physicist Philipp Frank, the philosopher Ehrenfels and the young Albert Einstein, then lecturing in Prague. Here Kafka heard papers on the theory of relativity, the quantum theory of Planck and the principles of psycho-analysis. Thus, shortly before he came to write his major works, he was introduced to the most momentous ideas of the new age—again a fact which belies the legend of Kafka the ignorant provincial.[10]

It is the common experience of Kafka scholars that even where they are aware of an obvious influence on Kafka's work it is not always easy to detect what Kafka has absorbed in his writings. One of the reasons for this is that Kafka was inspired not so much by the content as by the formal, analytical and methodological qualities of what he read. Kafka read Schopenhauer for his language, as he tells his young friend Gustav Janouch, Flaubert for his literary method, as Max Brod tells us, and in Kierkegaard he admired the 'Begriff des "Dialektischen"' ('concept of the "dialectical"'), and the 'Begriff der "Bewegung"' ('concept of "motion"'); 'Von diesem Begriff kann man geradewegs ins Glück des Erkennens getragen werden und noch einen Flügelschlag weiter', ('by this concept one can be borne away to the joy of understanding, and even a wing-beat beyond'); moreover he is awe-inspired by Kierkegaard's 'Denkrichtung' ('the trend of his thoughts')—'fast ganz abstrakt' ('almost entirely abstract')—and by 'das Durcheinander seiner an sich sinnlosen, beleidigenden, vielfach sich spiegelnden, gegenseitig aufeinander kletternden . . . Hilfskonstruktionen'[11] ('the chaos of his auxiliary constructions, in themselves meaningless, offensive, often mirroring one another, scrambling upon each other's shoulders . . .').

In his study of other writers Kafka instinctively looks out for the possibilities of style and perspective offered by their craft. His own art is determined by the urge to perfect the medium, to subject every word and intention to doubt and rigorous appraisal, and ultimately to exhibit in his works not

87

a philosophy but the very poetological foundations of his writing. In the knowledge 'dass ich . . . förmlich nicht genug Lungenkraft hatte, der Welt die Mannigfaltigkeit für mich einzublasen, die sie ja, wie die Augen lehren, offenbar hat' ('that I . . . simply didn't have enough lung power to inject into the world for my purpose the diversity which our eyes tell us it obviously possesses'), he learns to exclude contemplation of the world from his 'Stundenplan des Tages' (from his 'daily routine'), increasingly acquiring ascetic habits and pushing the act of writing in the direction of epistemology and of 'prayer'. Kafka's ambition is not to write about 'something' but to make every creative effort appear to be a unique approximation to truth. As many critics have pointed out his expressed desire is for a total or pure art, for literature that does not impress by its references to the external world but by the sheer force of its inner coherence.

At one level at least, comparison between Kafka and Einstein might very well begin by relating the former's purist attitude to literature to the latter's similarly purist attitude towards his own field, physics. According to Einstein, physical theories must not only not contradict empirical facts but also show, as far as their premises are concerned, 'naturalness' or 'logical simplicity'. As he explains in his 'Autobiographical Notes', the two demands Einstein made on physical theories are 'external confirmation' and 'inner perfection'. The latter he took so seriously that he could not help discovering a weak spot in his own theory of relativity:

> One is struck [by the fact] that the theory (except for the four-dimensional space) introduces two kinds of physical things, i.e. (1) measuring rods and clocks, (2) all other things, e.g., the electro-magnetic field, the material point, etc. This, in a certain sense, is inconsistent; strictly speaking measuring rods and clocks would have to be represented as solutions of the basic equations (objects consisting of moving atomic configurations), not, as it were, as theoretically self-sufficient entities.[12]

There are many parallels in Kafka's writing to the argument for 'inner perfection', and his wish 'to sit in the innermost room of a spacious locked cellar with my writing things and a lamp'[13] contains them all. If Einstein has become the symbol of theoretical thinking, remote from the problems of practical life, then Kafka has become the symbol of an art that is total in its opposition to practical living.

But it is not analogies of this kind I want to pursue. I am interested in an aspect of Einsteinian physics—and, I am glad to say, no knowledge of Lorentz transformations or field equations is required for my purposes—which has more than one relevant parallel in Kafka's art. I should like to argue that Kafka achieved something in the field of ethics and poetics that Einstein achieved in the field of physics.

If one can say, with Boris Kuznetsov, that 'according to Einstein concepts that fail to offer a basis for conclusions capable of being verified by observation are physically meaningless', then one can also say, as I shall try to demonstrate, that according to Kafka ideas or conceptions that fail to offer a basis for conclusions capable of being verified by experience are *ethically* meaningless, or absurd. If, secondly, Einstein's success as a modern physicist can be, and has been, interpreted as the result of his consistent reversal of orthodox ways of asking questions, then Kafka's success as a modern writer can be, and indeed has been, interpreted as the result of his 'total reversal of German idealism' (Erich Heller).[14] If, thirdly, one can define, with Philipp Frank and Werner Heisenberg, Einsteinian physics not as a doctrine about the objective motions of material bodies but as a doctrine about bringing order into our sense observations, then one can say of Kafka's poetics that it does not concern itself with the creation of fictional—in the traditional sense, humanly possible—worlds, or even with the problems of reflecting, shaping, and making intelligible the reality we know, but with a radical critique of our ways of making sense of the world. These three obvious points about Einstein, together with the perhaps less obvious 'transformations' from Einsteinian physics to Kafka's poetics, can best be demonstrated by an analysis of the idea of 'simultaneity' as we encounter it in both physics and the history of literature and ideas.

Most books on 'Relativity', including Einstein's own, begin

with a critique of the conception of simultaneity. In his well known, popular exposition of this theory Einstein invites us to assume that lightning has struck the rails on a railway embankment at two places $A$ and $B$ far distant from each other. We are then asked to make the additional assertion that these two lightning flashes occurred 'simultaneously'. If we now ask each other whether there is sense in this statement, we are very likely to answer with a decided 'Yes, of course'. After further reflection, however, it may occur to us that the matter is not as simple as it may appear at first sight. What do we mean, as physicists, by the concept of simultaneity, Einstein asks. And he answers:

> The concept does not exist for the physicist until he has the possibility of discovering whether or not it is fulfilled in an actual case. We thus require a definition of simultaneity such that this definition supplies us with the method by means of which, in the present case, he can decide by experiment whether or not both the lightning strokes occurred simultaneously. As long as this requirement is not satisfied, I allow myself to be deceived as a physicist (and of course the same applies if I am not a physicist), when I imagine that I am able to attach a meaning to the statement of simultaneity.[15]

We are now asked to add another body of reference to our present one: a railway embankment. We imagine a very long train travelling along the rails with the constant velocity $v$ and in the direction indicated in the figure below:

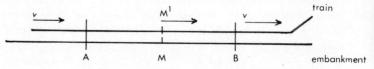

People travelling in this train will naturally regard all events taking place along the line in reference to the train. Now the following interesting question arises: 'Are two events (e.g., the two strokes of lightning $A$ and $B$) which are simultaneous *with reference to the railway embankment* also simultaneous *relatively to the train?*'[16] A rigorous analysis of the above experiment will

90

show that the question must be answered in the negative. Events which are simultaneous with reference to the embankment are not simultaneous with respect to the train, and vice versa, for the simple reason that the velocity of light is both constant and limited. Whilst the observer at $M$ will receive the light-signals emitted from $A$ and $B$ at the same time, i.e., simultaneously, the traveller at $M^1$ will see the beam of light emitted from $B$ earlier than he will see that emitted from $A$. The latter must therefore come to the conclusion that the two events are not simultaneous. The most natural definition of simultaneity, as far as the physicist (and by implication everybody else, as Einstein points out, not without a certain amount of relish) is concerned, leads to none other than the relativity of simultaneity, and more generally to the relativity of time.

Before we can usefully establish any analogies to Kafka, we must first try to understand the significance of Einstein's conclusion, as far as both its internal properties and its historical significance are concerned. With regard to the former it is enough for our purposes to note that Einstein's definition of simultaneity is an operational[17] or co-ordinative definition,[18] that is to say it is given by the co-ordination of an experiment with light-rays to a fundamental concept in physics. 'Simultaneity', as defined by Einstein, is not an intuitive concept, not even an empirical concept, in the ordinary sense, it is a *verified* concept. As a witty commentator pointed out, an idealist who insisted on his rights would have to modify Schopenhauer's 'The world is my representation.' He would have to say: 'The world is my verification.'[19] At this point Einstein's revolutionary thinking forces us, I think, to reconsider the whole stock of our inherited notions, concepts and ideas. If to the modern scientist the objective world is so obviously and inescapably 'the aggregate of facts verified by modern science, the world rendered by the conceptions verified by the science of our time'[20] then the question arises whether the principle of 'experimental verification' is not one that holds equally true outside physics, for example in the field of ethics, aesthetics and poetics. We shall see that in Kafka's work this question is both raised and answered in an unexpected way.

To make quite clear the implications of Einstein's achievement—so that we can measure it against Kafka's—we need to consider the concept of simultaneity before it experienced its Nietzschean 'revaluation'. We have the option of studying the matter either in the context of Newton's mechanics or of Kant's *Critique of Pure Reason*. I prefer the latter, simply because we now have a chance of disengaging ourselves from physics—after all an uncomfortable territory for the critic—and also because, as far as I can see, the relationship of Einstein's thinking to Kant's definition of simultaneity appears to have attracted little or no attention.

Kant discusses the 'principle of coexistence'—his term for simultaneity—in the context of what he calls 'the Law of Reciprocity or Community':

> Things are coexistent when in empirical intuition the perceptions of them can follow upon one another reciprocally, which . . . cannot occur in the succession of appearances. Thus I can direct my perception first to the moon and then to the earth, or, conversely, first to the earth and then to the moon; and because the perceptions of these objects can follow each other reciprocally, I say that they are coexistent.[21]

What follows in Kant's text is a definition of the concept of simultaneity that misses Einstein's own definition by a mere hair's breadth. Because time itself cannot be perceived, Kant continues, and we are therefore not in a position to gather, simply from things being set in the same time, that our perceptions of them can follow each other reciprocally, we require, in the case of things which co-exist externally to one another, 'a pure concept of the reciprocal sequence of their determinations . . ., if we are able to say that the reciprocal sequence is grounded in the object, and so to represent the coexistence as objective.' Besides the mere existence of A and B, there must be something 'through which A determines for B, and also reversewise B determines for A, its position in time, because only on this condition can these substances be empirically represented as *coexisting*.' In short, there must be mutual interaction between things before we are able to determine their possible co-existence. And here is Kant's extraordinary statement, which brings him so tantalizingly close to Einstein's 'thought-play' with strokes of lightning, trains and railway embankments:

> The light, which plays between our eye and the celestial bodies, produces a mediate community between us and them, and thereby shows us that they coexist. We cannot empirically change our position, and perceive the change, unless matter in all parts of space makes perception of our position possible to us. For only thus by means of their reciprocal influence can the parts of matter establish their simultaneous existence, . . . even to the most remote objects . . . I do not by this argument at all profess to disprove void space, for it may exist where perceptions cannot reach, and where there is, therefore, no empirical knowledge of coexistence. But such a space is not for us an object of any possible experience.[22]

After Einstein, it is difficult to imagine how Kant, or Newton, could have missed indulging in that little thought-experiment which would have made explicit to them the extraordinary implications of their statements. As we have seen, for Kant's definition of simultaneity notions of space and time can be disregarded; all that is needed are notions of interaction and influences, the sort of thing that allows for experimental verification. And of Newton it is said that his principle of the equivalence of inertial systems ($=$ special principle of relativity, i.e., the invariance of natural laws with respect to the transition from one inertial system to another) did not really require, for its practical application, the concepts of absolute time and space. One cannot help feeling that Kant and Newton would have understood Einstein perfectly had they been able to read chapters eight to nine of his *Relativity*. In the light of what had already been said, from at least the eighteenth century onwards, about the type of critical reasoning required for the discovery of the central points of 'Relativity' (Einstein himself acknowledges his debts to past thinkers, particularly to Hume, Kant and Ernst Mach), Einstein's argument for operational definitions sounds almost like a commonplace. In what respect then does Einstein differ from others? The simple answer seems to be that he not only restated the criterion of operational validity but applied it and made it work. We must allow a physicist to explain this further:

. . . before Einstein people had not considered the matter to any great extent, and probably only seldom if ever consciously formulated or applied the criterion. Einstein's revolutionary contribution consisted in his self-conscious use of it in new situations and in the way in which he applied it. What Einstein did was to make a more detailed analysis of the physical operations used in the measurement of length and time than had ever been made before. In doing this he uncovered necessary details which are always involved in any measurement of length, but which had formerly been ignored simply because of their universality, and because no one had had the imagination to formulate them or to see that they might be significant.[23]

What had become explicit by the time Einstein arrived on the scene was not merely of interest in itself but helped us to detect details in the conventional operations of science that were of immediate consequence for both theoretical and experimental physics.

What has all this got to do with Kafka? In order to answer this question we must make yet another detour, this time into the history of an old, typically Western and European idea: the category of totality, or the absolute, as it has appeared and reappeared in literature and thought since time immemorial— but more selfconsciously and polemically so since the latter half of the eighteenth century. It is also convenient to begin the argument somewhat before Kafka, and not with him.

Interestingly enough, it is not only physics which operates with the concept of simultaneity. It is also known to philosophy, literature and theology, where it has its own peculiar definition and history. On the whole we cannot expect to find, in the history of literature and thought, the exact equivalent to the physical term but have to rely on formulae like 'Einheit aller Erfahrung' ('unity of all experience', Hegel), 'Ko-existenz' (Kant) or 'das Gegenwärtige' ('everything apprehended in the same moment of perception', Goethe). Goethe, of course, offers us not only a variety of synonyms for 'das Gleichzeitige' ('the simultaneous') but the term itself. At the same time he emphasizes its central importance to human experience: 'The most important thing remains that which is perceived simultaneously because it is reflected in its purest form within us, and we in it.' This is a key sentence in the history of nineteenth-century thought and epistemology, an epigrammatic summary of what Goethe, Hegel and the whole age were eager to express: a sense of the simultaneity of idea and experience, in accordance with the belief in the pre-established harmony between the subjective and objective worlds.

As is well known, the young Goethe actually believed, with Spinoza, in the identity of 'being' and 'perfection', postulating, with Hegel, the eternal validity of the truly present moment. Reality is conceived of as a union of opposites, as God and world, mind and matter existing harmoniously and simultaneously. The later Goethe is less confident in this respect. 'Das Gleichzeitige' is no longer an a priori fact but rather a quality, a desired condition of the world. He speaks of the need 'das *Abenteuer der Vernunft*, wie es der Alte vom Königsberge selbst nennt, mutig zu bestehen'[24] ('to undergo bravely the *adventure of reason*, as the sage of Königsberg himself called it') as if there were some doubt as to whether what enters life through the phenomenal world is actually analogous to our reason. And frequently reason is not sufficient for the difficult task of yoking 'Idee und Erfahrung' ('idea and experience') together. The problem is that whilst 'in der Idee Simultanes und Successives' are 'innigst verbunden' ('in the Idea the simultaneous and the successive are intimately joined together'), the two are always separated from the point of view of experience. Nevertheless, we must not despair: 'Dessen ungeachtet bleibt unser ewiges Bestreben, diesen Hiatus mit Vernunft, Verstand, Einbildungskraft, Glauben, Gefühl, Wahn und, wenn wir sonst nichts vermögen, mit Albernheit zu überwinden.'[25] ('For all that, it remains our eternal aspiration to bridge this hiatus by means of reason, intellect, imagination, faith, feeling, illusion and, if all else fails, folly.') As we shall see, it was precisely the 'Albernheit' of the attempt which makes certain later writers, Kafka in particular, decide to reverse Goethe's scheme, and with it every single idea related to it. But what Goethe could not solve *qua* scientist (he speaks of the unresolvable 'Widerstreit zwischen Aufgefasstem und Ideiertem',[26] of a 'contradiction between what is perceived and what is imposed by way of ideas') he was quite happy to solve *qua* poet, and laconically he invites us 'zu einiger Befriedigung in die Sphäre der Dichtkunst [zu] flüchten' ('to escape into the sphere of poetry and thus attain partial satisfaction'). 'Gleichzeitigkeit' is now to be achieved through art, a kind of simultaneity which is defined, with a view to Hegel, by Hans-Georg Gadamer:

> Gleichzeitigkeit ist . . . nicht eine Gegebenheitsweise im Bewusstsein, sondern . . . eine Leistung, die von ihm verlangt wird. Sie besteht darin, sich so an die Sache zu halten, dass diese 'gleichzeitig' wird, d.h. aber, dass alle Vermittlung in . . . Gegenwärtigkeit aufgehoben ist.
>
> (Simultaneity . . . is not what is given in the conscious mind but rather . . . an achievement that is demanded of it. This consists in pursuing a thing until it becomes 'simultaneous'; that is to say, all mediated experience is transmuted into . . . present perception.

And Peter Eichhorn adds, in his book on *Idee und Erfahrung im Spätwerk Goethes*: 'Misst man das Spätwerk an dieser Forderung, so wird eine ungeheure Leistung der *Vergegenwärtigung* sichtbar.'[27] ('If one judges Goethe's late work by this criterion, one perceives a tremendous determination to draw all experience together into the present moment.')

I think it is safe to generalize from this statement, and to apply it to the mainstream of nineteenth-century literature and thought as a whole. This 'Leistung der Vergegenwärtigung' was so impressively demonstrated that it turned willy-nilly into a rather oppressive ideology by the end of the century. At this point in time writers were faced with a choice: should they accept the inherited belief that, to put it in its most general terms, there is an unseen order, and that our supreme chance lies in harmoniously adjusting ourselves to it, or should they side with the critics of this belief (Dostoevsky, the later Nietzsche) and expose the whole thing as 'Albernheit' or 'der grosse Stumpfsinn' ('the great stupidity')? As we know, Hofmannsthal and Rilke are the representatives of one kind of choice, Kafka and Trakl of another.

From the very start Kafka's work is a unique attempt to write
against the grain of traditional literature and its familiar
assumptions. His critique of the Chandos experience in
*Description of a Struggle*, his Dostoevskyan juxtaposition of two
modes of existence in *Metamorphosis*, and his reversal of the
scheme of the *Bildungsroman* and the picaresque tradition in
*America* are impressive examples of this. But it is really in *The
Trial* and in *The Castle* that we find Kafka's fully developed
'Critique of Heaven and Earth', to borrow a phrase from van
Leeuwen's book on Marx and theology. It is in these novels
that we find two of Kafka's well known aphorisms transformed
into a new kind of poetics. One of them is buried away in the
'Notes from the Year 1920': 'Some deny the existence of misery
by pointing to the sun; he denies the existence of the sun by
pointing to misery.'[28] The other we find in *Wedding Preparations*: 'The crows maintain that a single crow could destroy
the heavens. There is no doubt of that, but it proves nothing
against the heavens, for heaven simply means: the impossibility
of crows.'[29] The first one is easily recognizable as a typically
Nietzschean 'Umwertung' (revaluation) and belongs to the
field of ethics. The second, the more interesting one, has been
interpreted as a paradox, as if 'only in a metaphorical sense'
could it be said that 'the heavens and the crows . . . exclude
one another.'[30] But the aphorism is no more and no less of a
paradox than Einstein's critique of simultaneity. The apparent
unity of sky and birds (a pure sense impression) must not
deceive us into concluding that a similar unity exists between
heaven (the other meaning of Himmel) and man (the 'crows',
members of the family of the *corvidae*, in Czech *kavka*, pointing
to at least one particular man—or to 'an actual case', as
Einstein would say). Just as the constancy of the speed of light
is the limiting factor in the physical definition of simultaneity,
human existence as such is the limiting factor in the theological
definition of any relationship involving man and heaven. The
two do not merely exclude each other by way of a linguistic
paradox but by way of the very real limitations of human
existence. Kafka's aphorism is logical positivism applied to an
assumption of traditional theology.

Reasoning of this kind imbues Kafka's writing, often
polemically so, on all conceivable levels. This can best be

FRANZ KUNA

demonstrated through an analysis of the first chapter of *The Trial* and—with more complex ramifications—through an analysis of the Bürgel episode and the 'Aktenverteilung' ('distribution of the files') in *The Castle*.[31]

The first chapter of *The Trial* contains one of the most skilful attempts in literature to suggest how two different planes of reality are superimposed on each other, and how this affects the protagonist's consciousness. The passages in question emphasize the incompatibility of the court officials (representatives of an unfamiliar world) with things and characters from K.'s everyday life, and highlight the confusion resulting for K. The first hint of this comes when Frau Grubach almost enters the room where K. is talking to the warders:

> As he was re-entering the next room the opposite door opened and Frau Grubach showed herself. He saw her only for an instant, for no sooner did she recognize him than she was obviously overcome by embarrassment, apologised for intruding, vanished, and shut the door again with the utmost care. 'Come in, do,' he would just have had time to say. But he merely stood holding his papers in the middle of the room, looking at the door, which did not open again, and was only recalled to attention by a shout from the warders, who were sitting at a table by the open window and, as he now saw, devouring his breakfast.[32]

If one takes the figurative meaning of 'verhaftet' (e.g., 'einer Sache verhaftet sein', to be in the grip of something) then it is implied that landladies and transcendental matters do not go very well together. K. cannot bring someone from his normal everyday life into contact with his 'arrested' existence, and with officials from the court. It is also implied that the appearance of Frau Grubach drives the presence of the warders from his mind, since he is left standing in a state of stupor until his attention is once again attracted by a shout from them.

The exact nature of this incompatibility is made even clearer in another episode. While Josef K. is being interviewed by the Inspector, three employees from his bank (the counterparts of the three representatives of the Law) are also present in the room. K., although aware that they are there, does not recognize them until the Inspector brings their identity to his notice. Mortified by their presence, he immediately switches his attention to these three young men; but in doing so, and this is the significant fact, he forgets about the officials from the court and they depart unnoticed. K. realizes this himself a few minutes later:

> Then he remembered that he had not noticed the Inspector and the warders leaving, the Inspector had usurped his attention so that he did not recognize the three clerks, and the clerks in turn had made him oblivious of the Inspector.

The implication here is that the incompatibility of these characters is, despite their differences, not inherent in them, but results from an inability on K.'s part to incorporate them both into his consciousness at any one time. The bank clerks and the court officials do exist in the same room; it is just that Josef K.'s awareness of the one precludes an awareness of the other. Or to put it more directly, the one kind of reality blots out the other kind.

Josef K. has then a kind of double consciousness, which is to say he has to process reality into two separate worlds. The general nature of these two worlds is to some extent clear. The first is that of K.'s everyday practical existence. His work at the bank, Frau Grubach, his visits to the pub all belong to it. It is a world of carefully established and closely followed routine. The second world is one where totally different values and patterns of behaviour are valid—it is the world to which, for K. at least, the court belongs. That the world of the court is a world which is at best 'complementary'[33] to K.'s own can be assumed from the fact that K. cannot combine the two, and from the fact that the world of the court can only claim K.'s attention at moments when he is not deeply involved in his own world—for example, on waking first thing in the morning. Josef K. himself suggests this:

> In the Bank, for instance, I am always prepared, nothing of that kind could possibly happen to me there, I have my own attendant, the general telephone and the office telephone stand before me on my desk, people keep coming to

see me, clients and clerks, and above all, my mind is always
on my work and so kept on the alert; it would be an actual
pleasure to me if a situation like that cropped up in the
Bank.[34]

When K. reflects in the evening on what has happened earlier
in the day, it seems to him that the whole

. . . household of Frau Grubach had been thrown into great
disorder by the events of the morning and that it was his
task alone to put it right again. Once order was restored,
every trace of these events would be obliterated and things
would resume their old course. From the three clerks themselves nothing was to be feared, they had been absorbed
once more in the great hierarchy of the Bank, no change
was to be remarked in them.[35]

Characteristically enough, people uninvolved in these events,
like Fräulein Bürstner, K.'s fellow-lodger, cannot find the
slightest 'trace of disturbance'. What kind of world is it which
our normal routine prevents from taking hold of us? One
thinks of Conrad's Marlow steaming up his river in Africa:

I had to keep a look-out for signs of dead wood we could
cut up in the night for next day's steaming. When you have
to attend to things of that sort, to the mere incidents of the
surface, the reality—the reality I tell you—fades. The inner
truth is hidden—luckily, luckily. But I felt it all the same;
I felt often its mysterious stillness watching one of my
monkey tricks . . .[36]

The 'reality', 'the inner truth'—these are simply Marlow's
metaphors. What is watching the mystically inclined sailor is
the world of man's irrational and metaphysical desires and
ambitions. The same is the case with Josef K. The difference
is that whilst Conrad presents us, once again, with a modifica-
tion of a familiar Romantic scheme—the 'threshold' can be
crossed—Kafka is at pains to demonstrate the total division
between the seen and an assumed unseen reality. In *The Castle*
Kafka will go a step further. Not only will he relentlessly

concentrate attention on the logical steps taken by thinkers like Martin Buber when they move from the interhuman I-Thou meeting to the man/God I-Thou encounter—and I suspect the Klamm/K. relationship (or rather non-relationship) to be a parody of Buber's encounter-theology—but he will also expose the very notion of some purified, stable, spiritual, non-empirical divine/human encounter as so much nonsense. And he will give impressive examples of how there is no such thing as the simultaneous experience of seen and unseen realities.[37]

But there are other, perhaps less obvious but no less pointed, examples of Kafka's 'critical' intentions in *The Castle*. When Frieda criticizes K., in the course of her remarkable analysis of their relationship, for failing to utter her name with the same affection with which he utters the name of Barnabas, she is not being merely oversensitive but is expressing her acute and justifiable awareness of the lack of tenderness in K.'s dealings with her. K. sadly fails, it seems, to live up to Frieda's almost Hegelian vision of love. The feeling of love makes its appearance 'through the bodily members themselves', Hegel wrote, 'through a look, the facial expression, or in a still more spiritual way through the voice tones or a word.'[38] Bürgel similarly refers to opportunities in which more can be achieved 'by means of a word, a glance, a sign of trust . . . than by means of lifelong exhausting efforts'.[39] K.'s inability to demonstrate anything of the sort, in other words his failure to combine his spiritual ambitions with terrestrial happiness, is frequently attributed by Kafka's readers to what they call his opportunism and scheming mind. And indeed, it would be pointless to deny that Kafka was not also interested in portraying the appalling narcissism of the K.s, even in providing some kind of literary account of his own experience. Yet in the final analysis the scene just described reveals itself as a minor but nevertheless significant example of Kafka's urge to verify lofty notions of the compatibility of this phenomenal world and the beyond. If one accepts Emrich's suggestion, that Klamm stands, among other things, for impersonal or absolute Love, then it becomes clear that to K. the impossibility of combining Klamm and Frieda at any single moment of time is not the result of a personal deficiency but a fact of human experience in general. Moreover, as far as K.'s and Frieda's kind of loving is concerned (an all too human love, and the only one they know) the quest for Klamm acts as a divisive rather than a unifying factor.

There are also many passages of a more incidental kind in Kafka's work which reveal his constant urge to put traditional notions of the possibility of a harmonious order to the test. Josef K. in *The Trial* may wish to trust the 'officials', but a closer look at their *modus vivendi*, the way they 'were confined day and night to the workings of their judicial system', reveals to him 'their remoteness' and their inability to 'have any right understanding of human relations'.[40] Olga explains to K. that the 'gentlemen' from the Castle 'feel out of place in the ordinary world' and that the 'great gulf' which both villagers and Castle officials try to bridge does not exist after all.[41] Barnabas enjoys the distinction of being one of the Castle's messengers, but during the time of his affiliation to the Castle his real life is 'monotonous', 'unnatural' and 'herzbeklemmend'.[42] Frieda has always 'some sort of secret' (due to her 'alleged affair with Klamm'), but these are 'secrets that nobody could inquire into.'[43] She must therefore be taken, Pepi concludes, at her face value. K.'s plan to 'organize and supervise' his own trial, to draw up a plea which would contain a complete history of 'the whole of [his] life', is perhaps the most ironic and utopian analogue in Kafka's work to more traditional schemes of rationalism—if one ignores the possibility that Kafka is here parodying the claims and methods of contemporary psychoanalysis as well:

> Yet even though K. believed he could manage all this, the difficulty of drawing up the plea seemed overwhelming . . . No doubt it was a task that meant almost interminable labour. One did not need to have a timid and fearful nature to be easily persuaded that the completion of this plea was a sheer impossibility. Not because of laziness or obstructive malice . . . but because to meet an unknown accusation, not to mention other possible charges arising out of it, the whole of one's life would have to be passed in review, down to the smallest actions and accidents, clearly formulated and examined from every angle.[44]

When the narrator exclaims 'And how dreary such a task

would be!' he produces a typically Kafkaesque understatement, thereby highlighting the absurdity of the idea. Of the various phases of rationalism—such as seventeenth-century attempts to pierce the veil of the universe, Kant's attempts to detect basic and immutable categories of human understanding, and Hegel's absolute idealism—it is a generalized Newtonian mechanics to which K.'s reasoning most readily belongs. In the eighteenth century many men not only believed in the predictive power of Newtonian mechanics, as far as the future history of the universe was concerned, but also proclaimed its universal applicability, particularly with respect to the logical construction of concepts and the possibility of devising a unified view of the world, both in its physical and metaphysical aspects. In the light of modern physics the commonsense answer to Newton, that it is impossible to determine the co-ordinate and velocities of *all* the molecules of the universe (a precondition for making accurate predictions), is an understatement. And so is K.'s reason for ultimately abandoning the idea of drawing up a plea: the practical demands of human existence do not permit a full-time investigation of one's external circumstances and inner condition.[45] But even at this level both these rejections of the idea of a total accountability of what is happening in and around us are expressions of one and the same modern intention: not to allow abstract or absolute claims to override the demands of logical operations or of individual existence. Scientific operationalism and ethical existentialism are only two sides of the same coin, a fact which the typically modern separation of physical and moral criteria tends to disguise.

In order fully to appreciate Kafka's 'Copernican revolution' in literature, it is necessary to put his achievement in a historical context similar to the one we have reconstructed in the case of Einstein. The idealist tradition was of course responsible not only for pushing literature in the direction of both Olympian metaphysical heights and the cosy corners of 'Biedermeier' but also for giving birth to its opposite, what Dostoevsky called 'underground'.

Oddly enough, it was Goethe himself who expressed what in his day must have been a rather heretical attitude:

> Nach drüben ist die Aussicht uns verrant;
> Tor, wer dorthin die Augen blinzelnd richtet,
> Sich über Wolken seinesgleichen dichtet.[46]
> (From prying gaze what lies beyond is hid;
> A fool, who thither squinting spies
> And deems, his likeness fills the skies.)

He is more explicit in the following passage:

> Man is situated as a real being in the middle of a real world
> and is endowed with the faculties to apprehend and beget
> the real and beside it the possible. All healthy men have the
> conviction that they exist and that things exist around them.
> However there is also an empty spot in the mind, i.e., a
> place where no object is mirrored, just as in the eye there
> is a spot which cannot see. If a man pays particular heed to
> this spot and becomes engrossed in it, he will succumb to a
> mental disorder and divine here *things from another world*
> which are in fact unreal and have neither shape nor sub-
> stance but trouble him as hollow night-spaces and, if he
> cannot tear himself away from them, will pursue him more
> cruelly than phantoms.[47]

As Eduard Spranger comments: 'der reine Jenseitsstandpunkt
ist für Goethe keine inhaltsvolle Ausdrucksmöglichkeit. Das
schied ihn tief und tiefer vom Kreise derer um F. H. Jacobi
und von dem Jugendfreunde selbst.'[48] ('pure transcendentalism
was not for Goethe a meaningful possibility. This divided him
fundamentally and ever more clearly from the circle around
F. H. Jacobi and even from the latter himself, the erstwhile
friend of his youth.')

Does this mean that Goethe had lost all metaphysical
ambition, that he was accepting after all Kant's sharp distinction between 'das Erforschliche ... und das Unerforschliche'
('what can and cannot be investigated')? Of course not. In
making apparently radical epistemological statements (some of
them clearly reminiscent of operational definitions in modern
physics) he was merely expressing his distaste for purely ideal
(imaginary) quests of the Romantic type, and in the process
fortifying his own position. A revealing aspect of this position
is expressed in the following lines:

Hinauf! Hinauf strebt's.
Es schweben die Wolken
Abwärts, die Wolken
Neigen sich der sehnenden Liebe.[49]
(Upward! Striving upward.
The clouds float
Downward, the clouds
Bend to meet love's yearning.)

The idea of a human being striving upwards, and of mysterious, benevolent forces striving downwards, is taken up by Kafka in *The Castle* and, needless to say, repudiated. Klamm is compared to an eagle whose far-away gaze is 'downward-pressing' ('herabdringend'). But Klamm is irredeemably trapped by his own laws. Though he sometimes interrupts the silence of his existence by unimaginable cries, as if he too was crying out for K. as K. is crying out for him, he cannot break through the 'indestructible circles', which hermetically seal off his existence.

Unfortunately there is no room to analyse Goethe's position further, nor can we discuss here Romanticism's contribution to the critique of the idea of a pre-established harmony, or the kind of paradoxical tradition Professor Magill has discussed in a paper entitled 'Im Dienst der Wahrheit. Observations on some German prose fables'.[50] Let us move on to the most radical assault on metaphysics the nineteenth century was capable of, and begin the discussion with a passage from Dostoevsky's *The Brothers Karamazov*, in which Ivan Karamazov reviews, with quasi-Einsteinian logic, the relationship between God and the created world. In the passage in question Ivan begins by saying: 'If God really exists and if he really has created the world, then he created it in accordance with Euclidean geometry.' But he has second thoughts on this proposition:

'And yet there have been and there still are mathematicians and philosophers, some of them indeed men of extraordinary genius, who doubt whether the whole universe, or, to put it more widely, all existence, was created only according to Euclidean geometry. They even dare to dream that two parallel lines which, according to Euclid, can never meet on earth, may meet somewhere in infinity. I, my dear chap, have come to the conclusion that if I can't understand even that, then how can I be expected to understand God? I humbly admit that I have no aptitude for settling such questions. I have a Euclidean, an earthly mind. So how can I be expected to solve problems which are not of this world? I advise you, too, Alyosha, my friend, never to think about it, and least of all about whether there is a god or not. All these are problems which are entirely unsuited to a mind created with an understanding of only three dimensions.'[51]

If there is a visible, Euclidean world on the one hand and an invisible, non-Euclidean world on the other, then it is probably impossible to bring them into contact. They are not only incompatible but mutually exclusive, like crow and heaven in Kafka's aphorism. Ivan does not doubt the existence of a non-Euclidean harmony ('I believe in the eternal harmony into which we are all supposed to merge one day. I believe in the Word to which the universe is striving and which itself was "with God" and which was God, and, well, so on and so forth, *ad infinitum*.'), only he finds it impossible to accept it, and for very good reasons. A non-Euclidean harmony has no regard for the human, Euclidean world; like Sortini's letter to Amalia, it is a violation of it because it is not a moral harmony. As Ivan puts it, quite clearly foreshadowing the position of twentieth-century radical existentialism:

With my pitiful, earthly, Euclidean understanding, all I know is that there is suffering and that there are none guilty; that cause follows effect, simply and directly; that everything flows and finds its level—but that's only Euclidean nonsense. I know that, and I can't consent to live by it! I must have justice, or I will destroy myself. And not justice in some remote infinite time and space, but here on earth, and that I could see myself . . . surely I haven't suffered simply that I, my crimes and my sufferings may manure the soil of the future harmony for somebody else . . . I don't want harmony. For love for humanity I don't want it. I would rather be left with the unavenged suffering.'[52]

We shall see that Kafka, in *The Trial*, takes up Dostoevsky's argument once more, providing interesting proof of it. And the K. of *The Castle* recommends to Pepi, during the lengthy conversations which make up the final pages of the novel, that she should accept her low position and suffering in place of any striving for infinite things. What is above all remarkable in Ivan's and K.'s position is their ability to understand, and in K.'s case actually to accept, the consequences of 'non-Euclidean' logic. Nineteenth-century literature was, on the whole, an impressive affirmation of 'Euclidean' harmony, to stay with Dostoevsky's metaphor, and the more majestic passages in nineteenth-century Realism, its frequent 'hosannas', and staging of 'significant moments', provide ample proof of this affirmation. In Dostoevsky's words, the whole age was concerned with organizing 'a universal state'.[53] The idea of harmony was an axiom derived from 'European hypotheses.'[54] The typical nineteenth-century attitude is expressed in a poem by Walt Whitman, the defender *par excellence* of Euclidean harmony:

> Logic and sermons never convince,
> The damp of the night drives deeper into my soul,
> Only what proves itself to every man and woman is so,
> Only what nobody denies is so.[55]

Oddly enough, even Nietzsche agrees at times with this late nineteenth-century position, as for example when he says: 'die Wertschätzung der Logik beweist nur die durch die Erfahrung bewiesene Nützlichkeit derselben für das Leben: nicht deren Wahrheit.'[56] ('the esteem which logic enjoys proves only its usefulness for life as proved by experience—not that it is true.') The opposite point is made towards the end of *The Trial*: 'Logic is . . . unshakable.' True, 'it cannot withstand a man who wants to go on living.' But the desire to live vanishes once Logic has been encountered in its transcendental form and force, a logic that has nothing to do with the power of persuasion we associate with commonsense experience. In the absence of any real alternatives, Josef K. had to convince himself that Logic, in the former sense, was indeed unshakable and that there was no point, at the end of his 'Prozess' (in both senses of the word), in beginning it again. *The Trial* ends with an affirmation of a non-human harmony. K.'s last view is of his two executioners as they, 'cheek leaning against cheek' (one of Kafka's most extraordinary juxtapositions of sentimental imagery and sinister context), watch him die. Life under the shadow of this extra-terrestrial harmony is no more than a farce. K.'s way out is to demand his own annihilation, thereby carrying out what had remained a mere threat and blasphemy with Ivan.

*The Trial* is Dostoevskyan in its radical critique of a cosmic harmony that leaves single individuals, like K., high and dry; it is un-Dostoevskyan in its refusal to explore the possibility of what we have already got, human existence, any further. The sentence 'Logic is doubtless unshakable, but it cannot withstand a man who wants to go on living' is a brilliant example of what might be considered a striking parallel, in the realm of ethics, to Niels Bohr's principle of complementarity, a principle Einstein could not being himself to accept because it did not satisfy his demand for non-statistical natural laws, and ultimately his own craving for harmony. Yet it is the principle that will explain different manifestations of one and the same phenomenon, and conveniently remove what would otherwise be a position of stalemate between nature and the scientist. Kafka's sentence, however, as a statement on the complementarity of what 'Logic' demands and the human urge 'to live' (notice that equal weight is given to both), is, ironically enough, both an explanation for the actual stalemate between K. and the Law and a criticism of the existential dilemma we create for ourselves by inventing absolutes. *Hic Rhodus, hic salta!* If we are so fond of dealing with transcendental forces, as the nineteenth century has encouraged us to do (for the most thorough analysis cf. Dostoevsky's *Notes from Underground*), then 'die Logik ist transzendental' (Wittgenstein) as well. In a situation in which man has created for himself not the Greek 'shining fantasy of the Olympians' (Nietzsche) but a metaphysical Olympus with absolute demands, Logic cannot remain 'human'; it cannot remain a logic with no other purpose than to provide proof of 'die durch die Erfahrung bewiesene Nützlichkeit derselben für das Leben.' Unfortunately, it is also a logic through which human existence experiences its utmost degradation. Seen in this way, *The Trial* reveals itself as the most logical and therefore the most devastating critique of the nineteenth-century intellectual and metaphysical heritage which we have hitherto been offered. And I am not forgetting Dostoevsky's *Notes*. What is more, in *The Castle* Kafka even managed to take the critique a stage further, by well-nigh exploding the myth of a transcendental world, and by resisting the temptation to turn K. into a sacrificial victim. Though even in this novel the positivist methodology remains implicit, it nevertheless constitutes the hidden basis of *The Castle*.

In *The Trial*, on the other hand, Kafka could not resist throwing the whole weight of his narrative powers into one scale. At this point in time he is more interested in demonstrating the unshakability of the 'Logic' than he is in paying homage to its equally unshakable complementary force. In his fiction Dostoevsky did not, and could not, do even that. It is characteristic of his writing to dramatize rather than to analyse the contradiction he had himself so convincingly described in the *Notes*. Here is how Ivan Karamazov reacts to his own unshakable conclusions:

'I want to live and I go on living, even if it's against logic. However much I may disbelieve in the order of things, I still love the sticky little leaves that open up in the spring. I love the blue sky; . . . I love great human achievements, in which I've perhaps lost faith long ago, but which from old habit my heart still reveres . . . I want to travel in Europe, Alyosha, and I shall be going abroad. I know very well that I'm only going to a graveyard, but it's a precious graveyard . . . And I shall not weep from despair, but simply because I shall be happy in my tears. I shall get drunk on my own emotion. I love the sticky little leaves of spring and the blue sky—yes I do! It's not a matter of intellect or logic. You love it all with your inside, with your belly.'[57]

If we ask ourselves whether Dostoevsky's passionate awareness of the possibly 'non-Euclidean' quality of the universe had a decisive formal influence on his writing, then the answer must be, in my opinion, in the negative. In his novels the expression of non-Euclidean wisdom does not transcend the level of sentiment. In the final analysis it is no more than an admittedly powerful and unexpected symbol of what Dostoevsky was really interested in: the status and function of the irrational in human experience, as he tirelessly explores it in his otherwise 'Euclidean' narrative structures. Dostoevsky still flirted with the possibility of devising a logic in which there was room for 'sticky little leaves' so that they might lose their merely metaphorical qualities—something Kafka could no longer bring himself to do. Hence his distrust of metaphors, which according to him only deceive us into believing that such a logic is possible. Dostoevsky did not exactly believe that a rational poetics was possible in which the logic of the universe was revealed through specific, poetic imagery, but he could not conceive of an alternative either. Not until Kafka do we find in literature a non-Euclidean mentality that can in any sense be said to be an integral part of its poetics. Even Proust's and Joyce's relativization of time cannot be taken as anything more than an interesting analogue to Einstein's thinking on the matter. Proust's well known reference to Einstein, his suggestion that the presentation of a space-time continuum in his work has something to do with the time-space continuum in modern physics, must remain an unrealized metaphor. What is missing is the clear sense of the existence of an objective and a subjective order, and an even clearer sense of the need for experimental verification of whatever is said or assumed about the objective side of things.

In Kafka's work we find precisely this: a stubbornly upheld Kantian dualism ('konsequenter Dualismus', as Christian von Ehrenfels called it in his *Kosmogonie*, 1916), *combined* with an experimental attitude and a rage for verification, both of which he incorporated, selfconsciously but without further comment, in his work. Dostoevsky and Nietzsche discussed, analysed, dissected the Leibnizian idea of harmony, and ideas related to it, and furiously demanded its dissolution. But Kafka had the imagination to devise a narrative structure of which, as I hope my earlier account of the first chapter of *The Trial* has shown, the critique of untested metaphysical notions is an integral part. The very plot is an experiment in epistemology. K.'s experience in Bürgel's room leads him, or rather the reader, to the discovery that mystical states are no more than partial eclipses of human consciousness. There will always remain the flicker of a dream, not about anything sublime but about the very thing K. had tried to forget: his fight with an enemy who can never be got hold of. From the point of view of human experience, the idea of mystical consciousness, whether it is based on total transcendentalism or on an assumed simultaneous presence of the seen and the unseen, is a logical impossibility. Mystical states of various degrees of intensity merely betray various degrees of falseness, if we claim that such states betoken the actual presence of the divine. K. has no choice but to shut the door behind Bürgel, leaving him to his chatter and prattle, only then of course to be faced with the final lesson: the exposure of the activities in the Herrenhof as none other than a caricature of our own futile striving.

Kuznetsov describes Dostoevsky's rebellion against a cosmology in which the fate of a speck of dust was as immaterial to the motion of the planet as the fate of a single organism was to the life or death of the species. In Einstein's emphasis on 'actual cases', and more radically so in modern particle physics, the importance of macroscopic and microscopic events is reversed. But Dostoevsky's desire for a universal harmony in which individual fates will not be 'negligibles' is exposed as wishful thinking in Kafka's verified world once we have decided to leave our salvation in the hands of absolutes. At the time he was writing his great works, Kafka could not help but demonstrate, with all the masochism he was capable of, that individuals *are* 'negligibles'. Josef K. becomes the sacrificial victim of an extrapersonal harmony; Amalia, Ivan's counterpart, of very much the same thing; K. is likened to a 'blindworm', and considered a creature worse than a 'nocturnal moth', when he pushes his luck as a proud individual. His activities are said to produce, at best, grotesque imprints in the snow, but nothing more. And ultimately his file is destroyed through sheer official negligence. All this is suffered by an 'actual case', and the fact that the letter K. sounds more like a mathematical symbol than a name highlights, in an inescapably logical way, the 'actuality' of this case.

111

# Kimberly Sparks

## Radicalization of Space in Kafka's Stories

At the end of Nabokov's novel *Ada*, Dr Ivan Veen says, 'I cannot imagine Space without Time.' Then he adds that he can very well imagine time without space. ' "Space-Time," ' he grumbles, 'that hideous hybrid whose very hyphen looks phoney. One can be a hater of Space and a lover of Time.'[1]

Like any novelist with a strong sense of the public, Nabokov makes his excursion on time and space playful and mock-solemn, with Dr Veen playing Uncle Toby to his own Father Shandy. And just as Nabokov escapes any serious scholarly responsibility by dodging behind his wicked Dr Veen, so does Thomas Mann hide behind the gentle pomposity of Professor Kuckuck in the *Confessions of Felix Krull*. How else but in the ironic mode would one dare to recapitulate the history of the space-time problem all the way from Heraclitus to Einstein? Dr Veen does it, first disposing of Heraclitus' river of constant flux by turning it into what he calls 'water-closet time', then flushing his way through the history of the problem to end with a rejection of 'the artificial concept of space-tainted, space-parasited time, the space-time of relativist literature.'[2] At the finish Dr Veen allies himself with those anti-spatialists who are unable to fold a roadmap.

Professor Kuckuck is less perverse, but just as ambitious in his exposition. He delivers a serio-comic cosmogony to a non-paying audience of one in a dining car between Paris and Lisbon. He cannot know, of course, that his listener is actually a latter-day Hermes, the patron of novelists and the patron of liars and thieves; and he probably doesn't know that ideal travellers on ideal trains are often used in popularizations of the theory of relativity.

There are of course more solemn dissertations on space and time. The works of Hermann Broch are a good example and later in this essay I shall try to characterize what one might call Broch's will to geometry. Of all the literary approaches to the space-time problem, Broch's is the most responsible, although scarcely the most accessible. His is the most serious long-term consideration of what has become a major critical issue in the twentieth century, namely, the spatialization of time.

As the term is used in literary criticism, spatialized time is the very opposite of sequential time; that is to say, it is the opposite of chronicling or simple storytelling. In spatialized time the emphasis is on simultaneity, on the juxtaposition of large numbers of objects or emotions that are posited as co-existing in an instant of time. This generates a paradox when it comes to literature, since it takes a considerable amount of simple, linear time just to list the things that are supposed to exist in simultaneous equilibrium with each other.

As one American critic puts it, 'the reader may feel that although language arranges words one after the other, like beads on a string, this fact does not tell us very much, since literature always seems intent on a vision of the world which would free the mind from any such narrow and mechanical scheme. It may even be said that literature tends to destroy or neutralize time by "spatializing" as simultaneous elements the things which words name one by one.'[3]

Other modern American critics use categories derived from Lessing to talk about the space-time problem in modern prose; Joseph Frank, for example, whose long essay on 'Spatial Form in Modern Literature'[4] was the American rediscovery of Lessing as a critic. Frank investigates the stagnation of time caused by the modern novelist's obsession with the simultaneous reflexive relationships among large numbers of things going on at the same instant. Joyce's *Ulysses* is Frank's central example, as it is in Hermann Broch's essay fragment 'Über syntaktische und kognitive Einheiten'[5] ('On syntactic and cognitive entities'), where Broch addresses the problem of simultaneity in modern prose. Broch suggests that the sentence, in this case Molly Bloom's enormous pseudo-sentence, is the appropriate syntactical instrument for binding discrete experiences into simultaneous equilibrium. *Gleichgewichtsherstellung* is Broch's

113

term for the act of spatializing time, and *Gleichgewichtskon-stellation* is his word for the resulting image.

Much of the currency of the term 'spatialized time' is due to Henri Bergson, who, like Dr Veen, is an anti-spatialist. In differentiating between two kinds of duration Bergson confirms the notion of spatialized time in literature, albeit negatively. One sort of duration is for him 'the form which the succession of our conscious states assumes when our ego lets itself *live*, when it refrains from separating its present states from its former states.'[6] The other sense of duration, the spatialized one, is generated when 'we set our states of consciousness side-by-side in such a way as to perceive them simultaneously, no longer in one another, but alongside; in a word we project time into space, we express duration in terms of extensity, and succession takes the form of a continuous line or chain, the parts of which touch each other without penetrating one another.'[7]

Bertrand Russell puts down Bergson's ideas on time as the 'mere autobiographical observations of a visualizer', whose 'views depend on the predominance of the sense of sight in him.'[8] But perhaps it is just this visual dependence that has made Bergson so useful to the critics. In any event, Gaston Bachelard offers a gentler critique when he concludes that 'profound metaphysics is rooted in an implicit geometry which—whether we will or no—confers spatiality upon thought; if a metaphysician could not draw, what would he think?'[9]

Mechanical clocks as we ordinarily think of them are actually space machines, that is to say, they turn temporal sequence into spatial succession. The mathematician Hermann Weyl puts this more poetically when he talks about natural clocks in his book on symmetry. 'In one-dimensional time', he says, 'repetition at equal intervals is the musical principle of rhythm. As a shoot grows, it translates, one might say, a slow temporal [rhythm] into a spatial rhythm.'[10] It is a thought calculated to drive Dr Veen wild. 'That sort of gossip may be pleasing, especially when we are young', he says, 'but no one shall make me believe that the movement of matter (say, a pointer) across a carved-out area of space (say, a dial) is by nature identical with the "passing" of time.'[11]

Clocks and watches in literature always seem to stand on the border between collectively experienced time and individually experienced time. If a fictional character and the world outside him are attuned to each other, then a real-world clock will work for him. But the more out of phase a character is with his surroundings, the more useless a standard clock becomes. For the introverted fictional character a clock becomes an absurd instrument—decorative at best, at worst a constant reminder of his out-of-stepness. Think of the wheezing clock that threatens Dostoevsky's underground man, or the accelerating clock at the beginning of Kafka's *Metamorphosis*, or of the clock without gears that is adequate to tell the time for Jean Paul's Schoolmaster Wutz.

The disagreement of public and private clocks—and the attendant disjuncture of public and private spaces—is doubtless what led Heinz Politzer to choose the fragment called *Gibs auf!* (*Give it up!*) as the text on which to base his discourse on method in his Kafka book.

It was very early in the morning, the streets clean and deserted, I was on my way to the railroad station. As I compared the tower clock with my watch I realized it was already much later than I thought, I had to hurry, the shock of this discovery made me feel uncertain of the way, I was not very well acquainted with the town as yet, fortunately there was a policeman nearby, I ran to him and breathlessly asked him the way. He smiled and said: 'From me you want to learn the way?' 'Yes,' I said, 'since I cannot find it myself.' 'Give it up, give it up,' said he, and turned away with a great sweep, like someone who wants to be alone with his laughter.[12]

As far as spatialized time in literature is concerned, the more emphasis one puts on the *simultaneity* of events, the more *useless* becomes a device designed to picture the *sequentiality* of events.

There have been a number of conscious and wilful literary experiments directed at the apparent paradox of simultaneity and sequence. One of the most radical and beautiful of these is the Benjy chapter in *The Sound and the Fury*. Benjy is Quentin Compson's brother, but whereas Quentin is highly intelligent and overwhelmed by a too-finely developed sense of personal time (he is a freshman at Harvard when he commits suicide), Benjy is a gentle idiot, devoid of all sense of time and all sense of causality. The chapter in which we see the world through Benjy's eyes is a *tour de force* of almost pure spatialization. The sense of flow is completely thwarted. All events are juxtaposed and simultaneous because Benjy lacks the faculty to string them out in causal chains, and consequently all causal connectives—such as 'because', or 'therefore' or 'since'—are absent. Benjy can make no conceptual connections whatsoever, he can only associate bright shapes and smells and pains with his simple emotions; and the progress from emotional state to emotional state is always keyed associatively, never causally.

It will be worth considering one example of how Benjy experiences the world. Faulkner is obviously pleased with this passage as a minor technical victory, because he repeats it several times. Benjy is being taken to town in a buggy. Queenie is the name of the horse. The causal thread is simple: the buggy moves to town and turns slowly round the confederate war memorial in the town square. For Benjy, however, the trip becomes a series of discrete images that he cannot bind into a conceptual whole. And so the trees they pass seem themselves to flow and the light spaces between the trees are just bright shapes. As they slow down to turn round the statue in the square, the stopping of the one wheel is an event independent of the continued rolling of the other.

> I could hear Queenie's feet and the bright shapes went smooth and steady on both sides, the shadows of them flowing across Queenie's back. They went on like the bright tops of the wheels. Then those on one side stopped at the tall white post where the soldier was. But on the other side they went on smooth and steady, but a little slower.[13]

Benjy's apprehension of space is infantile, limited to the simplest geometrical relationship of 'nearby-ness.' He cannot even deal with the simple qualities of separation, spatial succession, enclosure and continuity. Piaget tells us that these 'are of a primitive character, forming that part of geometry called topology, [which is] foreign to the notions of rigid

116

shapes, distances, and angles, or to mensuration and projective relations.'[14]

A feeling for Benjy's infantile experience of space and time is just as important to an understanding of Kafka as is the sophisticated notion of the spatialization of time. More important, if possible, for in many if not most Kafka characters the sense of infancy and birth is just below the surface, and there is a constant confusion of bedrooms, sickrooms, nurseries and cells. These elementary spaces, and the hero's primitive, topological investigation of them, figure importantly in such stories as *The Judgment*, *Metamorphosis*, *A Country Doctor*, *In the Penal Colony* and in the novel *America*.

But there is a more primitive sort of clock that is appropriate to the more primitive sense of space that Piaget calls topological. Such a clock is made up of a collection of objects and the space that is used to house them. It can be referred to, for want of a better term, as a fetish clock or a junk clock. Mechanical clocks are Euclidean devices, dependent on rigid geometries and finely divided symmetries and precise rational rhythms. But for a simple mind, a mechanical clock is remarkable only for its shininess, or its ticking, or its association with father. For a childish mind a clock is a fetish, and like any other fetish it can be gathered into a collection of fetishes and stored in an appropriate space, which for a child or for an infant/ adult is almost always a bedroom or a transformation of a bedroom. And in the way such a collection behaves—whether it grows or shrinks, whether it becomes more orderly or less orderly—resides its ability to tell time.

An example of such a collection can be found in *The Life of the Cheerful Schoolmaster Maria Wutz* by Jean Paul. This particular collection is interesting for several reasons. First, the collection was made by a child, and children are the best collectors. We will see it, however, displayed on an old man's deathbed. Second, the collector was a claustrophiliac, a lover of small spaces, and the best collections come cramped for space. And third, the collection is the product of a desire never to grow up, underscored in this case by an almost anal refusal to part with much-handled treasures. In sum, this little collection is the residue of a species of innocent and gentle idiocy:

I must not forget that I promised to tell you about the objects our Wutz had about him on the bed. First of all there was a child's cap of green taffeta with one ribbon torn off; next, a child's toy whip on which there were still some flecks of gold; a tin wedding band; a box with the tiniest books imaginable; a wall clock; a dirty notebook and a bird trap the size of one's index finger.[15]

The objects in this pathetic collection are all highly charged with the memories of Wutz's childhood. He passes these souvenirs through his hands as another man might tell his beads. And their arrangement on the bed is not mere juxtaposition: Wutz's collection is in truth an ensemble with a peculiar kind of harmony.

But if Wutz's collection is the residue of an encapsulated world, a *petit monde* as Jean Paul puts it, the *grand monde* is never far away. And the values of the great world outside can also be concretized in ensembles of junk. When junk is emblematic of public values it becomes that kind of public fetish that is technically called 'kitsch'.

Flaubert presents both kinds of junk clocks in his story *A Simple Heart*, but where Jean Paul uses his narrator's pocketwatch to show us the disagreement of public time and Wutzian time, Flaubert actually sets the two clocks running counter to each other. The dynamic of the story is decay and disintegration, a pessimistic thought—but not a surprising one from a man who once said to George Sand that 'the whole dream of democracy is to elevate the proletariat to the level of stupidity of the bourgeoisie.'[16] The decay and disintegration that we see in the story is public decay, the diminution of a society's cultural and moral vigour. The decay is presented in terms of a public collection which is in a state of reduction. The receptacle for this particular inventory is the house of Madame Aubain, a widow who is presiding over the decline of a once wealthy family. The furnishings of her house have been culled from the fittings of the several houses which her family once owned. A two-sentence glimpse into Madame Aubain's parlour will at once convey the crampedness of the container:

Eight mahogany chairs were lined up against the white-painted wainscoting, and under the barometer stood an old piano loaded with a pyramid of boxes and cartons. On either side of the chimney-piece, which was carved out of yellow marble in the Louis Quinze style, there was a tapestry-covered armchair, and in the middle was a clock designed to look like a temple of Vesta. The whole room smelt a little musty . . .[17]

The gradual emptying out of Madame Aubain's house constitutes one clock by which the story is timed, and into this world in decline Flaubert inserts Félicité, a simple mind, an innocent and almost inarticulate creature whom Flaubert compares to the mute beasts of the fields. He makes her into a collector and as the Aubain house gradually empties out, Félicité transports souvenirs to her attic room—souvenirs, paradoxically, of experiences she herself has never had. It is a mark of Flaubert's affection for Félicité that he makes her so naive, so innocent, so ineducable that even this world in decay cannot corrupt her. For while the objects in her collection register on the educated reader as a chaos of tawdry, secondary cultural clichés, for her they are an inventory of fresh primary images, keyed to the emotions she has never been able to express. It is an ensemble of pure images because Félicité is an almost pure magpie, innocent of any ability to understand the world in conceptual terms. Her collecting principle is her capacity to be touched and dazzled. Here are the contents of Félicité's room:

This place, to which few people were ever admitted, contained such a quantity of religious bric-à-brac and miscellaneous oddments that it looked like a cross between a chapel and a bazaar.
A big wardrobe prevented the door from opening properly . . . There was a table beside the bed, with a water-jug, a couple of combs, and a block of blue soap in a chipped plate. On the walls there were rosaries, medals, several pictures of the Virgin, and a holy-water stoup made out of a coconut. On the chest of drawers, which was draped with a cloth just like an altar, was the shell box Victor had given her, and also a watering-can and a ball, some copy-books, the

119

illustrated geography book, and a pair of ankle-boots. And on the nail supporting the looking-glass, fastened by its ribbons, hung the little plush hat [that had belonged to Virginie].

. . .

All the old rubbish Madame Aubain had no more use for, she carried off to her room. That was how there came to be artificial flowers along the edge of the chest of drawers and a portrait of the Comte d'Artois in the window recess.[18]

Madame Aubain's collection measures the decline of a family, the loss of social and personal identity. Félicité's collection of fetishes times an elementary kind of growth, the simple imaging of a simple mind. Taken together, the parlour and the servant's bedroom—two antithetical spaces—form a kind of hourglass, with rubbish for sand and death for a stopping place. There are sophisticated ways of looking at such primitive topological clocks. One way—a very valuable way—is to examine the individual objects in a pathetic collection. This is the method of Freudian explication and it has characterized much of Kafka criticism. Just think of the speculation on Georg Bendemann's watch chain, or on the lady in the fur boa who means so much to Gregor Samsa, or even think of the piece of Veronese salami in Karl Rossman's footlocker.

But there is another way—a very modern way—and this is to examine the collection as a whole, together with the space it is housed in, in an attempt to get at the abstract sense of ensemble that underlies it. This critical concept has no easy label, but it has to do with the concept of entropy, which is part of the theory of thermodynamics.

The special usefulness of the entropy principle is its applic-ability to ensembles, to systems on any scale. Entropy and negative entropy, as measures of disorder and order, have tempted thinkers in various fields to appropriate the thermo-dynamic model and apply it to considerations of time and form. Some scholars have even called entropy 'time's arrow' because it reflects the statistical tendency of any collection of things to proceed from a state of differentiation and organiza-tion to a state of randomness. On the universal scale, the irreversible rise in entropy points towards a statistical chaos.

It seems somehow paradoxical to use elevated terms like 'entropy' or the 'spatialization of time' to get at the primitive sense of space and time that governs such childish creatures as Maria Wutz or Félicité or Benjy Compson, but the most elementary experiences of space and time are the hardest to formalize. And it is really the *infantilization of space* that sets Kafka's writing apart from the high intellectualizations of space that one finds in Goethe's *Novelle*, or in Kleist's *Michael Kolhaas*, or in Hermann Broch's *Die Schuldlosen*. The telescope with which the princess in Goethe's *Novelle* looks over into the past spatializes time in a complicated and symbolic way. To re-establish the spatial symmetry of the three market place scenes in *Michael Kolhaas* requires prodigious feats of memory on the part of the reader, and the Euclidean figurings of space in Broch's novels are extraordinarily complex, forcing the reader into a kind of quasi-mathematical speculation.

In Kafka, however, topological space dominates Euclidean space—land-surveyors to the contrary notwithstanding—and even his most conscious and apparently sophisticated characters experience space and time in primitive ways.

Georg Bendemann is an excellent example of this and *The Judgment* can serve as a paradigm for the way Kafka uses space. Georg is as mature, lucid and articulate as any of Kafka's characters. He has a room of his own, he has succeeded his father in business life, he is engaged to Frieda Brandenfeld—and he wears a watch and chain. He even has a friend—or the fiction of a friend—to whom he writes and towards whom he behaves in ways that show a highly developed sense of strategy and conscious dissimulation. Georg can speak and he can write, which seems at first to set him off from those characters who are unable to communicate in words. Kafka constantly equates the inability to speak with infancy or regression. Gregor Samsa loses the gift of speech immediately after his metamorphosis; the condemned man in the penal colony can't speak the language of the explorer and the officer; and Karl Rossman's 'first and most important task' in America is to learn English, for as his Uncle Jakob tells him, 'a European's first days in America are a kind of birth.'

On one level Georg Bendemann is conscious of the problem

of space—or spaces—for he suggests that he and his father exchange rooms, and he reflects on the other spaces in which he and his father meet: their common living room at home, the restaurant in which they take their lunches, the office—none of which we ever actually see. In fact, Georg's conscious musings on rooms reveal little of the way he really perceives space.

The unconscious structure of the story is a primitive spatial dynamic that expresses the contrary urges that Georg can never voice. *The Judgment* begins as it ends, with the dialectics of inside and outside, one of the most elementary geometrical oppositions, but one capable of being exaggerated, even radicalized, which is just what Kafka does. When it is introduced in the first paragraph of the story, the opposition of inside and outside seems bland enough, almost pleasant. It is a Sunday morning in spring and Georg Bendemann, a young businessman, is sitting at the open window of his room, looking out onto the river that parallels the street in front of his house, seeing the bridge over the river and the hills on the far bank. He has just finished writing a letter to a childhood friend, who is now living abroad.

The scene as Kafka sets it is bland to the point of pallor, as devoid of motion as it is of real colour. At first glance the scene would seem to be quietly natural, but Georg's room is only described as a 'Privatzimmer', and except for the desk at which he is sitting, no furnishings are mentioned, not even a bed, that most indispensable of props in a Kafka story.

The day itself has no qualities except for its name and its location in the spring. The house in which Georg lives is nondescript, one of a row of similar houses that stretch along the river. 'Leichtgebaut' (lightly built) is the only adjective that Kafka applies to them, a much less striking word than 'ramshackle' which the Muirs use in their translation.

If the reader can transpose the scene onto a canvas, he will see that the row of houses is but one of a set of four similar images in the first paragraph. The houses constitute a long, segmented, repetitive image, physically parallel to and visually analogous to the river. The metaphorical analogy is strengthened when Kafka writes that the houses 'sich hinziehen',—they stretch out—along the river. The bridge is a similar image, both visually and by metaphorical association, for not only is it sensibly associated with the river, and not only is it the same sort of long-oriented, segmental image—Georg focuses on the bars of the bridge railing at the end of the story—but it connects the houses and the river with the last in this set of images: the low undifferentiated hills on the other bank, hills whose only attribute is their 'schwaches Grün'. Again the Muirs choose too strong a word when they call it a 'tender' green.

The landscape is clearly a dead abstraction, a consciously chosen setting for the sealing of the letter to Georg's friend abroad. But even this framed action, set as it is in the tension between outside and inside, is retarded and muted. Kafka says of the letter that Georg 'sealed it in playful slowness'. There is no paper, no envelope, just the action of sealing. 'Verschliessen' is Kafka's word for it, and it is the most highly charged word in the paragraph.

Kafka himself says, in a letter to Felice, that the story is full of unadmitted abstractions. The concreteness of these initial images is minimized in favour of what Gaston Bachelard calls 'the drama of intimate geometry',[19] a simple opposition 'tinged with aggressivity'.[20] But even in their nakedness the houses, the river, the bridge and the hills suggest a family of similar images that are characteristic of a number of Kafka beginnings. They are all images of an apparent outside, but they nevertheless carry in them a strong sense of enclosure. When Gregor Samsa finally manages to open his bedroom door in *Metamorphosis*, the first thing he sees is a more elaborate version of the houses at the beginning of *The Judgment*:

> The light had meanwhile strengthened; on the other side of the street one could clearly see a section of the endlessly long, dark-gray building opposite—it was a hospital—abruptly punctuated by its row of regular windows.[21]

The apparent outside described in *In the Penal Colony* is a deep, sandy valley completely surrounded by naked slopes—a clear extension of the image of the low hills across the river from Georg Bendemann's window. And the bridge as portrayed at the end of *The Judgment* finds its extension and exaggeration in *A Hunger-Artist*. Not only does Georg hold onto the bridge railing 'as a starving man clutches food',[22] but the bars that support the railing are the root image for the hunger-artist's cage.

In their most radical form these long-oriented, repetitive images of an apparent outside become images of the body itself. In the first paragraph of *Metamorphosis* Gregor Samsa architecturalizes himself when he sees his 'dome-like brown body divided into stiff arched segments'.[23] And in *A Hunger-Artist* Kafka forces the visual equation of the hunger-artist's body and his cage.

In and of itself, the abstract opposition of outside and inside has nothing to do with time. Only when the spatial metaphor begins to evolve and vary itself does time become an issue. But it is a strange kind of time; it is not a time to be expressed in terms of causal logic, but rather in terms of a logic of association, the logic of the spontaneous succession of spaces.

Kafka makes this point in a telling way in *The Judgment*. He does it by extending in time a physical gesture that requires only a moment for its actual accomplishment. The gesture is easy to précis: Georg Bendemann seals the letter to his friend and sticks it in his pocket. There's nothing more to it than that, and yet a third of the total length of the story is devoted to getting the letter from Georg's desk to his pocket. What fills the intervening space and time is a digression on the theme of outside and inside that is as necessary to this story as the digression on Odysseus' scar is to the *Odyssey*.

With the letter in his hand, Georg falls into an automatic reverie in which he begins to harden and exaggerate the indeterminate spatial images of the first paragraph. The notion of outside enlarges from the view across the river to the immensity of Russia, the place to which Georg's friend has fled. But as in all Kafka stories, the outside is only an apparent outside and asylum turns into enclosure. Georg generates for himself the picture of his friend—jaundiced, wearing an alien beard, isolated from the German-speaking colony in St Petersburg, isolated even further by the solicitude with which Georg withholds significant news of home. And to make his friend's encapsulation final, George sticks the letter in his pocket.

Pockets are one of Kafka's favourite reductions of 'inside'.

124

Georg Bendemann's father even has pockets in his nightshirt. Karl Rossman has a secret pocket in which he keeps his passport, and Karl's clown companion, Robinson, has a white waistcoat with four little black-bordered pockets. But Robinson is a man without secrets, and so as he himself informs us, 'They aren't real pockets, they're just made to look that way.'

Having put the letter in his pocket, Georg moves farther inward. He leaves his room and walks down the short corridor to his father's room, where he will begin that terrible play of gestures that every reader of Kafka knows so well. The father's room is opposite to Georg's in every way. There are the obvious contrasts of 'Vorderzimmer', front room, and 'Hinterzimmer', back room, of light and dark, of open and closed windows. Even Georg mentions these. But what strikes one most is that in moving from Georg's room to his father's room there is a transition from a sterile space to a collector's space. The dark corner in which Mr Bendemann sits is adorned with mementos of his dead wife, and beyond these souvenirs can be seen the remains of his half-eaten breakfast, his spectacles and a newspaper. This particular collection is small and static because *The Judgment* is too short a piece for a collection to either grow or decay in. What is visible, however, is suggestive of decline and disintegration, a sense augmented by Mr Bendemann himself with his soiled underwear, his failing sight and his toothless mouth.

There are other collectors and other collections in Kafka, and almost always the collection times the regression of an immature hero. One by one the souvenirs of an unconquered adolescence disappear from Gregor Samsa's bedroom, and article by article the contents disappear from the footlocker that Karl Rossman brings as a portable home to the New World.

There is no need to go into the details of the grotesque charade through which Georg Bendemann and his father load association after association onto the topological framework of inside and outside, turning the bedroom into a birth-space, death-space, sexual space and judgment space. Nor is there any need to do more than allude to the special space-time effects that Kafka uses in this story—the radical perspective from which the cowering Georg looks up at his father looming over him with his fingers touching the ceiling, or the way the bedsheet unfolds in the air when it is thrown off by Mr Bendemann. The space and time of the victim always distort and stretch under the weight of authority, and these pieces of trick photography are easy enough to accommodate, like the slow motion apples in *Metamorphosis* or the frantic harbour traffic in *America*.

But we need to follow and understand Georg's headlong flight down the stairs, out of the door, across the street and onto the bridge. The re-establishment of the image of the bridge completes the spatial template of the story; it confirms the dialectic of inside and outside, the formal abstraction on which the story is built.

It is an abstraction which is so insistent that spatial symmetry in *The Judgment* completely dominates temporal flow, as it does in *A Country Doctor*, a story which proceeds even more obviously by the method of the spontaneous generation of spaces, a story in which time misbehaves even more than it does in *The Judgment*.

What is striking, however, is the degree to which the underlying abstraction of the inside-outside asserts itself in the longer stories, which have a much stronger sense of sequential time. *Metamorphosis*, for example, begins with Gregor Samsa in his bedroom and ends with his sister Grete stretching her liberated body in the open countryside. In between come infinite variations of inside and outside, ranging from picture frames to chests of drawers to the space under Gregor's divan to Gregor's body itself.

And for all its difference in tone and despite its picaresque sense of episode, the novel *America* is erected on the same simple dialectical abstraction. Karl's first action in New York confirms it; when confronted with an apparent outside, namely the open air of New York harbour, which is dominated by a huge and threatening motherly statue, he automatically retreats to an inside, the stoker's cabin. What follows is an endless set of spatial puns built on the same simple symmetry. The visions of outside shift from New York harbour to various balconies to the open road to the infield of the racetrack at Clayton to the mountains through which the train passes on its way to the Nature Theatre of Oklahoma. But they are all just apparent outsides, just as America itself is only an apparent asylum, a schlemazzle's paradise.

The inside spaces in *America* are the most intriguing; the labyrinth of the ship's passages and compartments are a kind of portable Europe with rooms varying from the stoker's airless cabin to the galley to the elaborately ceremonial inner space of the captain's cabin with its view of New York staring in through its triptych windows. 'Yes, in this room one knew where one was', reads the text. There is Johanna Brummer's tiny bedroom, where Karl has committed the thinly disguised incest for which he has been sentenced to America. There is Karl's bedroom in his uncle's house and there are proliferations of bedroom throughout the story. But what Kafka seems to enjoy most are the reductions of space that are less obvious translations of inside. Mention has already been made of Robinson's sham pockets, the secret pocket in Karl's suit and the footlocker in which Karl carries his souvenirs of home. But one of the most fascinating space machines in the whole novel is the American writing desk which stands in Karl's room at his Uncle Jakob's house. It is a wonderful creation with hundreds of compartments, and by cranking a handle attached to its side one could produce infinite variations on these compartments so that, as Kafka puts it, even the President of the United States could find a place for each of his state documents in it. It is a structure adequate to the complexity of the law.

The alternation of inside and outside in *America* produces the rhythms by which the novel is timed. The geometrical dialectic forms a clock which, like all clocks, translates spatial rhythms into temporal rhythms. And like all true clocks, it can only time the past. In Kafka this is good enough, for none of his characters ever has a future. Not even America can provide a time to grow in. It can only provide a time for infinite regression, for elaborations on a foregone past. New York is no truer an outside for Karl Rossman than is St Petersburg for Georg Bendemann's friend, for like all images of outside in Kafka, the two cities find their counter-image in a bedroom in Prague.

# Christian Goodden

## The Great Wall of China: The Elaboration of an Intellectual Dilemma

My reasons for choosing to examine *The Great Wall of China* are twofold. The first is that in spite of any structural weaknesses or narrative discontinuities which might detract aesthetically from the story, it has, like the excerpt 'Before the Law', a conceptual concentration and intellectual density which make it appealing in other ways. The fascination of this density might well explain Paul Raabe's claim that this story in particular was of central importance to Kafka himself.[1] The commentator in the story speaks for Kafka's and our own fascination when he says: 'I cannot go deeply enough into this very question.'

The other reason is that in spite of the innumerable references that have been made to this story, no critic—to this author's mind—has yet produced even a thoroughgoing exploration of the story, let alone a satisfactory one. Those accounts which do exist are either far too scant in their treatment or merely retell the story in an uncritical way. Others, such as those by Herbert Tauber, Hermann Pongs or Clement Greenberg, tend to view the story from a fairly exclusive Jewish viewpoint—a trap in the interpretation of Kafka which hopefully we have now learnt to recognize and avoid. *The Great Wall of China* is no more exclusively concerned with Jewish theology or the Diaspora than are any other of Kafka's works. Now this is not to say that Jewish elements might not be identifiable in the material of the story. Much of the power and brilliance of Kafka's art lies in the fact that his chosen concepts and motifs can cause resonances for readers in many more fields than one. And so in interpreting this or any other of Kafka's works we should be careful to bear in mind that any one metaphor, for example the 'Great Wall', can and probably does embody a multivalency which means that its significance can be interpreted in a number of ways.

Ostensibly at least, this story is about the building of a wall. Straightaway we notice that Kafka was careful to entitle the work *not* 'Die Chinesische Mauer' (as the Muirs' translation would have it) but *'Beim Bau* der Chinesischen Mauer', indicating that it is not the wall as a completed object which is being dealt with, but rather the on-going process of its construction.

This wall puts us in mind of another—the cemetery wall which K. mentions in *The Castle*. K. recalls a period in his childhood when he, like all the other boys in the village, tried to climb the wall. The exercise of climbing the wall is not the means to an end. It is the end itself. The objective could never have been to look over the top of the wall, for the children already knew what lay on the other side. They had even experienced the illusory goal, for by a side-gate they had already gained access to this place of rest, this 'Friedhof' which is the termination of all such activity. No, as K. admits in the anecdote, the real objective had something to do with the climb itself. It was the slippery wall and the anticipation and act of overcoming it which provided the spur for carrying on with the attempt. Thus, as the animal in *The Burrow* tells us, people like K. are really, if the truth be known, perpetually fascinated by the sheer difficulty of the attempt.

The suggestion that the completed wall could never have been meant to be the final objective, and that therefore the process of its completion might serve as a pretext for the fulfilment of some other ulterior motive, is confirmed by a variety of considerations. Consider, for instance, the wall's technical feasibility and also its efficacy as a means of defence—the purpose which, ostensibly, it is meant to serve. China, the territory which it is meant to defend, is so large, indeed to all intents and purposes so infinitely large—'the endless leagues of China' (p. 70)—that the wall would on the one hand have to be impossibly long, and would on the other take an eternity to construct. Notwithstanding these impossibilities the wall has been started. But, whereas one long incomplete stretch of wall might have afforded some protection, the wall has been started piecemeal, so that at no point can it even begin to serve its purpose, for at any point the enemy, which it is supposed to keep out, can come in. (cf. p. 67) As the commentator in the story observes, it is more than useless, for the individual completed pieces are simply left to be destroyed by the enemy. Compounding with these difficulties is another. Assuming that the wall was nearing completion or, indeed, had actually been completed, no single man, not even the planners, could verify whether the wall was complete or not, partly because of its impossible length, but also, again, because of its piecemeal construction. (cf. p. 67f.) Ironically, it is probably the nomadic enemy and not the 'Führerschaft' (leadership) which has the best overall view of the state of the wall. If there is one chink in the armour, they, like water pressing around a faulty dam, will know about it. And as with any means of protection in such circumstances, even one chink is logically the only difference between a useful and an inadequate device. As an illustration, consider a fence which only partly surrounds a flock of sheep. It is of as little use as no fence at all. It either protects and contains or it does not. The same is true of the Great Wall.

The length of the wall makes it vulnerable and hence inexpedient in another more subtle way. The very fact that it is extremely long means that there is more of it exposed to attack. In this sense it works against itself. Every extra unit of length does not improve the overall degree of protection: this is constant—the wall either protects or it does not. Each additional unit of wall lowers the 'effectiveness per unit' value, that is, makes the whole more tenuous or each unit weaker or thinner in relation to the whole.[2] This Law of Inverse Proportions can be seen at work both in Kafka's life and throughout his oeuvre.

There is another reason why the building of the wall can only be a token gesture and not a serious attempt at self defence. As the animal in *The Burrow* also knows, any elaborate or extensive system of defence actually constitutes a provocation, for far from deterring possible enemies it simply invites closer attention.[3] Just as K.'s sheer protagonism draws the vigilance and vindictiveness of both the Law and the Castle upon himself, so also the building of the wall achieves exactly the reverse of what is apparently intended. It betrays or advertises the presence of a vulnerable being who otherwise would remain unnoticed. But this very fact is most revealing. The real purpose of the building of the wall is to pinpoint the builder—pinpoint him, moreover, in both senses of the word. On the one hand it betrays him to the enemy's penetrating glance, much as the butterfly is betrayed to the pin of his collector, but on the other hand, during the process (and disregarding now any suggestion of wilful masochism) it draws attention to his existence.

Of all our considerations there is one which overrides the others and proves beyond doubt that the building of the wall simply cannot serve the purpose which it pretends to do. This concerns the unreality of the enemy. Seeing that there is no threat, there is no need to build a wall to offset it. Even if it was once thought that a serious threat existed, this is not sufficient reason for building a wall nowadays. The truth is that the reality of the enemy is exploded by the colourful, exaggerated, typically mythopoeic horror with which it is portrayed. As the commentator says, nowadays the enemy has no more reality than a popular fiction or hypothesis. He knows that with or without the wall (physically) he is equally safe:

> Against whom was the Great Wall to serve as a protection? Against the people of the north. Now, I come from the south-east of China. No northern people can menace us there . . . We have not seen them, and if we remain in our villages we shall never see them, even if on their wild horses they should ride as hard as they can straight towards us—the land is too vast and would not let them reach us, they would end their course in the empty air. (pp. 73f.)

Moreover, this is not a local immunity, for the threat cannot be said to be any more real anywhere else. Characteristic of the unreality of the enemy, there is everywhere an infinite distance between the threat and the threatened.[4] From this might be inferred that the people who live in the north, those people who theoretically are exposed to the threat but who probably know that the enemy is non-existent, doubtless talk in their way about a barbaric and mysterious 'Südvolk'—a long-range extra-territorial threat which exists somewhere beyond their southernmost counterparts. Moreover, it might also be inferred that they too send off armies of men for no real reason to build a wall in the south, just as the southerners build in the north.

No doubt the same is true of the easterners and westerners. The entire nation is engaged in building a wall against an enemy which can only exist, so to speak, beyond its ken. This extraordinary arrangement would explain the strange project that ultimately the whole of China should be encompassed by wall. So, as the commentator mocks, the enemy cannot consider itself the cause of so much activity: 'Unwitting peoples of the north, who imagined they were the cause of it!' (p. 74) There remains, therefore, the 'strange conclusion' that the Wall was started as 'something inexpedient'. (p. 72)

The inexpediency of this activity is, however, only apparent. Closer scrutiny shows that the building of the wall is not quite the totally senseless activity which it might seem to be: 'and yet in one respect it has much to be said for it'. (p. 72) What is it that can be said for it? What justification can there be for believing in the existence of an enemy or authority which evidently does not exist? What are the ulterior motives for building the wall, and what purpose can it really serve? We should not underestimate the difficulty of answering these questions. At every point they touch upon imponderables which, as the commentator admits, are 'einzigartige Unklarheit' ('unique in their obscurity'): 'The limits which my capacity for thought imposes upon me are narrow enough, but the province to be traversed here is infinite.' (p. 73)

As an aid to procedure let us view the inexpediency of the building of the wall in terms of the characteristics of a quest.[5] We may define the most common type of quest as a *modus vivendi* which is psychologically and existentially comfortable. This comfort is guaranteed by the selection of an impossible goal or the recognition of some unreal and therefore implacable foe. In the case of the former there is no end to the measures which must be taken to achieve the goal, and in the case of the latter there is no end to the counter-measures or measures of appeasement which must be taken to avert or assuage the foe. In our story both the activity and counteractivity are happily united in the building of a wall. On the one hand the completed wall would be impossibly long, and on the other its construction points to an enemy whose unreality guarantees implacability and hence impossibly lengthy counter-measures. So the psychological and existential comfort must have been assured for quite a few years. Indeed, if it is accepted that the decision to build a wall has always existed right back into prehistory: 'I believe that the high command has existed from all eternity, and the decision to build the wall likewise.' (p. 74), it can also be assumed that the comfort too has been assured since time immemorial.

Moreover, we are led to believe that even though most people have now seen through the deceptive mechanism of such a quest, it is still an acceptable mode. And this brings us to the message of the story. This message is an exhortation by the commentator that we continue to accept the quest as a *modus vivendi* irrespective of whether we question it or not. Questioning the quest is not the danger. The exercise of criticizing the dishonesty of the building of the wall is academic and probably harmless. The danger is that because of this, or indeed for any other reason, the quest will be renounced: 'To set about establishing a fundamental defect here would mean undermining not only our consciences, but what is far worse, our feet.' (p. 81)

This brings us back to the comfort which must be guaranteed. Now the comfort of the quest is not the rock-bottom premise which our argument so far has made it seem, for it itself relies upon another premise—the prior assumption that the pre- or post-quest experience is less comfortable or, to put it the other way round, is even more unfortunate, than any misfortune invoked through the quest. Thus the commentator assumes that the psychological and existential benefits of building the wall outweigh the benefits of not building it. Or, in other words, he assumes that the shortcomings of the quest are slighter than those which would be incurred if the wall-construction was abandoned or if it had never been started. Here, then, we can make a retrospective explanation. The building of the wall, or quest, was started as the preferable alternative to an extra-quest predicament.

In order to test this premise, and thereby understand the arguments based upon it, it should next be asked what it is like to experience this extra-quest predicament. The commentator in our story likens the experience to that of a river which overflows its banks. (cf. p. 293) Note how the river metaphor approximates to our quest-motif. So long as the river flows on contained within its banks, it enjoys direction, an illusion of progress and a sense of definition within certain limits. As soon as it exceeds its banks, it loses all these and becomes expansive, diffuse, formless and lifeless. This is the danger, so we are warned, which would accompany a renunciation of the quest. To be outside the quest as a *modus vivendi* would be to experience the existential predicament of the river beyond its banks. There is no longer a river with a source and a goal, but an aimless, undifferentiated, chaotic, featureless mass. (cf. p. 293) Bearing this in mind, and recalling also how we likened the Great Wall to a fence which surrounds a flock of sheep, we can now begin to appreciate the wall's real purpose. It is not meant, as is pretended, to keep wolves out; it is meant to keep the flock in. The danger is not that hostile 'Nordvölker' will invade the boundaries, but that the boundaries will be overrun by the subjects from within. This is the threat to which the existence of the Chinese nation is exposed. To exist extra-murally, that is, in the pre- or post-quest predicament, is to prefer an unlimited freedom and nothingness to something limited and ambiguous, something which whilst, admittedly, imposing certain formal restrictions, does at least afford the comfort and security of a well-ordered life. This insight places the reader in a good position to understand a sentiment which crops up in many of Kafka's works. Two examples will suffice here. In *America* we learn of the worthlessness which Karl Rossmann associates with his freedom as he embarks on his quest for a position in life. In *The Trial* the advocate echoes the commentator in *The Great Wall of China* when he says that it is often better to be in chains than to be free.

The profound discomposure caused by the intimation or actual experience of this extra-mural nothingness is also mentioned in Kafka's oeuvre. It is like the discomposure of the child who sits alone in the dark and must sing to keep up his spirits. Or like the discomposure of the animal in *The Burrow* who likewise sits alone in the dark and who, in an effort to cheat his sense of unrest, first supposes an enemy and then elaborates a burrow to defend himself from it.[6] And the same is true in *The Great Wall of China*. The wall is being built to stave off discomposure. Thus, to refine the original statements, it can be argued that the real reason for the building of the wall is as follows: it was instituted (like a quest) as a collective escape from a disconcerting nothingness into a palpable form of existence.

This is an existential reason of a negative nature. We can see how the wall—viewed positively—is meant to contain and orientate the lives of those within it. The building of the wall and the (perpetual) anticipation of its completion give to existence both at the individual level of the subject and at the collective level of the nation or empire a sense of purpose and a *raison d'être*. The wall is the vehicle through which the visions and aspirations of the people are expressed: 'The humble credulity with which their [the builders'] reports were listened to, the confidence with which the simple and peaceful burgher believed in the eventual completion of the wall, all this tightened up again the cords of the soul.' (p. 70) Apart from allowing the possibility of fulfilment of these functions, the wall serves another purpose. As has been said, it does not protect those living under its shadow but rather contains them.

This notion of being contained by both the wall and the framework of the quest is a subtle one which demands elucidation. In terms of Kafka's river analogy the builders of the wall are strengthening the river-banks of their existence, so that on the one hand they do not spill out and on the other (and conversely) so that they maintain the original shape, formation and direction of their existence.[7] The wall is like the banks of a human river. Between them existence is given 'Umrisse' (boundaries) and 'Gestalt' (form). With these comes a sense of 'eigenes Wesen' (individual identity). So the wall is a kind of defining agent. It draws attention to the identity of the subject. This is what was meant by the proposition that the real purpose of the building of the wall was to pinpoint the builder in his activity. The building of the wall, like the mechanism of the quest, embodies that process whereby the creative subject points to himself and identifies himself in terms of something outside himself. It does not matter whether this is achieved through building and contemplating a wall or in resisting a fictional foe, so long as the gaze bounces back on the self, or, in the case of the enemy, the resistance makes the resister self-aware.

In this way the subject can be seen to be in league with his enemy. Although he fears him, at the same time he cannot do without him. Presumably this is what Nietzsche meant when he wrote: 'Wer davon lebt, einen Feind zu bekämpfen, hat ein Interesse daran, dass er am Leben bleibt'. ('He who has committed his life to fighting an enemy has a vested interest in keeping him alive.')[8] Seen as a collective artifact or 'Volkswerk', the wall is the object in which the whole community recognizes its collective national and imperial identity. The wall is the symbol of their co-existence, of their peculiar way of life and of their particular 'Weltanschauung'. It is a cornerstone which perspectivises their way of life, the object which gives it coherence and substance, or, to use T. S. Eliot's term, their central 'objective correlative'. It is in this sense that the building of the wall is to be seen as a lasting 'Einigungsmittel' (means of unification). It is a further instance of the human capacity (or weakness—depending on how one looks at it) to realize and believe in a sign—'die Vorstellungs- oder Glaubenskraft beim Volke'—'faith and imaginative power on the part of the people'. (p. 80)

Just as the building of the wall conceals its real function, so also does the postulation of an enemy. Of course, on the face of things the enemy is a necessary party to the ostensible function of the wall. The wall cannot appear to be built as a defence if there is no apparent enemy for it to fend off. But as has been suggested, the enemy may have nothing more than subjective reality. However, it is exactly in the guise of a mental fiction that the enemy fulfils its real function. Like the wall, it keeps a check on the state of the subject. But whereas the wall provides an existential cornerstone, the postulation of an enemy provides a moral and even an intellectual cornerstone. And just as the wall contains the subject existentially, so also the enemy acts as a guardian or deterrent—a kind of moral and intellectual wall which is meant to keep the subject from straying from the straight and narrow. The commentator in the story gives us only a single example. But its implication, which probably for aesthetic reasons is left unworked, is clear enough: 'When our children are unruly we show them these pictures, and at once they fly weeping into our arms.' (p. 73) The enemy is the bogey-man with which parents threaten unruly children—the moral and intellectual big stick which is wielded to keep the little people of the empire in order. Remembering that the enemy has in effect mere subjective reality, it can be seen that the postulation of its authority (and this goes for all authorities in Kafka's oeuvre) is really a self-devised exercise in moral and intellectual restraint—a conclusion which abounds with implications of contingency and relativity.

During the earlier consideration of the integrity of the wall, conclusions were reached which, it could be objected, forced the issue. On the one hand the invulnerability of the wall varied in inverse proportion to its length and on the other the wall either contained or it did not. In other words, it was claimed that integrity did not come in half measures. From another perspective, it might be said that the perfect wall would be an unbroken ring of infinitely small circumference. The mistake, to continue in the logic of this vein, is to equate perfection with elaboration—a mistake which nearly all Kafka's protagonists make. Now if these considerations do appear somewhat forced, it should be added that they are being forced in order to derive principles whose relevance obtains not so much to practical expressions of the quest, but rather to its more general and abstract expressions. In particular we were anticipating that moment when we could apply insights into the nature of the wall to such relatively abstract expressions of the quest as the quest for knowledge or intellectual pursuit in general. We anticipated, in other words, transferring and applying information gained at one end of a spectrum of abstraction to the other.

In *The Great Wall of China* these considerations arise in the following way. The commentator tells of a Chinese scholar who likened the wall to the Tower of Babel. Of this towering edifice it was said 'that the tower failed and was bound to fail because of the weakness of the foundation.' (p. 71) Forestalling any objection that what applies to the Tower does not necessarily apply to the wall, the commentator quickly adds that the analogy is both meaningful and useful for (and this is an important confirmation of the possibility of working any spectrum of abstraction) there is a truth in the observation which is at least valid intellectually. (cf. p. 71) It is in this realm, the realm of the physical quest as a metaphor for intellectual pursuit, that there is something worth following up. And it is with this in mind that Kafka's works should be read, particularly the stories such as *The Great Wall of China*, *The Burrow*, *Investigations of a Dog*, *The Village Schoolmaster* and *Josephine the Singer*.

If, then, we think of the quest for knowledge and of its increasing complication, or, indeed, of the ramifications in any one of its many compartments (one thinks of K.'s conversations with the Superintendent in *The Castle*), it can be seen that every new addition does not necessarily strengthen the whole structure, any more than extension of the wall or burrow improves its overall integrity. More precisely, it does strengthen the whole, but only as a perpetuation and consolidation of one way of doing or seeing things; it is merely a more complete corroboration of what went before, and of whose integrity there is no guarantee. That, as pointed out earlier, in the discussion of the institution of the quest, is a prior assumption, the validity of which goes unquestioned. What it does do, therefore, is throw the researcher back on his premises, make the builder ever more aware of the intervening distance and of the increasingly slender, remote and tenuous foundations on which the entire intellectual edifice relies. It is these fundamentals which need resurveying, not the steps and refinements that have and will be made from them.

Of course, if the possibility of error in these subsequent steps is once admitted, the door is opened to a whole new range of horrors. Perhaps important omissions have been made; perhaps, in concrete terms, the wall of knowledge has been built piecemeal, and perhaps there are holes in it which to this day have gone undetected: 'In fact it is said that there are gaps which have never been filled in at all . . . on account of the extent of the structure.' (p. 67) Or perhaps at some or at many points in the prosecution of this quest wrong forks have been taken[9]— something which can only be judged after the event, and even then only comparatively.[10] Or perhaps the whole movement to date has been quite erratic and arbitrary.[11] And then consideration of this mode implies consciousness of others. But with a relativistic insight one knows for better or worse that on these other tracks too, at a similar point of remove and with the same

historical perspective, the same doubts, the same awareness of
self in a forward position, the same cosmic weight of responsibility and indecision would beset the perpetuator. An appreciation of this position could be called a crisis of consciousness.

This feature, which relates consciousness to the historical
length of a quest, is a most productive one. Happily, it also has
a satisfying commonsense appeal about it. It is, after all, quite
natural that prolonged activity of any kind (assuming that it
does not tranquillize the protagonist in such a way that, like
the 'Bürger', he becomes 'still und einfach' or worse) should
cause one to stop and wonder, is this a reasonable pursuit? Is
the effort worthy of the goal? Is it the best suited to the task at
hand? And so on. With the added conviction that the idea is
intuitively sound, this feature can be explored further. If, for
instance, we now apply to this relationship the principle which
we observed earlier, namely the Law of Inverse Proportions,
we can see that not only is consciousness related to the quest in
that prosecution of the latter stimulates the former, but that in
addition, the relationship is such that the greater the extension
of the quest, the greater the critical awareness of it, and particularly the critical awareness of the self involved in its activity.
To put it another way, the longer the history of the quest, the
greater and more numerous the doubts which attack it. If this
observation is interpreted, the result is a statement about the
relationship between consciousness and the quest which is
evolutionary in nature.

This evolutionary aspect is well embedded in *The Great Wall
of China*. Alongside the building of the wall there has been a
corresponding development of critical awareness of it. It
transpires that it is really this and not the actual physical construction of the wall which absorbs the commentator. The story
as told by him is a treatise upon the historical elaboration of an
intellectual dilemma, what has in this essay been called a crisis
of consciousness. To put himself right again with the reader he
quickly introduces: 'Meine Untersuchung ist doch nur eine
historische' ('My inquiry is purely historical'). In the early
days of the wall, construction must have been done unconsciously, that is, nobody stopped to question the project's
integrity. Without the metaphor, the course of knowledge,
intellect and belief must have been started without considera-

tion of its wisdom and direction. This is not surprising if it is remembered, by reason of the argument above, that the initiators of the quest could not logically have been aware of the initiation. Subsequently it was naively assumed that a 'Führerschaft' must have started it and that therefore this authority must be in control. Later, as the quest began to have an appreciable history, and as one or two doubts could no longer be suppressed and ignored, this control-authority was found to be lacking—incredibly so. Eventually it was found to be legendary and mythical, and scholars began to write treatises likening the wall to the Tower of Babel—a similar construction which expressed man's religious sentiments and his relationship to God.

In those days the people with the insight must have been few. Their voices must have sounded heretical. They probably experienced the same savage, irrational reaction that, in our own history, great isolated intellectuals like Copernicus and Galileo experienced. Perhaps this accounted for their rarity. Many more might have harboured the insights but might have kept them secret or suppressed and ignored them with 'betretenes Schweigen' ('embarrassed silence')[12] either for fear of censure or because they themselves found the insights intolerably disturbing, both intellectually and existentially. (cf. p. 293) Nowadays, with a great historical perspective and an equally great and irrepressible awareness, it is likely that the doubters and disbelievers, if they were honest with themselves and broke their 'betretenes Schweigen', would form the majority. The uncertainty about this latest atmosphere, the doubt about the safety and wisdom of such an admission, is reflected in the equivocation of the commentator's own comments and also, as will be seen, in his ambiguous position: 'One can perhaps safely discuss it now . . . no lightning flashes any longer from the long since vanished thunderclouds, and so I may venture to seek for an explanation of the system of piecemeal construction which goes farther than the one that contented people then.' (pp. 72f.)

Naturally enough, the association of critical awareness with the quest has led to the question of whether the quest as a procedural mechanism should be continued or rejected. It has been suggested that the dilemma that this choice poses constitutes a crisis of consciousness. Eventually one cannot fail to recognize that as a *modus vivendi* the quest and all it entails is deceitful. It moves with its premises unquestioned, its methods ill-considered and *ad hoc*, and its aims and direction pretending to be under control. Yet at the same time one cannot help but appreciate the powerful arguments in its favour—arguments which we have examined in detail and which lie implicitly in the commentator's advocacy of the mode. Basically these revolve around the assumption that one accepts the quest and gives credence to its goals because this affords the quester a sense of existential, moral and intellectual definition. Now this is undoubtedly beneficial, but with one crucial qualification —a qualification of time. What was beneficial and satisfactory for those at an earlier stage of the quest is not necessarily appropriate for those at a later stage. The cultural inheritance of former times is not necessarily the most suitable for a critical awareness which claims to be more highly evolved. Great-grandfather's religious beliefs, moral precepts and intellectual bases for judgment are not necessarily the best for the present-day. As Freud wonders: 'Wir sollen glauben, weil unsere Urväter geglaubt haben. Aber diese unsere Ahnen waren weit unwissender als wir, sie haben an Dinge geglaubt, die wir heute unmöglich annehmen können.' ('We are supposed to believe because our great-grandfathers believed. But these our ancestors knew much less than we do. They believed in things which nowadays we could not possibly accept.')[13] To prefer such a mode, when consciousness has seen through the delusive element of it, is to place personal and collective comfort before intellectual integrity. To continue in it side by side with one's knowledge and insight is to live hypocritically, practising what Orwell has called 'double-think'; one knows something not to be the case yet pretends to believe that it is and behaves as if it were. This type of critical, or hypocritical, existence has been called a life based on the philosophy of 'as if'.[14] This philosophy admits the nature of fictional and religious truths, but defends them for practical reasons.

Now this is exactly the position of the commentator and his contemporaries in *The Great Wall of China*. Their late historical position makes it inevitable that many will be conscious that they base their lives on a fraud. Yet knowing this they either refuse to believe it or pretend that the discovery had never been made. Thus, as far as the wall and the 'Führerschaft' are concerned, they know that the heart or substance has been discredited (intellectually) in both, and that therefore the mythical superstructure of their existence has been toppled, and yet they continue to build what Martin Greenberg[15] would call their 'lying symbolical' wall, behaving as if nothing had changed: 'We builders of the wall know that it was not so and hold our tongues.' (p. 74) Similarly, when an official visits the commentator's village and tells that an Emperor reigns quite other than the one in whom they believe, they refuse to believe the official, dismissing his information with barely concealed smiles. Whilst the official is there, however, and this is symptomatic of their whole attitude, they behave *as if* nothing were wrong.

The full ambivalence of the villagers' attitude is neatly and paradoxically expressed in the parable *Eine kaiserliche Botschaft* ('A Message from the Emperor'). In this it is clear that the Emperor was dying and is now dead, yet in spite of this the villagers persist in believing in him and waiting for his antique 'Botschaft'. This way in which the people living 'as if' prefer the illusions of the past to the truth of the present is perhaps best illustrated by an anecdote which tells of an episode from the commentator's youth. During some religious celebration a beggar enters the house, much as Nietzsche's 'tolle Mensch' ('madman') enters the famous market place,[16] bringing news from another province which is most disturbing to those present. Amidst derisive laughter the evidence is destroyed and the beggar ejected. The beggar like Nietzsche's 'tolle Mensch' might well have said 'Ich komme zu früh . . . ich bin noch nicht an der Zeit',[17] for a generation later, that is, when the commentator has grown up, we read of the overriding impression that an incontrovertible truth had been ignored and denied: 'And though—so it seems to me in recollection—the gruesomeness of the living present was irrefutably conveyed by the beggar's words, we laughed and shook our heads and refused to listen any longer. So eager are our people to obliterate the present.' (p. 79)

So, as Kafka has expressed it in his fragment *Gib's auf!* (*Give it up!*), the quest and all it stands for must be renounced.

Its main claim is disqualified by the fact that during the time of its institution a new element has evolved, namely that of critical consciousness. The intervention of this puts a different complexion on the face of the problem. The quest is seen as a deceitful procedure. Apart from this, continuation of the quest by the quester who knows its claims to be disqualified, yet who behaves as if they were not, means that his life is out of gear with reality. The quester, like the commentator, inhabits a world of archaic make-believe which is quite other than the world of the here and now. Worse, there is a division within the man himself. He thinks one way and acts contrariwise. There tugs within him an existential and psychological allegiance to the quest and an intellectual or critical allegiance to a truth which threatens to shatter it and undermine himself. A widening of this division would mean a magnification of the divided, dislocated type, which writers like Hofmannsthal and Musil have contemplated in their literature of crisis—the kind of disintegrating figure who no longer embodies unity of body and mind.

The claims of the quest can be further invalidated by looking at the whole problem the other way round. Thus, instead of examining the (ambiguous) benefits which the quest as a *modus vivendi* claims to offer, we should examine the extra-quest 'predicament' to which the quest claims to be the preferable alternative. Is it not true that counter-arguments for a life outside the quest have always been overlooked? What is wrong with the truth that there is no 'Führerschaft', that aims and directions are uncontrolled, that ultimately participation is in a haphazard, arbitrary, cosmic experiment? On what authority is an existence outside the definition of the quest to be rejected as intolerable? Have not the possibilities of exploiting this so-called 'disconcerting nothingness' always been ruled out automatically and out of habit?

These questions point beyond themselves to another. This concerns the basis from which the pro-quest arguments are made. There is a premise in these arguments which—both in this essay and in the account of the commentator—has remained largely unquestioned. It is assumed that the extra-quest predicament is uncomfortable both now and at all times. Yet this is unsubstantiated. For this predicament, this existence beyond the confines of the wall or the burrow or the Castle or the 'Law', has been experienced neither by critical minds nor by minds which have been independent of the habit of the quest. Moreover, as has been argued, this could never have been the case, for critical awareness comes only towards the end of the quest. The decision to opt for this mode can never have been taken, for the option and therefore the decision has always and only existed exclusive of any others: 'the high command has existed from all eternity, and the decision to build the wall likewise.' Thus, much rather than present dire pictures of the extra-quest predicament, both the reader and the commentator should talk in terms of the possibility of readjusting the mind so that it can achieve equanimity outside the quest, just as it did within. The question is whether, to use Erich Heller's expression, the mind will mind having itself disinherited of the paraphernalia of the quest, upon which it has for so long relied.

To answer this question would be to find an answer to the dilemma or critical choice which has emerged. Apart from the difficulty of finding an answer, it would in any case be highly speculative. Such speculation exceeds both the brief of this essay and also the material of our story. Nevertheless a couple of pointers can be singled out. One, which is perhaps the underlying premise to emerge from the interpretation in terms of a quest-motif, concerns the inevitable expansion of consciousness. It is to be hoped that eventually this will annihilate all traces of the quest and its intellectual dishonesty, leaving the critical mind free to readjust itself to its new-found freedom.[18] The other concerns one or two remarks made by the commentator which are revealing in that they show a discrepancy between his official decision and his personal opinion—a discrepancy typical of the philosophy of 'as if'. It seems that the commentator agrees with us in spite of himself. His official conclusion is that, having gained an insight into the crisis, he will pull back from the brink, for the consequences of investigating further would be not merely morally and intellectually dangerous, but existentially disastrous: 'To set about establishing a fundamental defect here would mean undermining not only our consciences, but, what is far worse, our feet. And for that reason I shall not proceed any further at this stage with my inquiry into these questions.' (p. 81) If the commentator and the

author, Kafka, have one and the same voice, this is an odd
conclusion for a Kafka story. For above all we associate Kafka
with inflexible intellectual rigour and honesty, and an ultimate
desire to establish the truth.[19] So it is all the more gratifying
that a final impression, the one which seems to shine through
the commentator's decision and contradict it, is in the spirit of
both Kafka's philosophy and our own. We know of his lasting
and consuming interest in the question of the quest: 'I cannot
go deeply enough into this very question.' And again: 'The
desire to trace the causes of these phenomena . . . has always
teased me and teases me still, and the building of the wall is
itself essentially involved with these problems.' (p. 75)
Further, we know that whilst he perhaps advocates the quest
as a matter of (momentary) necessity, he does not consider as
virtuous the attitude which attends it. (cf. p. 80) On the contrary, it is 'eine Schwäche beim Volke' ('a weakness of the
people'). But above all else we note how the commentator's
official decision is trivially but crucially qualified by the one
word 'vorderhand'. Whilst not proceeding any further 'for
the time being', he tacitly recognizes that the quest will and
must be continued, if not now, then later and if not by himself,
then by someone else.

# J. J. White

## Endings and Non-endings in Kafka's Fiction

Some itinerant wise men once came upon a statue which, as most of them could see, had not been completed. Some said it was almost finished, others thought the work only half carried-out; though a few could not even tell whether it was finished or not. When they compared this statue with others by the famous sculptor, many found the unfinished work inferior, simply because it was incomplete. Pointing to torsos from bygone days, some stated that they considered certain kinds of incompleteness better than any final work could possibly be. Others remembered the beautiful figurines which the great artist had also fashioned, and judged that his skills lay in miniature work. And one man, who recalled that the artist came from a distant tribe renowned for its incomplete works, saw in the unfinished statue an embodiment of the infinite sense of longing peculiar to that people.

Attention turned to why the artist (long since dead) had failed to finish the work. Perhaps he had deliberately given up in order to show the problems of completing such a task. Some claimed the fragmentariness was not intentional, that he had simply died before being able to finish; others that he had not decided what final shape the stone should receive. One wise man even suggested that it was because the great man was by nature not interested in perfecting works, for he had left many statues incomplete. However, most of those present proceeded to examine the shape of the nose and ears on the unfinished statue, comparing them with the noses and ears of other statues (which the artist had finished and sold at market), apparently unperturbed by the statue's condition.

Kafka's readers will appreciate that this cautionary tale, reflecting critical reactions to the varying degrees of completion in Kafka's works, has no single moral. For some it will be self-evident that one should distinguish between finished and incomplete works; for others this may, in Kafka's case, appear a mere pedantic irrelevance. Fragmentariness or completeness are for some matters of factual description, independent of value-judgment, whereas for many the one state remains axiomatically better than the other. Thus it has been forcefully argued that Kafka's 'failure to bring any of his major works to completion' can 'legitimately be taken as the basis for the most devastating criticism' of his 'version of reality', that the un-finished state of, in particular, his greatest novel, *The Castle*, 'both artistically and philosophically represents an impasse'.[1] Yet it was not only major works that Kafka failed to complete: in Max Brod's words, 'die Tagebücher wimmeln von Plänen, Skizzen, Anfängen, das Allerwenigste ist ausgeführt worden.' ('The diaries abound with plans, drafts, beginnings, only the smallest amount has been carried out.')[2] At a conservative estimate, four-fifths of Kafka's literary work is fragmentary, in one sense or another, it has been claimed.[3] However, the real issue is not so much one of quantity; it concerns the different types and effects of fragmentariness and non-ending—as well as varieties of completion—to be found in Kafka's fiction.

There is admittedly a background of non-literary factors here which it would be unrealistic to ignore, although their role is largely a matter of speculation. Kafka's enforced habit of nocturnal writing (where exhaustion often conflicted with his desire to write in long stretches); his actual method—the inspirational opposite of many a writer's frequent reworking of material—which at its best could allow him to declare, 'when I arbitrarily write a single sentence, for instance, "He looked out of the window", it already has perfection',[4] but could also often let him embark on something, only to give up once things took a disappointing turn, rather than go back and revise; such relative imponderables, together with hindrances of illness, acute self-criticism, the vicissitudes of personal relationships, and the eventual ravages of a fatal disease, all have a bearing on the unfinished state of his works. And yet, over and above these biographical complications, there are features of Kafka's writing which make its unfinished (or completed) state also a matter of intrinsically literary concern.

The idea that Kafka did not finish a large portion of his work simply because he was not interested in endings can be emphatically rejected. His letters and diaries reveal a deep concern for how fictions end. The conclusions to specific works by himself[5] and by others[6] probably attracted as much critical comment from Kafka as any aspect of literature—not to mention many personal recriminations about the difficulty of terminating work-in-progress. Kafka's diary, for instance, at one point contains an illuminating comparison between the conclusion of Flaubert's *Education Sentimentale* and that of the Pentateuch, of which Kafka observes: 'This dying vision [of the promised land] can only be intended to illustrate how incomplete a moment is human life, incomplete because a life like this could last for-ever and still be nothing but a moment.' (p. 394) The echoes here of much of Kafka's own work reveal how vital the question of ending was to him as a writer.

Three features of Kafka's work have been frequently cited as relevant to the problem of endings. The vividness of the central metaphors tends, according to Günther Anders and Martin Greenberg,[7] to contribute either to an anticlimactic conclusion or to an endless predicament. Eliseo Vivas, one of the first to submit that the handling of endings (and in particular a failure to terminate) was central to an evaluation of Kafka's work, has suggested that because of his heroes' 'stubborn empirical method'[8] (in the face of largely metaphysical challenges) the novels could not effect a successful transition to an ending. Vivas charges that the heroes 'refuse . . . to solve their problems by the only means that such problems can be solved . . . through the valid claims of religious intuition in certain ranges of experience', and Kafka in turn fails to end by 'transcending' the characters' limited perspective.[9] Yet this argument at most throws light only on some stories; elsewhere the very limitation of viewpoint in fact enables the writer to close after disposing of the central figure. Interminability has also been diagnosed as the result of that archetypal Kafka-situation of never-arriving,[10] or its concomitant: never-arriving at a decision. Yet it is doubtful whether the plot's failure to arrive, either physically or syllogistically, must necessarily always be causally connected with an inability to complete structural patterns.

One approach to this aspect of Kafka's writing is to start with works that were successfully terminated, before going on to some of the unfinished ones. In doing so, we need to question the orthodox image of a Kafka who *could have* finished certain works (if he had wanted to, or had been given the time, or—possibly—if he had had a greater honesty or mastery of his material). Such premises have led at one level to fanciful specu-lation about what the end of certain works could have been, and on a more complex plane to a measuring of fragments against complete works (often on the basis of unspecified criteria). A perhaps natural curiosity about an ending that, in some cases, actually existed (only to be lost or destroyed) or, more frequently, could conceivably have been written, given favourable circumstances, can become detrimental to a direct investigation of the works themselves. So too can the common assumption that finished pieces are inevitably better than fragments (or vice versa) or that *all* finished works—or even *all* fragments—are of the same order of complexity and merit. With Kafka things are not that straightforward. To appreciate why not, it may help to begin, not at the beginning or at the end, but near the middle.

In December 1914, when struggling with the writing of *Der Dorfschullehrer* (*The Village Schoolmaster*) (soon to be abandoned), Kafka made in his diary a number of observations about organic form, including the statement 'that the story, if it has any justification to exist bears its complete organization within itself even before it has been fully formed.' (p. 322) When trying to dispel misgivings about a particularly recalci-trant work, Kafka was wont to resort to accounts of some ideal goal. In the passage mentioned, one finds him theorizing about a conceivably organic *Novelle* form in which the end clearly evolves from the foundations of a successful beginning.[11] It is unlikely that he is thinking in a vacuum here: the description suggests that Kafka had in mind that work of his which very strikingly displays from the outset a 'fertige Organisation in sich' ('complete organization within itself') and about whose ending he never had any qualms: *The Judgment.*

In recent investigations of the fragment as an art form, two points have repeatedly emerged which throw some light on Kafka's thought-process here: first, that fragments can be considered to relate to completed works as reality would to some utopia,[12] and second, that there is a strong tendency to view fragments as prefigurations of completed whole forms (rather than in isolation)[13]—a predisposition which can be exploited as part of the genre's particular aesthetic effect.

In Kafka's diary-entry, one can observe his thoughts going elegiacally back to the relative utopia of a disciplined *Novelle* form, his dissatisfaction with the unfinished *Village Schoolmaster* project being at the same time conditioned by the kind of exemplary achievement that *The Judgment* represented. Thus, to understand Kafka's later endings and non-endings, one must first consider the organic structure and ending of *The Judgment*.

But what and where *is* the end of *The Judgment*? In a way, the end already starts at the beginning, a paradox which is a token of the work's organicity. In another sense, the end begins with the father's judgment. And whilst we can agree with J. P. Stern's remark, when referring to the arbitrary authority of Bendemann's father, that 'In an important, not accidental way [*The Judgment*] is fragmentary. That last gap between crime and punishment is never quite closed . . .',[14] we can nevertheless still note that the gap here differs structurally from those to be found in later works. It functions as the work's 'Wendepunkt' ('turning-point'), dramatically externalizing or making explicit much that has hitherto lain symbolically below the surface. The ending proper, though, which may in one sense commence with the story's beginning and in another with the father's judgment, really comes to fruition in the last three paragraphs.

Here Bendemann rushes downstairs and out of the building to throw himself from the bridge. But in place of the rapid end which the rhythm and pitch of the previous, 'action' paragraph invite one to expect, comes a relative slowing of pace, verging at times on *tableau*:

> He still held on, with a gradually weakening grip, and glimpsed between the bars of the balustrade an omnibus which would easily drown the sound of his fall: he called quietly: 'Dear parents, I have always loved you', and let himself drop. At this moment an almost endless stream of traffic crossed the bridge.[15]

This closing section channels attentions towards various objects that crystallize what has gone on before, it includes retarding sentiments and symbolic details revealing the *Novelle*'s organic unity.

Synthesized here we find the logical conclusion to a governing quest for judgment (begun on page one with Georg's visit to his father), which now unequivocally follows his condemnation, with an immediacy of acceptance alien to later works. We feel the hero's sense of being condemned, as he peers through the bars ('Geländerstangen'); here finally he expresses love for his parents and tacitly acknowledges, even with relief,[16] the charge of guilt. He 'let himself' drop. The last sentence of all manages to dramatize his father's indictment in a shift of focus, a distancing of the reader from Georg's fate[17] which reflects the earlier: 'Now you know what exists in the world around you, until now you only knew about yourself.' But the conclusion does more than recapitulate and synthesize the entire work so far, it specifically points back to the *Novelle*'s beginning. Writing once of *America*, Kafka noted that a lot still had to happen, 'before the circle closed in the desired way',[18] and it is this closing of the circle that one perceives as so effective in *The Judgment*. Walter Sokel has analysed the role of the bridge and in particular the river at the beginning and end, revealing much about the contrast in mood and narrative style at these two points. His reading can be supplemented with various further small details: the story *starts* with an image of Georg *ending* a letter—its *volte face* is signalled by his father's description of how the friend in Russia destroys such letters; the phrase *'gerade* einen Brief . . . *beendet'* ('just ended a letter') is taken up at the end with the reference to a *'geradezu unendlicher* Verkehr' ('an almost endless stream of traffic'); and the 'spielerische Langsamkeit' ('playful slowness') of Georg's initial actions is also not without parallel at the end.

For all this, the image of coming full circle will hardly do justice to *The Judgment*'s final sentence, for this not only draws things together and points back to the work's beginning, it also transcends the rest of the tale. The ultimate image of traffic transcends Georg's previous claustrophobic world, just as Georg has been lifted out of his self-centredness (although this wider perspective was hinted at in the first paragraph of the story). The 'endless stream of traffic', taking up the previous punning reference to a bus 'which would easily drown the sound of his fall' (cf. Biblical Fall and German noun *Fall* = 'case'), forms part of an end which, in terminating Bendemann's life, also acknowledges and rejoices in the incommensurability—and perhaps outward indifference—of the world around him: 'endless' is the penultimate word.

In contrast to such a complex conclusion, Kafka criticized *Metamorphosis* for its 'unreadable ending', a reaction often ascribed to dissatisfaction on his part with the narrative perspective of the events related after Gregor has died. Yet if the final pages failed to satisfy their author (as has been argued) primarily on grounds of viewpoint, it would seem surprising that he should favour a comparable shift at the end of *Ein Hungerkünstler* (*A Hunger-Artist*). In any case, as Hartmut Binder has pointed out,[19] there is no strict adherence to Samsa's perspective throughout, hence the ending annoyed Kafka for other reasons (reasons which it could be important to consider with an eye to later works).

There are at least three stages to the ending of *Metamorphosis*. First comes Gregor's own end; as life ebbs away from him, we are offered the sentimentality of a deathbed scene, only to be pulled up short by the arrival of the Samsas' servant. Then comes a series of reactions to Gregor's death: the servant's callousness contrasting with the family's largely mixed feelings —Frau Samsa's 'tremulous smile', the description of all three Samsas as looking 'a little as if they had been crying' and of their reaction not as one of unmitigated relief, but only '*as if* relieved'. This anticlimactic phase of contradictory emotions acts as a transition to the final, 'real' ending: the excursion to the countryside, with its more positive images of harmony among the Samsas and a 'confirmation of their new dreams and excellent intentions . . . at the end of their journey' in the visually gratifying impression of Grete's nubile body.

Knowing of Kafka's own self-confessed 'dislike of antitheses', one may wonder whether the difficulties of this ending do not stem from the fact that the part after Gregor's death is built too schematically on contrasts with what has gone before: Grete's body versus Gregor's carcass, the 'Butcher's boy' with his meat-load after Gregor's slops and emaciation, emancipation from the lodgers after dependence on them, freedom of movement and harmony after restriction and isolation. Frank Kermode's suggestion that 'ends are ends only when they are not negative[20] but frankly transfigure the events in which they were immanent'[21] seems to sum up the difference between *Metamorphosis*'s final scheme of negations[22] and *The Judgment*'s transcending of what has happened before the end.

Kafka may also have found the optimism of this comparatively epilogic (Beissner) ending unconvincing, although after what has just occurred its idyllicism in fact reads deliberately hollow and is clearly no answer to the experiences of the Samsa family. (One is reminded of Josef K.'s slamming the door on the whipping scene at one point in *The Trial*.) This concluding 'utopian' outing, which some have criticized as a false improvisation and others have praised as a deliberate satire of the Samsas' myopic values, also raises problems of transition. One finds this reflected in the various gradations of the end: a harsh contrast between sentimentality and crudeness, followed by a mixed mood and a final falsely utopian episode. Yet whilst *Metamorphosis* may not possess the kind of conclusion which closes the circle in the satisfying way that *The Judgment*'s does, it manages to prepare for its final disjunctive elements by making them function as part of a definite emotional release for the family: a metamorphosis of their previous conditions (and the *Metamorphosis*-idea, together with the sub-division of the narrative into parts and the occasional infringement of perspective, all contribute to this new kind of non-organic disjointedness). In other works around this time, discontinuity —the presence of some hiatus between the main body of the work and its conclusion—assumes more radical proportions.

Towards the end of *In the Penal Colony*, after the Officer has been destroyed by his 'remarkable piece of apparatus', and before the European Traveller visits the Tea House, comes a marked caesura in the narrative. Whereas the collected works show this simply by a double-space between paragraphs, the first edition (and Paul Raabe's recent *Sämtliche Erzählungen* volume, p. 121) makes the break more pronounced by the inclusion of the asterisks which Kafka had himself suggested inserting. Similarly, when originally published as a fragment, *The Stoker* also displayed such a visible seam in the narrative:

between the stoker's interrogation and Karl's subsequent departure from the ship. The use of such a hiatus to register large narrative divisions is quite common in German, but contrary to established practice, Kafka's use of it does not belong to some recurrent pattern. It comes in both cases only once—just before the end, as a token of what is in effect a disjunctive closure. Hence, since there is no real transition to it, one has the impression of what Kafka once called a 'Schluss von aussenher' ('superimposed conclusion'), not evolving organically from the work, but remaining more tentative, almost a *finis ex machina*.

One can trace certain parallels between this kind of hiatus (in *The Stoker* and *In the Penal Colony*) and the last parts of *America* and *The Trial*. Manifestly, both works have difficulty in effecting a coherent transition from their main corpus to an already existent (and by extension to the case of *The Castle*: envisaged) ending. The present qualitative leap from the body of these novels to 'The Nature Theatre of Oklahoma' and the execution chapter ('The End'), respectively, involves more, in the former case, than simply our awareness that Rossmann mentions adventures not yet described—including 'Unternehmen 25'—and that, in the latter, Josef K. displays an acquiescence which did not seem to be emerging in the Cathedral episode, as if some change in him had occurred 'offstage'. Kafka may try to relativize the artificial optimism or pessimism of these finales by what Heinz Politzer once called 'substituting theatricals for valid religious content',[23] but this does not solve (indeed, it can even exacerbate) the practical difficulties of effecting a transition to them.

Ultimately, the problem of finding or securing an ending is often linked with judgment and death, although a certain confusion can arise between the widespread thematic importance of mortality in Kafka's works and the actual, more limited presence of deaths in them.

One needs to distinguish between stories which actually do end with a death (such as *The Judgment, Metamorphosis* and *A Hunger-Artist*) and various incomplete works to which death might conceivably have furnished an ending—including *America, The Castle* and *The Burrow*. Of approximately seventy finished works, only five portray an actual death at the close.

Significantly, Kafka is often unwilling or unable to end precisely those works which entertain death as a *possible* conclusion. Probably the most complex instance of such an impasse in his early work is the novel *America*.

Although Kafka once noted that in the end Rossmann would die, it is left unclear whether this would be before or after his 'Naturtheater' recruitment—or whether even (in any final version that he would write) the hero would still die. As has also happened in the case of *The Burrow*, critical opinion has tended to divide on this question simply by opting for one of the possible endings rather than concentrating on the significance of the novel's apparent reluctance to conclude with any actual death-scene. The ending in fact chosen for *America*: departure on a journey—by no means out of keeping with Kafka's proposed title for the novel of *Der Verschollene* (The Man who disappears)—seems an overt refusal to consign his hero to the death mentioned in the diary. And in the manuscript, Kafka renders even this type of ending more tentative by separating it from the rest of the chapter by drawing a line (his normal indication of a new chapter division) across the page between the recruitment and the beginning of the train-journey, a ploy which is surely in the same diffident vein as the asterisked ending of *In the Penal Colony* or the hiatus-closure of *The Stoker*.[24]

Works where Kafka can be seen struggling against what one novelist recently referred to as 'the tyranny of the last chapter, the final, the "real" version'[25] invariably involve important issues of acceptance—at times even of death. The problem of transition and the presence of an organic, or any kind of ending depends predominantly on the hero's (and by extension, the author's) willingness or reluctance to accept or give a verdict. In some cases, a birth-to-death pattern reinforces expectations of some organic completion within a framework of existential guilt, with the work commencing symbolically, in the case of *The Trial*, with a '*birth*day' and ending with execution; or with a kind of rebirth and cycle of infantility to death, in *Metamorphosis*. But the pattern may still not always be completed: it would be premature to assume that *America*, which activates comparable paradigmatic expectations with statements like 'The first days of a European in America might be likened to a re-birth', would by that token necessarily conclude with Karl Rossmann's death.

Much more could obviously be said about the problem of engineering an end or a transition under such circumstances, but this dilemma represents only one side of a much larger issue. To complete the picture, it is necessary to turn to works in which Kafka has in various ways managed to resolve this challenge. For, in Günter de Bruyn's words, 'somewhere one has ultimately to make an ending, if the heroes do not die.'[26]

Kafka's finished works include many familiar modes of ending, some employed with utter conventionality. Certain time-honoured closing gestures of recapitulation—the adding of an epilogue, an abrupt termination to some short impression begun *in medias res*, or the closing enumeration of a series of rhetorical questions—are common enough conclusions, not only in the *Betrachtung* cycle, but even in the *Landarzt* collection. But with a measure of irony, Kafka can also be found harnessing traditional types of ending to more complex effects than they had by and large engendered hitherto. Thus, the final sentence of the story *A Country Doctor* may well remind one of the moralizing fable's didactic conclusion: 'Once one has followed the false ringing of the night-bell—one can never make amends for it'. Yet compared with some transparent moral, this lapidary statement turns out to be a Chinese Box of a conclusion, raising as many questions as it seems to answer. What is this night-bell? What does it mean to follow its call? (One is thrown back across the enigmatic story in search of answers.) And how double-edged, and even resigned, this conclusion appears, if set alongside that of the didactic fable! By offering a moral that does not conceptualize the fictional incident, but remains, with the possible exception of the verb 'make amends', within the tale's world of images, Kafka's story concludes without letting abstract sentiment simplify the complexity or compromise the symbolic logic of his vision. Similarly, *On Parables* (Kafka's elusive parable about the nature of the genre) rejoices in a triumphantly delivered *Pointe*, but one of such a devious order that it is closer in form to the riddle than to many of its more overtly didactic forerunners.

In general, one might distinguish between those finished

works which, due to their relatively unproblematical material, Kafka experienced little apparent difficulty in ending (many of the *Betrachtung* pieces would appear to come into this category); those which end skilfully without betraying their central enigmas and paradoxes; and stories, of which *The Judgment* might arguably be considered the only good representative, where the ending both satisfies and transcends our prior expectations.

There is a school of thought which holds that endings are by definition the Achilles Heel of fiction. George Eliot has remarked that 'conclusions are the weak point of most authors'[27] and E. M. Forster once expressed the view that 'nearly all novels are feeble at the end'.[28] Clearly, one should not lose sight of this wider dimension of fictional activity when considering Kafka's particular problems and solutions. And bearing in mind that he could hardly, with his mind and material, indulge in that 'distribution at the last of prizes, pensions, husbands, wives, babies, millions, appended paragraphs and cheerful remarks' which Henry James[29] (and, following in his wake, *Aspects of the Novel*[30]) saw and satirized as the novelist's (literally) last resort, one can appreciate how general problems of ending will be compounded by the nature of that for which an end is being sought. In Kafka's personal opinion: 'The only really difficult and insoluble problems are those which we cannot formulate, because they have the difficulties of life itself as their content'.[31] With him, as with possibly few writers to such an extent since Kleist, fictional endings are inextricably bound up with metaphysics, theodicy and even apocalypse, but with a further complication created by his particular conception of time according to which 'it is our conception of time that makes us call the Last Judgment by this name. It is in fact a kind of martial law'.[32]

One way out of this virtually insoluble predicament is to make the refusal to adopt a terminal position, to judge or accept a verdict without equivocation, part of the ending itself, if there is to be one, that is. Instead of (in Samuel Beckett's phrase) 'finality without end', Kafka succeeds in much of the work of his middle and late phases in finding various expressions of an 'end without finality'. This solution can already be witnessed in the part of *In the Penal Colony* where the European

157

Traveller eventually makes for his boat to get off the island as fast as he can. Unfortunately, here certain issues have become overrefracted. From the outset the Traveller has been called upon to judge the punishment-apparatus (which is why it is being shown to him and explained). But since, within a structure of symbolic displacements and secondary elaboration, this very machine then passes judgment in kind on the Officer and even on itself towards the end, there is a sense in which the Traveller's reactions have become superfluous (except in the way it lets the man indict his whole culture through his ostrich-like actions). In *A Country Doctor*, on the other hand, a comparable concluding motif is far more successfully used. Here, the doctor's diagnosis is of greater importance than the Traveller's proved to be. Having evasively abandoned Rosa in her hour of need and been offered a second chance to reach a decision about what is, in symbolic terms, the same dilemma, he once more hedges on the moral issue and attempts to escape, seeking a happy end, as it were, for himself: 'now it was time to think of saving myself'. But this time he finds himself condemned to wander forever.

As Dorrit Cohn has demonstrated, the sense of endlessness in such a conclusion is related to the use near the end of a certain kind of present tense which becomes, in her words, 'a direct grammatical signal for the story's open-ending. It signifies that the speaker's past experience is his present plight, that it ends in infinite regress.'[33] An ultimate sense of infinite regress can also be achieved by other stylistic means, such as closing on a rhetorical question, the future tense (of prophecy) or the infinitive.[34] Such devices belong to Kafka's repertoire of strategies for erecting what Cohn once characterized as the 'einmal-niemals dialectic'[35] of certain stories: i.e., the situation where something happened *once* in the past, after which things will *never* be the same again.

Still, it can be queried whether it is not fundamentally the author's predilection for seemingly interminable, open-ended[36] situations, rather than their reinforcing grammatical tokens, which creates so often that sense of an 'end without finality'. Every reader of Kafka no doubt draws on a private store-house of images of infinite regress and unending tasks in Kafka's works. The journey without end is common to both *The*

*Huntsman Gracchus* and the final part of *Der Kübelreiter* (*The Coal-Scuttle Rider*) and some, like Hermsdorf, would even attribute it to *America*. Through his reputedly endless series of Doorkeepers guarding the Entrance to the Law, the labyrinths of corridors, alleys and interminably convoluted discussions, Kafka seems to be continually playing with the notion of infinity (with that ultimate court, the Last Judgment, in permanent session just around the corner and just out of reach). Words like 'finally', 'ultimately', 'for good', 'forever' and 'in the end' abound in Kafka's writings, with an invariably tantalizing nuance to them, for little has any real finality, even at the end. 'Confessions', we are told, 'became most comprehensible when they were retracted'.[37]

If it is true, as one critic has suggested, that in much modern writing 'a full stop may be avoided, but there will [still] be a close: a false fullstop',[38] then in many instances Kafka's 'false fullstop' is the product of authorial sleights-of-hand, reinforcing pre-existing impressions of a predicament that could continue virtually *ad infinitum*, and yet not robbing us entirely of a closure. It is one of Kafka's underestimated accomplishments that his stories gradually discover and evolve ways of successfully closing 'without finality'; and this in a sense holds true for many of his apparent 'fragments', as well as the published work in the *Landarzt* and *Hungerkünstler* collections.

'When faced with Kafka's work the word "fragmentary" takes on a meaning that deviates from the traditional connotation' Max Brod once suggested in his Postscript to *Description of a Struggle and the Great Wall of China*. This is rather an understatement, since it can acquire a whole range of connotations depending on what part of Kafka's work one has in mind. There are fragmentary trial exercises, insignificant drafts, paralipomena, and many tangential sketches for the novels (not all of which, as Brod rightly warns, should be endowed with the status of unfinished chapters). But there are also substantial and yet incomplete works (unfinished either because *the* ending is still lacking, or more often because they contain a continual proliferation of potential endings and refuse to cut the Gordian Knot of paradox). Clearly, only some of these 'fragments' are of any great literary value. Yuri

159

Tynanov's suggestion[39] that one is at liberty to view the literary fragment as a genre in its own right (independent of holism and intentionalism) is particularly appropriate to some of the pieces of a substantial length, where the striking fact is that they have not been *finished* (rather than never really got started), and where the lack of an ending is palpably a product of the material itself, giving a fragmentariness that is motivated rather than disjunctive. For all the many cultural differences of detail and premise, this kind of GENERIC FRAGMENT bears certain marked resemblances to the *non finito* in the plastic arts, to a Romantic work like *Heinrich von Ofterdingen* or Robert Musil's *The Man Without Qualities*, rather than to Novalis's *Fragmente* or to those of many a *fin de siècle* Impressionist.[40]

Kafka described the limited degree of finality to a number of his early works' conclusions with a tentativeness that found its aesthetic correlative in the fragment form. *America* he called 'fast endlos' ('almost infinite'). And whilst he wrote of *Metamorphosis*: 'My little story is finished', he added guardedly, 'but today's ending does not please me at all.'[41] 'After the first draft [of *America*] is completed, what a difficult, perhaps impossible, task it will be to bring the dead sections at least partially to life',[42] he writes in 1913. Often enough one finds Kafka describing projects as only 'vorläufig aufgegeben' ('temporarily abandoned'). And eventually, reflecting this hesitation about finishing, or giving up forever, comes a cluster of works which commentators have themselves often cautiously described as 'apparently' or 'seemingly not completed' (counterparts of Kafka's own equivocations). These generic fragments treat subjects which are either by their very paradoxical nature not terminable in any usual way, or else about which the narrator does not apparently wish to present a final conclusion. They are thus incomplete—fragmentary in more senses than one—but also include a measure of rounding-off, for all that. By dint of at least having such a 'false fullstop', they differ from many Romantic and Impressionist types of fragment—and from many other of Kafka's own fragments. The group includes *The Village Schoolmaster, Blumfeld, an Elderly Bachelor, The Great Wall of China, Investigations of a Dog* and *The Burrow*.

The idea of a 'false fullstop', a sense of inconclusiveness and yet a gesture of closure, can be observed in the case of *The Burrow*. This fragment, as Heinrich Henel's analysis demonstrates, concludes by means of the strategic positioning, in the final complete sentence, of a certain leitmotif, present at two prior turning-points in the work: 'All remained unchanged'. Henel argues that because of this element of rounding-off, one would probably not even realize (without extrinsic information) that the work was, in the loose sense, a fragment. But comparing the concluding leitmotif with certain analogous closure-patterns in music,[43] and thus concentrating primarily on formal factors, Henel perhaps goes one step too far towards aligning *The Burrow* with Kafka's more definitively terminated works. For if one examines the actual wording of the leitmotif, 'all remained unchanged', words so reminiscent of the end of another generic fragment: the 'So he lived on . . .' of Büchner's *Lenz*, one can appreciate how it in fact generates an equally strong sense of 'end without finality'. For whilst the formal pattern of the leitmotif-structure creates a semblance of closure, albeit one that has proved deceptive in two previous cases, the words themselves (like the three dots that follow them in the printed text) militate against any impression of finality. These are the two, contradictory components of the 'false fullstop'. One finds further examples of it, in varying degrees of pronouncedness, in published stories from Kafka's lifetime too; for the distinction between works that had been tentatively finished and those that are provisionally abandoned is in many instances practically non-existent.

Dorrit Cohn has called *A Country Doctor* a story that 'ends in infinite regress', a point which is true of the final paragraph's essential content, but needs to be modified to take account of a certain terminal complexity. For in reality the conclusion negotiates a careful course between what could have been a genuine open-ending (with the story's earlier line 'Never shall I come home' as a potential statement of infinite wanderings) and the token ending which the final words still give to the work (suggesting an analogy, discussed above, with the moral).

Another potentially open-ended work, *Investigations of a Dog*, plays a similar *endgame* in its concluding assessment of interim gains made: 'immerhin Freiheit, immerhin ein Besitz' ('nevertheless freedom, nevertheless a possession'). The dog's 'interminable wandering' is interrupted to give a retrospective *Bilanz* (balance). And in this example, that mood of only provisional termination is very much governed by the concessive 'immerhin', as tentative a word as Kafka's ubiquitous 'vorläufig' ('temporarily').

On the whole, Kafka's generic fragments not only find ways of imparting a sense of fragmentariness, an air of provisionality usually combined with a sense of closure, they also tend (whilst the narrative progresses) to play with our expectations about possible outcome. The absence of any real ending often means in fact a series of hints at possible endings along the way. Thus, in a declaration of his dogged determination, the narrator of *Investigations of a Dog* at one point states: 'Ich werde es voraussichtlich aushalten bis zu meinem natürlichen Ende' ('I shall probably hold out till my natural end'). The duplication of 'aus' here (vor*aus*sichtlich *aus*halten') intensifies a central irony, for the adverb is of course tongue-in-jowl: the dog has little prescience and his life, like his account, finds no 'natural end'.

When bachelor Blumfeld, returning home one evening, finds two celluloid balls bouncing up and down in his living room, like a true Kafka-hero he does not ask what it all means, but simply how long it will last, for, he is pleased to conclude, even 'the unusual must have limits'. In his concern about how long the balls will continue to bounce, he posits limits and then has to readjust them as they prove either false or impractical. He imagines a dog would make short work of the balls, but since one cannot be procured, this idea too is dropped—at least 'temporarily'. And so, as he weighs up the further solutions open to him, poor Blumfeld finds himself in the predicament of the man in the music-hall joke who tries to throw away his boomerang: if he gives his balls to someone, there is a distinct likelihood that they will bounce right back to their 'master'. Still, after surveying various ways of ejecting his uninvited guests (whose removal from the scene would presumably constitute not only a definitive end to the story—just as their discovery marked its beginning—but also a verdict on their importance), Blumfeld hazards an attempt. Having locked the balls in his wardrobe, he promises them to a neighbour's child as a present, on the clear condition that they are only collected in his absence. Whether or not this ruse works we are not told, for Blumfeld goes off to work, never to return during the fragment—though the fact that his two assistants there in many ways resemble the balls does suggest his escape has been only illusory.

It would be relatively easy to have constructed an ending (within a framework of endlessness) using an image such as embarking on an interminable journey, since departure—even into the infinite—possesses a certain incisiveness, a fact well exploited at the end of *America* and *A Country Doctor*. The bouncing balls, on the other hand, remind Blumfeld of an experiment in perpetual motion. Any end to their movement is not easy to predict. Compared with those archetypal images of unending motion, the toiling of Sisyphus or the Danaids with their sieves, the double-bouncing movement of the balls is, as Blumfeld learns, difficult to interrupt, whereas the point where Sisyphus's single boulder reaches the foot of the hill regularly suggests a juncture. Kafka has selected an image of continuous oscillation which provokes curiosity in us, and of course in Blumfeld, about the outcome. By then removing Blumfeld from the scene, he finally opts for the kind of denial-motif we know from earlier works. He may, in doing so, avoid the surrender to a false ending, such as one finds in the film *Le ballon rouge* (in many ways a close relative of *Blumfeld*), but the fragment is perhaps too resistant to any sense of closure. Its final sentence is a reference to Blumfeld's assistants at work, although it could apply equally well to the balls: 'But they are over-apprehensive, and without any tact keep trying to protest their real or imaginary rights'.[44] This misses the lapidariness of *A Country Doctor*'s final statement and even the tentative ending of the fragment *The Great Wall of China*.

Indeed, the degree to which this Chinese fragment has been finished or left incomplete is as vexed a question as that concerning the Great Wall's actual completion. Malcolm Pasley's recent English translation, based on a critical study of the manuscript, has revealed that Kafka in fact crossed out the tentative ending most of us know from all the hitherto printed versions and continued the fragment in a new direction (with the arrival of a boatman). In essence, this means that Kafka first wrote an inconclusive ending for the fragment, was then dissatisfied with even this gesture of a conclusion, provisionally restarted the work and then gave it up.

The title's stress, *Beim Bau* . . ., (*Building the Great Wall* . . .), points to the Wall's incomplete state (though, retrospectively, from a time when it could in theory have been finished). The first sentence, 'The Great Wall of China was finished off at its northernmost corner', proves doubly inconclusive: for the ambiguous formulation, in conjunction with the 'System des Teilbaus' ('system of piecemeal construction'), could imply that this is the *only* point of completion, and in any case, the narrator elsewhere admits to coming from the South where even rumours about what is happening in Peking cannot be verified. Any answer to this problem is more likely to be a mark of the reader's impatience than a reliable fact, for Kafka's fragment deliberately toys with expectations of what has happened and how much we can ever ascertain.

In terms of the story, to try to understand is like attempting to build such a wall: 'the province to be traversed [intellectually, that is] here is infinite.' Similarly, 'the whole of China was to be walled round' yet China is believed to be 'infinite'. The narrator mentions the people's impatience to see the wall finished 'in its complete perfection', but sees such a project as a 'hard toil which . . . could not reach completion even in the longest life-time'.

There is therefore a difference between this Great Wall and the biblical Tower of Babel, with which the narrative connects it, viewing it as a possible foundation for some new, more ambitious Babel-project. In spatial terms, both represent attempts at transcending the seemingly infinite: at putting a wall around the endless expanse of China or building an infinitely high tower. In temporal terms, however, the Babel undertaking is terminated conclusively (if not as planned), whilst the other remains open-ended (as far as mortals and critics can tell). The Bible's 'So the Lord scattered them abroad from thence upon the face of the earth: and *they left off* to build the city' (Genesis, XI, 8) stands in contrast to the uncertainty about whether the wall, which has been deemed finished despite possible *lacunae*, *is* complete.

Hence, granted the incommensurability of the subject-matter, one wonders whether the narrative can in fact plausibly terminate. Actually, it emphatically refuses to complete the wall (or itself) or to have the task simply abandoned in either case.[45]

There was an aptness to many of Kafka's unfinished works first being presented to the public in the thirties under the collective title of *Beim Bau der chinesischen Mauer* (*Building the Great Wall of China*), for this image is central to the incomplete nature of his enterprise. Kafka often applied building and excavation metaphors to his literary work, but it is this striking notion of a 'Teilbausystem' ('piecemeal construction') that successfully catches two particular features of his literary fragmentariness: its linearity, and the quality of seeming to end many times over without ending definitively—of leaving the door open to hope. In most three-dimensional forms of art, fragmentariness is not concentrated in the same way at a point of break-off; the sense of incompletion is more diffuse. Hence, only literature (and music) can really exploit the temporal features of fragmentariness to any great degree: the playing with conjectures about endings, an unwillingness thereby to indulge in, or deny fully, any traditional conclusion, and the linearity common to both the form and such recurrent motifs as the quest, the journey or the long task, all of them crucial to Kafka's concepts of time, judgment and human frailty.

Kafka was not the kind of writer who could declare, as a recent Donald Barthelme character did, that 'Fragments are the only forms I trust.'[46] But some of the fragments he wrote after ceasing to struggle to attain the organic kind of ending of a work like *The Judgment*, show that he could produce an intermediate form—neither with, nor wholly without, an ending— worthy of being considered alongside the more traditionally terminated prose works. It may well be that Kafka's own historical perspective made him more critical of such generic fragments than a present-day reading public, conversant with experimental notions of the shape of fiction, would be. Yet towards the end of his life, in *A Hunger-Artist*, one finds him treating various aspects of this problem (in terms of the artist's relationship to the public) with much humour and insight into the dilemma of ending.

For the hunger-artist who wanted to go on fasting without. end, all present feats remain mere fragments of the utopian grand fast; he feels his art could be radically prolonged, continuing (with no limits set) 'to unimaginable extremes'. He wonders frequently why the public has so little patience with such a time-consuming undertaking. His chief complaint—that a 'premature termination of fasting' has been imposed upon him—is voiced in terms very reminiscent of Kafka's own remarks on the problem of ending. Only his impresario realizes that the public will demand false limits of the artistic performance in order to understand it. So, in response, a maximum of forty days is decided on. Ultimately, the hungering nevertheless has to stop, for even if the artist had wanted to go on forever now that public interest has waned, his life-span is finite. 'The fact that our task is exactly commensurate with our life gives it the appearance of being infinite' Kafka suggests in the third octavo note-book (*Wedding Preparations in the Country*, p. 95). Such a seemingly endless undertaking will, like the Great Wall of China, always remain finite and fragmentary within a single lifetime. And so the narrator has to report of his hero's art (and his story): 'even it came to an end'.

# Ronald Gray

## Kafka: A Critical Essay

James Thurber relates, in 'University Days', how he passed all his other courses as an undergraduate, but could never pass botany. This was because all botany students had to spend several hours a week in a laboratory looking through a microscope at plant cells, and he could never see through a microscope. All he could see when he put his eye to one was a nebulous milky substance. 'I see what looks like a lot of milk', he would tell his instructor. As a result. he finally took what was called a 'deferred pass', waited a year, and tried again. His professor returned from vacation, brown as a berry, and eager to explain cell-structure to the new class. Thurber took out his microscope, and again did not see anything. ' "We'll try it," said the professor grimly, "with every adjustment of the microscope known to man. As God is my witness, I'll arrange this glass so that you see cells through it or I'll give up teaching." ' But though they tried every adjustment of the microscope known to man, with only one of them could Thurber see anything but blackness or the familiar lacteal opacity, and that time he saw, to his pleasure and amazement, a variegated constellation of flecks, specks, and dots.

'These', says Thurber, 'I hastily drew. The instructor, noting my activity, came back from an adjoining desk, a smile on his lips and his eyebrows high in hope. He looked at my cell drawing. "What's that?" he demanded, with a hint of a squeal in his voice. "That's what I saw", I said. "You didn't, you didn't, you didn't!" he screamed, losing control of his temper instantly, and he bent over and squinted into the microscope. His head snapped up. "That's your eye!" he shouted. "You've fixed the lens so that it reflects! You've drawn your eye!" '

The experience of that instructor is familiar to all of us who read or write what is slightingly called 'secondary literature', particularly when it is about Kafka. With the greatest of pains, and with no obviously crooked intent, the undergraduate or Ph.D. student, or colleague, has produced a yet more unlikely version of what Kafka is about, and we despair, all of us, of ever arriving at that moment when our own clear vision will be recognized for what it is. Perhaps it is because everyone is drawing his own eye that such agreement as there is about Kafka exists. Human eyes are pretty much alike, and this may account for the kind of observation often heard, that Kafka is typical of twentieth-century man, portrays the crisis of our times, demonstrates our degeneracy, shows us Everyman. Why Kafka is singled out for this representative role is, after all, unclear. Why not Mann, or Lawrence, or Proust, if it has to be a novelist at all? Why not a soldier or politician? Which part of the twentieth century is Kafka typical of, and does the world he represents include Peking? Curiously, those who maintain that Kafka is only to be understood in terms of Prague in the final years of the Austro-Hungarian Empire are not averse to claiming for him a universal status, a harmony or identity between his microcosm and the macrocosm.

The bibliographies of 'Kafka-literature' cover several hundred pages of titles from all parts of the globe, and there are as many critical interpretations as there are titles. The variety of views expressed in the essays within this collection shows how little consensus has been achieved. Are we driven to the conclusion that we are all talking about a different experience of Kafka, that no true communication is possible, and that discussion is fruitless?

A possible avoidance of that unwelcome thought was offered in the most recent piece of Kafka criticism I happen to have read, which was Professor Roy Pascal's review of my book, *Franz Kafka*, in the *Times Literary Supplement*. Professor Pascal put forward the eirenic proposition that 'Kafka's novels are "open parables", that is, we must assume that they have a meaning, and that this meaning is ambiguous'. Such a definition does get us out of some of our difficulties. If we acknowledge first that we are merely assuming a meaning, we are not necessarily claiming objectivity, and if we are content to assume also that the meaning is ambiguous, we avoid some disputes. If we could use some word like 'multivalent' (but we can't) to translate the German *vieldeutig*, and substitute that, we could avoid them all. The question is, whether Professor Pascal's definition (as modified by me) helps us any more than Professor Thorlby's* in attaching any particular value to Kafka's work. A totally ambiguous writer, read by readers making totally different interpretations, would not give us a common focus. No doubt Kafka's work does owe a lot of its reputation to its being an object of dispute, as well as to being mysterious. It is like *Hamlet*, in that. Yet without some greater measure of agreement than has been achieved as yet, we face continual frustration.

We cannot be content with our position if all we can say is that Kafka—like Ossian, in his day?—became intellectually fashionable, an 'elitist' author, as the current jargon has it, for a certain period in the twentieth century, although no one could agree whether he was a sign of health or decadence, what he was really writing about, or whether he was a writer of distinction at all (for even that has been denied). Here a better solution to our differences begins to show itself, though we are a long way yet from settling them. Can we, in short, advance any reasons why Kafka is a writer who matters more to us than toy Nietzsches like Hermann Hesse? Or, since there are, I know, people who still (or again) take Hesse seriously, can we say why Kafka matters more to us than C. P. Snow?

We can begin to see a little more clearly, I think, if we question the ease of Professor Pascal's apparent assumption, that ambiguity is necessarily a valuable quality in a writer. I may do Professor Pascal an injustice there, but let us suppose that his definition was partly meant to express a value. We are, it is true, prone to see ambiguity as characteristic of poetry, in particular, and very often of prose too. I have no quarrel with William Empson on that score. On the contrary, I would like to remind you more precisely of what Empson said, in his *Seven Types of Ambiguity*, which was carefully qualified, not indiscriminately in praise of all seven types wherever found. 'Belief in ambiguities', he wrote, 'is liable to produce a sort of doctrinaire sluttishness. One is tempted to set down a muddle, in the hope that it will convey the meaning more immediately.'

But there is no making a virtue of ambiguousness. The

* See, 'Anti-mimesis: Kafka and Wittgenstein', pp. 59ff.

'practice of trying not to be ambiguous', to quote Empson again, 'has a good deal to be said for it. It is likely to lead to results more direct, more communicable and hence more durable, it is a necessary safeguard against being ambiguous without proper occasion, and it leads to more serious ambiguities when such occasions arise.' That insistence on the safeguard against being ambiguous without proper occasion is not much heeded in Kafka criticism—or in much writing about literature at all. On the contrary, not being ambiguous is often regarded as rather disgraceful. Professor Pascal in the *Times Literary Supplement* article called it 'consoling', which has seldom been thought an admirable quality, for some reason, since Nietzsche's day. The widely accepted view is that every occasion is proper for ambiguity. But if we examine that closely we shall be left with no grounds for saying anything definite about Kafka at all. We shall merely be left with a world from which value will have vanished, and in which no distinction between Kafka and Snow will any longer be possible.

You will see why it was that, when I was asked to write a book about Kafka, I put first my reasons for regarding him as a prose-writer worthy of the name. This is something we cannot afford to be ambiguous about, and no one who reads the early criticisms of Kafka's 'serpentine' prose—criticisms made before he had any reputation to speak of—will doubt the need for a case to be made. Beside William Sansom's pastiches, or Edgar Allan Poe's melodramatics, as I sought to show, Kafka stands out in his precision, detail, irony, sobriety, unpretentiousness, humour, lack of condescension, matter-of-factness.

But it also seemed important to contrast his prose at his best with the kind of writing he was capable of perhaps in some moment of desolation, when his own critical ability was least able to make itself felt, and which he only allowed to stand because of a half-conscious, half-unwilling desire that all his work should in any case be destroyed. What was published during his own lifetime, clearly after his appraisal, seldom has the faults of some of the unwieldy narratives which he handed to Max Brod only with the request that they be burned. *Metamorphosis* seemed to me the finest of his stories for its completeness (not by any means usual in Kafka), its symmetry, its controlled flow, and for many other qualities which would lose their essence by being reduced to a single word. That preference for *Metamorphosis* did not mean I was immune to the compelling power of *The Castle* or *The Trial*, and if Kafka had not attempted such ambitious themes as those of the novels he would hardly have gained the reputation he has. But I also instanced the kind of writing in which, at times, Kafka's confidence deserted him, the repetition of qualificatory words, the stumbling and confusion, the sheer boredom of many passages in both of the major novels, where all thought of conscious control has gone. He was not always able to confront his phantoms with the 'quiet critical ability' he proposed for himself. Those of us with less to fear have little idea what such control must have required of him.

These were not criticisms peculiar to me. Martin Walser has spoken of the boring quality in the novels, and Malcolm Pasley describes the 'chief characteristic—and perhaps the weakness' of Kafka's last works as 'the endless play with possibilities . . . the tireless building of hypotheses'. A reviewer in *Life and Letters* complained as early as 1930 of 'a continual procession of involuted and endless sentences, . . . unparagraphed pages', while as late as 1945 an editorial in the *Times Literary Supplement* confessed that Kafka was 'frequently tedious'. If I have allowed more weight to such criticisms, it is partly because they are usually ignored in the attempts to do everything else with Kafka but read him.

But I have met a criticism, since my book appeared, which takes account of what I was trying to do, and yet advances objections which deserve consideration. It came in a generous review in *The Spectator* (November 1973), from Dr Frank Field, who was broadly in sympathy with me and yet added that perhaps my 'narrowly aesthetic approach' was not wholly satisfactory. (I would for my own part not accept 'aesthetic' as a description, if it suggests mere attention to tinglings of the nerves, and excludes that listening for the whole man in Kafka that I was trying for: but that is a side-issue.) 'After all,' Dr Field added, 'had Kafka gone on writing stories like *Metamorphosis* he might have remained relatively unflawed as an artist, but would he be remembered as the major writer he

171

RONALD GRAY

undoubtedly is? . . . Is not the breaking-down of all these
checks and controls in Kafka's later work the reason why
novels like *The Trial* and *The Castle* possess their compulsive
and almost hypnotic power?' If I understand this rightly, Dr
Field was saying that Kafka's willingness to expose himself,
defenceless, to his own particular experience in all its hideous-
ness is what makes the two novels compelling—we are attracted
by that very ardour of self-abandonment (rather as Bürgel is
in the Castle interview, when he tells the helpless K. in effect,
that supreme power is his for the taking?), and that willingness
is ultimately what makes them great. If I unwittingly misrepresent Dr Field there, it is still in the vein of much of what
Kafka himself said. At times, Kafka removes the possibility of
discrimination entirely from human judgment—'the world can
only be regarded as good from the place at which it was
created'. Yet at other times he either speaks of employing his
'quiet critical ability', or allows himself the luxury of imagining
that all yielding to evil may be only a prelude to a sudden
reversal, an *Umschlag*, to the good. When he is in the first
mood, he fiercely declares some passage he has just written in
his notebooks to be worthless—though without saying to
himself why, and without destroying it. Here we can only
watch helplessly his self-laceration. In the second mood,
however, there should be some means by which we can see for
ourselves his success—and there is: comparing his best work
with the rest, we are able to distinguish it. Dr Field's point,
however, would seem to be made more in the spirit of the
third mood: like Kafka, we accept the heights and the depths,
and do not complain even if depths are only depths of tedium,
since these may lead at length to the great reversal. But they
cannot in themselves be the great reversal, and that no such
reversal ever came in the course of Kafka's writing is clear.
The castle remained inaccessible, and the court condemned
K. (if it was not his own self-condemnation, reflected by the
court) to a shameful death. By contrast *Metamorphosis* puts
without obfuscation the sheer truth of the degradation Kafka
was fated to endure, with great subtlety and power to move.

The question Dr Field seems to me to beg, is whether
'major' writer is a term that can be sustained. That Kafka
has been a major influence cannot be denied. He has at any

rate influenced such writers as Camus, Sartre, Michaux, Beckett, Peter Weiss, Kasack, Canetti, Rex Warner, Susan Sontag, which is a longer list than we could produce for the influence of Thomas Mann or Robert Musil. Yet with all possible admiration for Kafka's audacity, tenacity, sincerity, sense of humour, we have to admit that the case for placing him alongside the greatest names in the history of the novel has rather been taken for granted. After some fifty years, the assumption Dr Field now makes deserves a closer look.

With whom shall we compare Kafka, as a novelist and short-story writer? Not with Tolstoy, since he has nothing of Tolstoy's breadth or compassionate insight into complex relationships, nor with Dostoevsky, to whom he is closer, since Dostoevsky's intensity is capable not only of sustained con-centration, the construction of massive works, but also of being contained within a great framework, with hundreds of char-acters and many different points of view. In that regard Dostoevsky is closer to Tolstoy. One of Kafka's limitations, singled out by Friedrich Beissner as a characteristic, even, is his confinement almost entirely to a single point of view. This at once places him in a group of novelists that does not include, for example, Thomas Mann, Lawrence, Balzac, Flaubert, Dickens, in whose hands the novel became a wide panoramic structure, not all-embracing but at any rate able to provide a vast range of experiences of innumerable people with minute accounts of the circumstances in which they lived. As Lawrence said, 'Only in the novel are all things given full play'. He was of course speaking of that particular kind of novel, and of the potentiality, rather than, necessarily, of actual novels. But his point is clear: so far as the novel with a broad sweep is con-cerned, there is a chance for development and a real living quality. The full consequences of an action can be explored as they never can in drama: 'The novel will not let you get away with anything', as Lawrence also said. And to quote him a third time: 'Let us learn from the novel. In the novel the characters can do nothing but live. If they keep on being good, according to pattern, or bad, according to pattern, or even volatile, according to pattern, they cease to live, and the novel falls dead. A character in a novel has got to live, or it's nothing. We likewise, in life, have got to live, or we are nothing.'

Kafka hardly uses the novel in that sense. *The Trial* progresses from its startling opening through some fits of dullness, relieved by the grim fascination or evocativeness of such chapters as 'The Wnipper', or 'In the Cathedral', to its scarcely bearable conclusion. But there is little sequence. Events rarely have consequences. Characters rarely reappear a second time, not even Fräulein Bürstner, who seems at first so important, so closely associated with the whole cause and nature of the arrest. Kafka *could* 'get away with anything', simply because he does not attempt to show interrelationships, because he can ignore consequences. It is significant that both *America* and *The Trial* have final chapters that come after a gap in the writing. One does not know or feel why these particular endings should come, and Kafka is not, apparently, able to tell us. On the other hand, he does not write to a formula, a point in which he differs profoundly from Hesse. As he makes K. say of the Deputy Manager, 'He must realise as often as possible that K. was alive, and that like anything else that was alive, he was capable of surprising him some day with quite fresh capacities, however harmless he might seem today'. That at least is in the spirit of Lawrence's words on the novel. Had Kafka not felt the truth of it he would not have gone on to write such a different novel as *The Castle* is, or any other of the varied stories that make nonsense of attempts to find a single key, an overall pattern to his work. Such a pattern can be found in some writers. Kafka had far less certainty of direction, was more experimental, and that uncertainty is not only the distinctive thing about him, it is also what gives his works life.

But when uncertainty is itself elevated to a principle, it is what stifles his life, as he saw for himself. Uncertainty, doubts, the complete refusal of any consolation could and did become an absolute demand, something which nailed Kafka to a single position. In his desperation he was inclined to think that such ruthless disregard of comfort could in itself be an acceptable mode of life. And yet as he said, 'The Negative alone, however strong it may be, cannot suffice, as I believe it can in my unhappiest periods. For when I have mounted the smallest step, and am in some sort of security, however dubious, I stretch myself out and wait, not for the Negative to step up and join me, but for it to pull me down again. So it's a defensive instinct, that doesn't tolerate the provision of the smallest lasting comfort for me, and, for instance, smashes the marriage bed before it has even been set up'. (How close Kafka is here to Bürgel, stretching himself in bed at the thought of possibly releasing K.—who embodies the Negative—but being at once frustrated and exultant at K.'s falling asleep. K., unlike Kafka, could never take a 'Bürgel view' of himself.

Often in Kafka's work what he calls the Negative can be seen at work in just that way. Olga, in *The Castle*, in telling K. about the impossible demand made on her sister Amalia by the official Sortini, maintains that 'Amalia, while she did not love Sortini, perhaps did love him all the same', although there is nothing to show this beyond Amalia's violent rejection of him. This principled uncertainty is easily dismissed with the reflection that people who are in love know very well whether they are in love or not—like hunger, it is not something you can doubt having. It is a marked characteristic of Kafka's style, however, to qualify almost every statement with words like 'it is true . . . but', 'it must be confessed', 'perhaps', and 'for that matter', and in such a way that in places scarcely anything is held to. A favourite limiting expression even in the early stories, though its use increases with time, is *gewissermaßen*, 'to a certain extent', which shows the negative principle at its most powerful. On some occasions the retreat from definite statement becomes so compulsive that not only Olga is made to say that certain kinds of villager 'are to a certain extent extremely' appetizing for Castle officials, but the landlady says Klamm 'to a certain extent did not at all' summon Frieda to him a second time. Here the practice of not trying to be ambiguous would have served Kafka well, as he would have seen, had he ever revised his manuscript for publication.

These are no more than instances of a habit of mind which occasionally leads to slackened attention in the writing. I would like to look now at a more essential instance, which cannot of itself demonstrate anything about Kafka's work as a whole, but which does occupy such an important position in the construction of *The Trial* that I believe my point will seem not only clearer but more generally valid. I am thinking of the story, 'Before the Law', which is related by the priest to K.

175

in the cathedral, and which seems at first about to bring him the comfort and the resolution of his difficulties that he wants. It comes at a climactic position in the admittedly incomplete novel. It is offered by the priest when K. begins to feel that at long last one member of the court organization is showing him some consideration, but not in order to comfort him, rather in order to prevent him being deceived about the court. (Later, it is true, the priest combats K.'s interpretation, according to which the man in the story, whose situation somewhat resembles K.'s own, is deceived.)

The brief parable is in its outline simple enough. The man from the country comes to the gate of the law, but is told by the fearsome sentry that he cannot now be admitted, though he may, he is also told, attempt to get in despite this prohibition. There are, however, the sentry says, even more fearsome men at the inner gates, and the man sits down for many years, never attempting to go further. As he is about to die, he sees the 'inextinguishable glory' of the law blaze out from the innermost recess. At the same instant, however, the sentry tells him that this gate was meant for him alone, and that he is now going to close it.

Taken alone, this presents no difficulties. It may be felt as grim, or poignant, or an accurate allegory of Kafka's own situation, but it does not present a problem, unless we suppose that arrival at the intended gate implies a right to go in unhindered, and there is nothing in the story that suggests that, nor is there generally in similar 'quest' narratives. (What is meant by going in at the gate, and what it would be like to arrive at the law, is not defined either, but it seems to be something similar to discovering the nature of the charge against one, as K. fitfully tries to do in *The Trial* as a whole.) For the priest, however, a host of problems arises. He asks whether the sentry is really knowledgeable about the situation behind his back, whether he feels sympathy for the man from the country, whether he admires him, whether the man is deliberately deceived by him, whether he really deceives himself by his vanity. He asks whether the sentry has ever been in the interior recesses, whether he is really subordinate to the man whom he seems to dominate, whether the man is in reality more free than the sentry, since he is free to come and go as he pleases, even whether the sentry is able to shut the door which, on his own showing, is 'open as always'. K. is totally confused by these questions, and by the arguments and counter-arguments the priest presents, though the priest merely presents, and pretends to prove nothing. Since the priest ends by saying that according to one school of thought the validity of the sentry's utterances is proved by the fact that he is a servant of the law (which one might also doubt, as a fact, if one chose), K. concludes that the only meaning of the story is a negative one. Since the priest has already 'proved' that the sentry cannot be speaking the truth (but he hasn't: he has only suggested why he may not be) K. sees an impossible contradiction, for the servant of the law cannot be the purveyor of untruth. But K. does not leave it at that: he goes on to assume both that the sentry is a true servant of the law, and that he is lying: 'A wretched conclusion', said K. 'lying is made the universal rule'.

This in itself does not follow from the priest's comments. Nor is it even K.'s own settled view, for Kafka adds an explicit rider to this effect: 'it was not his final judgment'. It is merely an expression of despair, brought about more by the priest's befogging speculations than by any cogency in his argument. The questions the priest asks are not such as could possibly be answered from the story, for a work of fiction cannot tell us more than is actually there: we cannot know how many children Lady Macbeth had, or whether Hamlet was really killed by the allegedly poisoned sword of Laertes—for all we know, Hamlet may be shamming, and get up and walk off as soon as the curtains have closed. To ask whether Werther shot himself or was really shot through the window by Lotte's husband, or whether, as James Thurber speculates, Duncan was not killed by Macbeth at all, but himself, having suspected treachery, killed Lady Macbeth's father and substituted the body for his own ('had he not resembled my father as he slept . . .'—little did she know) is to ratiocinate in a void. In real life there may be more facts to discover; in fiction there are none, and what the author does not say is not evidence.

The whole structure of confusion superimposed by the priest has no more real persuasive power than an argument in a dream might have. It flows on, as dreams do, with all the

177

appearance of an argument, but completely without basis. Yet such is the hypnotic power of the writing here that I have always had the greatest difficulty in persuading students, and others, that K.'s conclusion is not only Kafka's own—despite the added disclaimer on K.'s behalf—but borne out by the sequence of thought in this section of the novel.* The story is regarded as both highly problematical and tending to show an unbearable paradox at the root of the universe, at which I am driven to repeat that there is no problem at all. The man from the country simply fails to enter, and we do not know why.

Our 'willing suspension of disbelief' does frequently result, when we read Kafka, in our submitting to something like hypnosis. We tend to accept the priest's view that the man from the country is not free to pass the gate, even though it is clear from the story itself that he is free, if he is able to take the risk. We tend to accept K.'s view that the judges are licentious, since we are told that the law-book he discovers contains an obscene picture, though the picture described does not seem obscene. We may not ask ourselves how the needle on the machine in *In the Penal Colony* becomes a great spike, when it is seen protruding from the officer's head. Often this is right of us: there is no more reason for that transformation than there is for transformations in dreams, and much of Kafka's work is to be experienced as a dream. Yet from time to time there is a semblance of something different, a reference to 'the world-order', or a suggestion that the cruel gods are about to return. Here we need to be aware whether we are experiencing one kind of world or another.

In the case of 'Before the Law' the negative conclusion, or semi-conclusion, has more the appearance of a wilful negativity than an attempt at conveying the quality of a dream. Kafka seems intent on, or habituated to, allowing the operation of the principle that only uncertainty is valid, despite the brilliant clarity of his story. I cannot go along with the view that Kafka 'stated inconclusiveness conclusively'.

It would be an exaggeration, though, to say that Kafka held to a principle of uncertainty at all times. By contrast with Samuel Beckett, whose characters take it for granted that all

* This part of my paper was hotly contested for almost the whole time allowed afterwards for discussion.

prospects, including the audience, are equally boring, Kafka's sense of humane concern is varied and rich. The comedy that plays round the figure of K.'s uncle, the moving account of Gregor Samsa's mother pleading with his father for Gregor's life, the beautiful natural scene by the river a few moments before K.'s execution, the tenderness of K.'s relation with Frieda, his gentleness towards Pepi—all these are moments of a kind that Beckett feels no compulsion to write about. Kafka seems to be, though subject to much the same demon as Beckett, infinitely more subtle in his exploration.

If, on the other hand, we look back to Baudelaire, as another writer close to Kafka, and much closer than Mann, Lawrence, Balzac, or even Dickens are (though a comparison between Lawrence's *Woman Who Rode Away*, and *In the Penal Colony* would be fruitful, too), one striking fact comes to mind. There is, of course, strictly no comparing a poet with a novelist, though both Baudelaire and Kafka embarked on something like religious quests, in an inverted sense, looking for the suffering in existence with a passion that other people apply to salvation. One would certainly have to allow, in any comparison, for the fact that whereas Baudelaire's accounts are of experiences of gruesome sights seen, Kafka's are more often curious and even contrived inventions of his own, spun on literary models: they are very often produced from his reading, rather than from life. (The wound in the boy's side in *A Country Doctor* is contrived to look like a rose; the machine in *In the Penal Colony* seems based on the one in Poe's *The Pit and the Pendulum*, one of Titorelli's paintings is based on Michelangelo's Moses, many reminiscences of *David Copperfield* find their way into *The Trial*.) But it is not so much these comparisons that I want to bring forward, as those moments in Baudelaire when the word 'great' comes to mind without any troubling of the conscience—such a moment is the one at the end of 'Un Voyage à Cythère', where the poet, having recognized that the promised land, the island of Venus, contains nothing but a gibbet, with the hanging image of his own corpse, concludes:

> Ah, Seigneur, donnez-moi la force et le courage
> De contempler mon coeur et mon corps sans dégoût.

179

There exists in short what James Smith, in a recent post-humously published volume (*Shakespearean and Other Essays*) called 'Baudelaire's heroism'. He can be compared to those peasants whom Wordsworth describes as reduced by poverty to 'the pleasure which there is in life itself', 'reduced that is', Smith comments, 'to finding a pleasure in mere existence, to that flicker of interest and hope without which any life is inconceivable. Yet, whether because of conscience or mere healthy instinct—whatever the name, the thing is wholly admirable—they do not wish not to be. Nor does Baudelaire', Smith concludes, 'reduced by spiritual rather than physical deprivation to a similar state; he clings firmly to what little life is left.'

Much the same could be said about Kafka. The difference I have in mind is that Baudelaire's plea for strength and courage, and the passion with which that plea is made, are unthinkable in Kafka. And as for Proust, similar also to Kafka in some of his concerns, the 'summons to a superterrestrial joy' which he speaks of in *Du Côté de Chez Swann* are not even hoped for in *The Castle* and *The Trial*. The only joy mentioned is very ambiguous. We note that K. feels joy only when, his arms rigidly held to his sides by the arms of the two executioners, something of their feeling passes over into himself. As for the castle, at its least malevolent it is no more than a being calmly contemplating the world in front of it. In Kafka we find acquiescence, patience, comprehensive surveillance to ensure that no false move has been made, no false hopes entertained, even a certain calculatingness—these are more typical of Kafka than passion or courage or joy. This again derives perhaps from the systematic mood in him—a paradoxical mood, since its chief aim is to assert the absence of system, but it is present all the same, and it destroys all passion as it destroyed Kafka's marriage bed. The plea that Josef K. would make would not be for the strength and courage Baudelaire prayed for, but rather for the ability to take his own life. (I am thinking of the passage at the end of *The Trial* where it appears that there is some superior being, perhaps a god, as K. believes, who requires suicide and at one and the same time withholds the power to commit the act. K.'s fault, as he sees it, is that he cannot live up to these expectations. He fails, by his own standards, to do the required deed, and take his life.) Nothing as ambitious as Baudelaire's desired contemplation without disgust emerges from Kafka's pages.

With that I have arrived at a clue to why Kafka seems to me less than a major writer. My reasons may be thought suspiciously like T. S. Eliot's, when he spoke of Goethe as a writer whom it was important to have read because of his European standing, though also in a certain sense 'provincial'— I mean (though any borrowing from Eliot has been unconscious till this moment) that Kafka's limitation to a single standpoint is itself, while it operates, a tethering of his range. He was, when all is said, a novelist who completed no novel, and barely a dozen short stories of considerable power, who did not write in any great tradition of European novel-writing, who had no great plan such as Joyce had in *Finnegans Wake* or Proust in *A la Recherche du Temps Perdu*: vast, completed projects rather than haunting sketches of what might have been. But there is further the limitation of what Kafka aims for, the fact that a celebration of life is something that he can never permit himself. The refusal is less abrupt than in Beckett, but it is there all the same, systematically there much of the time. In Baudelaire, celebration is always a potentiality— could Kafka conceivably have written the poems on wine in *Les Fleurs du Mal?* In Kafka, the glimpse of a girl ready for love and marriage, at the end of *Metamorphosis*, becomes for him, in his diary, a source for self-recrimination, as though it were sentimental, or perhaps consoling, to have ended on that note. And when the machine of torture in *In the Penal Colony* destroys itself, he is not content to leave it in the ruins of its self-destruction, but devises an ending—with which again he is discontented, and which reads as though it were awkwardly tacked on—to suggest that somehow the deviser of the machine will come again to restore it to activity. Guilt, as the officer in the story says, is always indubitable: that principled attitude becomes Kafka's own, here, and damages him as a writer.

Yet the distinction of Kafka's prose at its best is quite unlike the prose of a systematizer like the Marquis de Sade, for whom no alleviation is ever worth consideration: as Simone de Beauvoir says, even de Sade's admirers will admit that his work is for the most part unreadable. However close Kafka

181

may seem to de Sade in a small section of his work, no such admission could in his case conceivably be made. He is, at his best, a fastidious writer for whom any solecism, any degree of melodrama, sentimentality, is out of the question, and his real claim to fame is not a matter of contention, as it is with de Sade, but rather of reminding ourselves of where he stands in the many mansions of European literature. By comparison with Novalis, for example, he impresses by his lack of ghoulish relish and insubstantial emotion, though *Heinrich von Ofterdingen* is clearly in the line from which *The Castle* springs. He is often compared with Kleist, but though he shares Kleist's chaotic vision, he has none of Kleist's passionate intensity, nor his capacity for ludicrous exaggeration. It is through the comparison with Kleist that one becomes aware how uncontrived Kafka's situations generally are. Where Kleist will fly in the face of any likelihood to establish one of his paradoxes, Kafka seldom gives the impression of devising a situation to illustrate a theory of ambiguity. Gregor Samsa's transformation, though far more fantastic than Kunigunde's in Kleist's *Käthchen von Heilbronn*, does not seem at all contrived. Here, Kafka's complete assurance—knowing his own condition—gains one's assent in a way that Kleist usually manages not to do, by his stridency.

How did Kafka come by his reputation? That Max Brod had a very large hand in it is obvious. It may even be held that Kafka would not have become widely known outside Germany if Brod had not canvassed him intensely for twenty years and more after his death. That he became, paradoxically, a symbol for writers during the French Resistance is another chance that promoted interest in him, and his work clearly does have a great affinity with much European and American literature since 1945, particularly with French, but also Swedish; there have even been echoes in Persia and Japan. That affinity does not stretch to such authors as Solzhenitsyn, Brecht, Orwell, Pasternak, or Faulkner.

Yet when we ask what is distinctive in Kafka beyond his sober preoccupation with the almost total darkness into which he was born, we must point chiefly to that small body of work which surely is capable of keeping him read for generations still to come. He will be remembered for the calmness of mind with which he confronted his dereliction, though with less positive claim than men in a similar state, for instance St John of the Cross or Gerard Manley Hopkins. He never transcends affliction, and even regarded any kind of triumph with abhorrence. There was no 'and yet', *kein 'und doch'*, as he reminded himself on the final page of his diary. His most significant and telling image is that of the officer who lies on the machine of torture and remains, unlike his predecessors, untransfigured: the face is unaltered—'it was, as it had been in life. The lips were pressed firmly together, the eyes were open and had the expression of life. The look in them was calm and convinced. Through the forehead went the point of the great iron spike'.

Just as apposite is the answer given by the hunter Gracchus, certainly a kind of self-image, 'I am here. More than that I do not know. More than that I cannot do. My ship is without a rudder. It is running before the wind that blows in the lowest regions of death'. The quality in Kafka that will endure comes from his ability to go on quietly meeting that conviction. Like the helmsman in Conrad's story *The Nigger of the 'Narcissus'*, when the ship is being blown round the Cape with her yard-arms in the water and no prospect of staying afloat, in his best writing Kafka still 'steers with care'. For Kafka there is no sequel, though for Conrad's helmsman there was a triumphant return to the land he came from. Yet our admiration goes uncompelled to the careful holding of a course when the hurricane has struck, even when there is no prospect at all of survival, and to have created so highly wrought a story as *Metamorphosis*, with its articulation, its rounded view of the family in which the horror takes place, its scrupulous wording, was the work of an unquestionable master. 'I am here', says Gracchus; the officer's eyes 'had the expression of life'—but Kafka does more than either of these, he gives life to this death-in-life, holds it up so that we see it distinctly and with no scrap of embellishment. We must simply get used to seeing it for what it is, and that is all.

183

# Notes

WALTER H. SOKEL

1. cf. Wilhelm Emrich, *Franz Kafka*, Bonn, 1958, p. 260.
2. For a detailed discussion of the Oedipal structure of *The Trial*, I should like to refer the reader to my book, *Franz Kafka: Tragik und Ironie*, Munich-Vienna, 1964, chapters 7 and 8.
3. The exception is the fragmentary chapter, 'Zu Elsa'.
4. *Hochzeitsvorbereitungen auf dem Lande und andere Prosa aus dem Nachlass*, New York, 1953, p. 115. This volume will be referred to as HL. All translations from Kafka in this essay are my own.
5. cf. also Emrich's view, p. 265, that the purpose of the trial is K.'s taking issue with himself and coming to understand himself.
6. Quotations from *The Trial* are taken, in my own translations, from this edition: *Der Prozess*. Roman, New York, 1946 (1935), 5th edition, which will be referred to in the text as P.
7. cf. Ingeborg Henel, 'Die Türhüterlegende und ihre Bedeutung für Kafkas "Prozess"', *Deutsche Vierteljahrsschrift für Literaturwissenschaft und Geistesgeschichte*, Vol. XXXVIII (1964), p. 61. Although I disagree with Ingeborg Henel's formulation on this point, the pioneering contribution of her article should be emphasized.
8. HL, p. 48.
9. Beda Allemann's analysis of the novel ('Kafka. Der Prozess', in *Der deutsche Roman*, ed. Benno von Wiese, Düsseldorf, 1963, Vol. II, pp. 234–90.) assumes that the plea cannot conform to K.'s real (and impossible) task of justifying his existence 'fundamentally' because it would 'only contain a justification after the fact,' which is futile for the problem of his trial. However, if K.'s task is to discover his guilt, the impossibility of the plea is based on the necessary self-deception and duplicity involved in the attempt to justify all his past actions in retrospect. Allemann's assertion that the court is not at all interested in K.'s plea is of course unprovable. It is based upon the analogy between the Deputy Manager and the court which lacks persuasiveness because the Deputy Manager is the character at the opposite pole of K.'s trial, as K.'s choice of the court over the Deputy Manager's invitation shows.
10. In addition to '*Prozess*', the word '*Verfahren*' ('procedure') is used to designate K.'s trial.
11. cf. Emrich's view, p. 281, that Kafka by his treatment of the lawyer and Leni expressed his own rigorous rejection of the idea of help from another.
12. HL, p. 89.
13. cf. also Emrich, p. 261.
14. This circumstance has been pointed out by Heinz Politzer, *Franz Kafka. Parable and Paradox*, Ithaca, New York, 1962, p. 177.
15. Although Ingeborg Henel specifically states that the doorkeeper by his very existence points to the entrance at the same time as he forbids it,

she curiously fails to mention the passage in which he does so explicitly. Emrich does point out that the doorkeeper invites the man to enter, but he draws from this fact a conclusion very different from the one pointed out here. For Emrich the contradiction between prohibition and invitation indicates the dichotomy between 'official' and 'private person' present in all of Kafka's bureaucrats, p. 268. According to Emrich, the officials want to break out of the rigidly determined order of their service into a 'freer' existence. In contrast to Emrich, I hold that Kafka's restriction of the narrative perspective to the protagonist compels us to consider only the function their characters possess for the protagonist. Their own 'wishes' are inaccessible to us, as they are to K.

16. cf. Michel Carrouges, *Kafka versus Kafka*, tr. Emmett Parker, University, Alabama, 1968, p. 39. The original version *Kafka contre Kafka* appeared in Paris (Librairie Plon, 1962). Carrouges refers here to an article by Michel Cournot (*L'Arche*, Nr. 23) who suggests that the use of the name Franz for the arresting warder points to Kafka's participation in the carrying out of K.'s arrest.

17. cf. *Briefe an Felice und andere Korrespondenz aus dem Nachlass*, ed. Erich Heller and Jürgen Born, New York-Frankfurt, 1967, pp. 535, 546, 511. See also p. 289, where the ability to be decisive is ascribed to Felice, but by implication found wanting in the writer himself.

18. HL, p. 196, and *Briefe 1902–1924*, New York-Frankfurt, 1958, p. 195.

19. HL, pp. 166f.

20. The multivalence of the ending is very well discussed by Politzer, p. 217.

21. HL, p. 43.


J. P. STERN

1. I think in particular of Günther Anders, *Kafka: pro und contra*, Munich, 1951, English trsl. by W. A. J. Steer, London, 1960.

2. Note dated 25 February 1918, in *Hochzeitsvorbereitungen auf dem Lande*, ed. Max Brod, New York, 1953, pp. 120–1.

3. *The Blue Book*, Oxford, 1958, p. 17.

4. *The Disinherited Mind*, Cambridge, 1952, pp. 164–5.

5. I follow the text of Max Brod's edition, New York, 1964; the translations are my own.

6. *Justiz und N-S Verbrechen: Sammlung Deutscher Strafurteile wegen national-sozialistischer Tötungsverbrechen, 1945–1966*, vol. vi, Amsterdam, 1971, p. 417.

7. Quoted from M. Broszat, *Der Staat Hitlers*, Munich, 1969, p. 412.

8. *Ibid.*, p. 422.

9. Quoted from Karl Peters in *Deutsches Geistesleben und Nationalsozialismus*, Tübingen, 1965, pp. 160f.

10. See Gesetze des N-S Staates, ed. U. Brodersen, Bad Homburg, 1968, p. 41.

11. H. Picker, *Hitlers Tischgespräche im Führerhauptquartier*, ed. Percy Schramm &c., Stuttgart, 1963, pp. 326, 467.

12. 'Brief an den Vater' [1919] in *Hochzeitsvorbereitungen auf dem Lande*, ed. cit., p. 169.
13. Anthony Thorlby, *Kafka: a Study*, London, 1972, pp. 54f.
14. Max Brod, *Franz Kafka: eine Biographie*, New York, 1946, p. 210.
15. See J. P. Stern, *On Realism*, London, 1972, p. 93.


W. G. SEBALD

1. The Muirs' translation of this passage ('of having spoken my mind freely to a great man', p. 53) is misleading. In order to render the 'mächtig' more accurately it is probably advisable to use a combination of words like 'great and powerful'. Page references to quotations from *The Castle*, if they are not my own, refer to Franz Kafka, *The Castle*, tr. Willa and Edwin Muir, Harmondsworth, 1971 (1957).
2. Christian Enzensberger, *Grösserer Versuch über den Schmutz*, Munich, 1970, p. 49.
3. *Ibid.*, p. 39.
4. *Ibid.*, p. 51.
5. cf. *Wedding Preparations in the Country*, ed. Max Brod, London, 1954, pp. 60f.
6. cf. Martin Buber, *Die Erzählungen der Chassidim*, Zurich, 1949, p. 418.
7. 'Temptation in the Village', *The Diaries of Franz Kafka*, ed. Max Brod, Harmondsworth, pp. 280ff.
8. Buber, *op. cit.*, p. 201.
9. cf. my article on 'The Undiscover'd Country: The Death Motif in Kafka's *Castle*', *Journal of European Studies*, Vol. II, 1 (1972), pp. 22–34.
10. *Wedding Preparations in the Country*, p. 58.
11. Jakob Wassermann, *Mein Weg als Deutscher und Jude*, Berlin, 1921, p. 36.
12. In his *On Kafka's Castle*, London, 1973, pp. 81 and 213.
13. Buber, *op. cit.*, p. 365.
14. *The Diaries*, p. 400.
15. Gustav Janouch, *Conversations with Kafka*, 2nd revised and enlarged edition, London, 1971, p. 110.
16. Martin Walser, *Beschreibung einer Form*, Frankfurt and Berlin, 1972, p. 18.
17. *Tagebücher*, Cologne, 1957, p. 172.
18. S. Beckett, *Molloy*, London, 1966, p. 115f.


FRANZ KUNA

1. George Steiner, *Language and Silence. Essays 1958–1966*, London, 1967, p. 34.
2. Martin Greenberg, *Science and the Shabby Curate of Poetry. Essays about the Two Cultures*, London, 1964, p. 148.

3. *Ibid.*, p. 149.

4. cf. Boris Kuznetsov, *Einstein and Dostoevsky. A Study of the Relation of Modern Physics to the Main Ethical and Aesthetic Problems of the Nineteenth Century*, London, 1972, p. 22, where the author notes a basic feature of Dostoevsky's realism: 'it was *experimental*. Dostoevsky verified his initial conceptions by placing his heroes in extremely testing circumstance.' As I hope to show, this statement is even more applicable to Kafka. I should like to acknowledge at this point my debts to Boris Kuznetsov's stimulating book, particularly as far as its method and his skilful comparison between Einstein and Dostoevsky are concerned, and for constructive criticism to my colleagues Peter and Wendy Bell, Raymond Hargreaves, Martin Hollis, Martin Scott-Taggart, and Cedric Williams.

5. Philipp Frank's biography of Einstein, most of his other books on the interrelationships between science and philosophy, and Boris Kuznetsov's *Einstein and Dostoevsky* are laudable exceptions.

6. Philipp Frank, *Einstein. His Life and Times*, New York, 1972 (1947), p. 84.

7. Max Brod, *Streitbares Leben*, Munich, 1960, p. 253.

8. Max Born (ed.), *The Born-Einstein Letters*, tr. Irene Born, London, 1971, p. 4.

9. Angel Flores and Homer Swander (eds.), *Franz Kafka Today*, Madison, 1964 (1958), p. 61.

10. Klaus Wagenbach, *Franz Kafka in Selbstzeugnissen und Bild-dokumenten*, Hamburg, 1964, pp. 70f.

11. Franz Kafka, *Briefe, 1902–1924*, ed. Max Brod, Frankfurt a.M., 1966 (1958), pp. 224ff.

12. Einstein, 'Autobiographical Notes', reprinted in *Albert Einstein: Philosopher-Scientist*, ed. P. A. Schilpp, New York, 1951 (1949), p. 59.

13. Erich Heller and Jürgen Born (eds.), *Letters to Felice*, tr. James Stern and Elisabeth Duckworth, London, 1974, p. 156.

14. I would risk the generalization that it was in fact Einstein and Kafka who for the first time acted decisively, and with enormous consequences for their respective fields, in the spirit of Kant's 'Copernican revolution'. For many reasons one would like to add Wittgenstein's name here. But what Erich Heller has said in his essay on 'Wittgenstein and Nietzsche'— 'that the *Tractatus* participates in a pre-Kantian metaphysical faith'— makes me believe that this cannot be done.

15. Albert Einstein, *Relativity. The Special and the General Theory*, tr. R. W. Lawson, New York, 1961, p. 22.

16. *Ibid.*, p. 25.

17. cf. Gaston Bachelard, 'The Philosophic Dialectic of the Concept of Relativity', in *Albert Einstein: Philosopher-Scientist*, p. 571.

18. cf. Hans Reichenbach, 'The Philosophical Significance of the Theory of Relativity', *ibid.*, p. 294.

19. Gaston Bachelard, *op. cit.*, p. 570.

20. *Ibid.*, pp. 570f.

21. Immanuel Kant, *Critique of Pure Reason*, tr. Norman Kemp Smith, London, 1963, p. 233.

22. *Ibid.*, pp. 235f.

23. P. W. Bridgman, 'Einstein and Operationalism', in *Albert Einstein: Philosopher-Scientist*, p. 336.

24. Goethe, 'Anschauende Urteilskraft' [1820], *Goethes sämtliche Werke*, Jubiläumsausgabe, Vol. 39, p. 34.

25. Goethe, 'Bedenken und Ergebung' [1820], *ibid.*, p. 35.

26. *Ibid.*

27. Peter Eichhorn, *Idee und Erfahrung im Spätwerk Goethes*, Freiburg and Munich, 1971, p. 120f.

28. *Description of a Struggle*, tr. Willa and Edwin Muir, London, 1960, p. 291.

29. *Wedding Preparations in the Country*, tr. E. Kaiser and E. Wilkins, London, 1973 (1954), p. 41.

30. Peter Heller, *Dialectics and Nihilism. Essays on Lessing, Nietzsche, Mann and Kafka*, Massachusetts, 1966, p. 229.

31. The following paragraphs on *The Trial* are based on a similar analysis in my *Kafka. Literature as Corrective Punishment*, London, 1974, pp. 116ff. For a full analysis of the Bürgel episode, and the scene of the 'Aktenverteilung' see pp. 160–7.

32. *The Trial*, tr. Willa and Edwin Muir, Harmondsworth, 1971 (1953), p. 11.

33. I use the term in the sense of Niels Bohr's 'Complementarity Principle', which modifies 'Heisenberg's relation of indeterminacy' by stating that 'position' and 'momentum' are two different aspects of a small mass in much the same way that the particle properties and wave properties are two aspects of the photon. In Bohr's sense the term 'complementarity' does not suggest the possibility of removing this duality but refers instead to what 'positivistic' philosophy had already stated, that science cannot discover what actually happens in the world but can only describe and combine the results of different observations. As is well known Einstein could not agree with this view and thought it 'a mistake to permit theoretical description to be directly dependent upon acts of empirical assertions as it seems to me to be intended, [for example] in Bohr's principle of complementarity.' (Einstein, 'Reply to Criticisms', in *Albert Einstein: Philosopher-Scientist*, p. 674.) As I hope will become clear by the end of this paper, the Kafka who wrote *The Castle* is once more far removed from Einstein's position, his ultimate decision to allow notions of 'unity' and 'harmony' to override the empirical evidence of quantum-mechanics.

34. *The Trial*, p. 27.

35. *Ibid.*, pp. 24f.

36. Joseph Conrad, *Three Short Novels*, ed. E. Weeks, New York, 1960, p. 40.

37. cf. my analysis of the Bürgel episode in *The Castle*, in *Kafka. Literature as Corrective Punishment*, pp. 160ff.

38. Quoted from Jack Kaminsky, *Hegel on Art*, Albany, 1970, pp. 90f.

39. *The Castle*, tr. Willa and Edwin Muir, Harmondsworth, 1971 (1957), p. 245.

40. *The Trial*, p. 132.

41. *The Castle*, pp. 184f.

42. Muir's translation (*op. cit.*, p. 213), 'heart-breaking life', is misleading.

What is meant is a situation in which Barnabas's functioning as a normal human being is dangerously restricted. Thus the word contains not only the usual metaphorical sense of 'anxiety-ridden' but also in a very literal sense the notion of 'restricting the heart'.

43. *The Castle*, p. 273.
44. *The Trial*, pp. 141ff.
45. cf. *The Trial*, p. 142.
46. Quoted from Eduard Spranger, *Goethe. Seine geistige Welt*, Tübingen, 1967, p. 234.
47. *Ibid.*, p. 242.
48. *Ibid.*
49. Goethe, 'Ganymed'.
50. Publications of the English Goethe Society, New Series, Vol. XLIII, ed. F. M. Fowler, B. A. Rowley and A. C. Weaver, Leeds, 1973, pp. 57ff.
51. Quoted from Boris Kuznetsov, pp. 51f. I have based some of my arguments on his penetrating analysis of this passage.
52. *The Brothers Karamazov*, tr. Constance Garnett, London, 1961, (1912), pp. 250f.
53. *Ibid.*, p. 265.
54. *Ibid.*, p. 240.
55. Quoted from Philipp Frank, *Philosophy of Science*, Englewood Cliffs, N.J., 1962, p. 2.
56. 'Aus dem Nachlass der Achzigerjahre', *Werke in drei Bänden*, ed. Karl Schlechta, Munich, Vol. III, p. 556.
57. Quoted from Boris Kuznetsov, *op. cit.*, pp. 98f.

KIMBERLY SPARKS

1. Vladimir Nabokov, *Ada*, New York and Toronto, 1969, p. 543.
2. *Ibid.*, p. 541.
3. John Lynen, *The Design of the Present*, New Haven and London, 1969, p. 20.
4. *Sewanee Review*, Vol. LIII; 2, 3, 4, 1945.
5. Hermann Broch, *Gesammelte Werke*, Vol. VII, Zürich, 1955.
6. Henri Bergson, *Time and Free Will*, New York, 1910, p. 100.
7. *Ibid.*, p. 101.
8. Bertrand Russell, *A History of Western Philosophy*, London, 1946, p. 830.
9. Gaston Bachelard, *The Poetics of Space*, Boston, 1969, p. 212.
10. Hermann Weyl, *Symmetry*, Princeton, 1952, p. 51.
11. Vladimir Nabokov, *Ada*, p. 541.
12. Franz Kafka, *Description of a Struggle*, New York, 1958, p. 201.
13. William Faulkner, *The Sound and the Fury*, New York, 1929, pp. 11–12.
14. Jean Piaget and Bärbel Inhelder, *The Child's Conception of Space*, New York, 1967, pp. 8–9.
15. Jean Paul Friedrich Richter, *Life of the Cheerful Schoolmaster Maria Wutz*, in *Nineteenth Century German Tales*, ed. Angel Flores, New York, 1959, p. 31.

16. Cited by Harry Levin in *The Gates of Horn*, New York, 1966, p. 287.
17. Gustave Flaubert, *A Simple Heart* in *Three Tales*, Baltimore, 1961, p. 17.
18. *Ibid.*, p. 49.
19. Gaston Bachelard, p. 218.
20. *Ibid.*, p. 212.
21. Franz Kafka, *Selected Short Stories*, New York, 1952, p. 35.
22. *Ibid.*, p. 18.
23. *Ibid.*, p. 19.

CHRISTIAN GOODDEN

1. *Franz Kafka. Sämtliche Erzählungen*, Frankfurt a.M., 1972, p. 404. The quotations in English are taken from *Metamorphosis and Other Stories* (which also contains 'The Great Wall of China'), tr. Willa and Edwin Muir, Harmondsworth, 1970, and all page references refer to this edition.
2. If these considerations seem somewhat forced, their pertinence will become clearer later. We are primarily trying to derive principles whose relevance and applicability are greater to less concrete and more abstract considerations.
3. For a closer examination of this and related observations the reader is referred to my article in the *Journal of European Studies*: 'Two Quests for Surety: A Comparative Interpretation of Stifter's *Abdias* and Kafka's *Der Bau*', Vol. 5, No. 4, 1975.
4. This infinite distance is a key element in the parable *A Message from the Emperor*. As long as the Emperor remains an object of speculation, for evidence of his true nature can never reach the subject, the subject can go on believing in him. Note, incidentally, the religious connotation in 'der Bote' = both messenger and Apostle. The same is true of, say, Klamm in *The Castle*. He and his credibility remain intact only as long as and in so far as there is confusion about his identity. There is a certain continuity here among all Kafka's authorities—be they the Castle, the Law, Klamm, the Doorkeeper, the Emperor, the 'Führerschaft', the 'Nordvölker', the enemy in *The Burrow*, etc. This is not to say that they are identical. Some are real, some figments of the imagination; some are benevolent, some hostile. What is common to them all is their function. Their function is to guarantee the possibility of certain (mythological) processes.
5. One of the main disputes to arise during the Symposium concerned the question of interpretation and approach. In subscribing to the more positive view, which not only saw the necessity and value of interpreting Kafka's works, but also recognized that no one interpretation need exclude any other (with the qualification that some interpretations could become manifestly more far-fetched than others), I would like to point out that not only is employment of a quest-motif a non-exclusive approach to the works (the quest has existential, religious, psychological etc. aspects), but that also as a multivalent interpretative medium it embodies criteria for evaluating the relative 'far-fetchedness' of any one interpretation. For example, the quest

190

has only remote political implications (see note 7.) and in terms of a quest-motif any interpretation which claims politics to be a central feature of Kafka's works is far-fetched. Also during the Symposium there arose the concept of choice. It was generally agreed, I think, that at the bottom of many of Kafka's works there lay a choice. *The Great Wall of China* is no exception. As I point out in my essay, the story contains an exhortation that the wall continue to be built, the 'Führerschaft' believed in etc. But the question which emerges is whether these activities should be continued or renounced. Herein lies the choice—a momentous choice upon which the life and life-style of the people of the Chinese Empire appear to depend.

6. Or like Pepi's ill-case in *The Castle* when she says that the worst thing is not her eternal drudgery, but rather the intermittent lulls in activity, when she and the other servant girls nearly die of fright and wait for the order that never comes. Or the discomposure that K. feels when he craves for a confrontation with Klamm, his personal enemy or god, and yet is forever denied this and is the more disastrously delivered over to the debilitating nothingness which cheats him of the feeling of security and vitality that is afforded to those, including himself, who quest for the Castle.

7. Incidentally, it can be seen from this that the building and consolidation has an entrenching, conservative, perhaps politically repressive aspect to it. Note, for example how the 'Bürger' are 'still und einfach'. They put their trust and hopes in the building of the wall (quest) with an uncritical and submissive naiveté.

8. Nietzsche, *Gesammelte Werke*, ed. Karl Schlechta, Vol. 1, *Menschliches, Allzumenschliches*, Munich, 1954, p. 700.

9. In a very similar evolutionary analysis Robert Musil uses just this image. He writes, in *The Man without Qualities*, that perhaps we have taken 'die falsche Abzweigung' or have got onto the wrong track: 'auf eine falsche Strecke geraten' (*Der Mann ohne Eigenschaften* ed. Adolf Frisé, Hamburg, 1969, p. 32).

10. There is something logically insuperable here. As the animal in *The Burrow* knows, it is a mistake to have only one example of something, and to use it exclusively. Ideally, the animal would like two entrances to his burrow, so that he could enter his burrow and watch himself enter from the other at the same time—an impossibility. Similarly, in terms of entering upon other courses of action, one can only take one at a time, never knowing whether this is the right course except with hind-sight. Janouch reports Kafka as having said: 'One only knows the rightness or wrongness of the road when one has reached the goal' (*Conversations with Kafka*, 2nd ed., London, 1971, p. 173).

11. An arbitrariness in the form and direction of existence is best illustrated by the closing lines of *Der Jäger Gracchus* (*The Huntsman Gracchus*). Note that this story was written just before *The Great Wall of China*.

12. This is exactly the reaction of a group of villagers in *The Castle*. In pointing out a discrepancy between his own observations and the villagers' delusions about the nature of Klamm, K. threatens to destroy their beliefs with an unpalatable truth. Their reaction, which is a mixture of laughing disbelief, embarrassed silence and self-evidence, shows that they know this.

The same reaction greets the intellectual dog in *Investigations of a Dog*. When he asks about the origin of the earth's nourishment, he is greeted with feigned incomprehension and is answered by 'if you haven't got enough to eat, we'll give you some of ours'—an irrelevant and infuriating answer. Above all, the intellectual dog wants the other silent dogs to admit that they know what they know.

13. Freud, *Gesammelte Werke*, ed. Anna Freud *et al.*, Vol. XIV, 'Die Zukunft einer Illusion', London, 1948, p. 348.

14. cf. *Ibid.*, p. 351.

15. *The Terror of Art*, London, 1971, p. 49.

16. cf. Kafka's: 'While far away in front in the market square at the heart of the city, the execution of their ruler is proceeding.' (*The Great Wall of China*, p. 76).

17. Nietzsche, Vol. 2, 'Die Fröhliche Wissenschaft', p. 127.

18. The expectation of this is given explicit utterance in Kafka's very last story *Josephine the Singer*. Josephine, another example, like the Great Wall or the 'Führerschaft', of the 'lying symbolical', must be annihilated.

19. Kafka writes in his Diary for 25 September 1917: 'Happiness only if I can raise the world into the pure, the true, and the immutable.' cf. the passage in *Investigations of a Dog* in which the intellectual dog says that he sought out loneliness and fasting 'to achieve truth and escape from this world of falsehood'. (p. 121)

J. J. WHITE

1. Eliseo Vivas, 'Kafka's Distorted Mask', in his *Creation and Discovery. Essays in Criticism and Aesthetics*, Chicago, 1955, p. 68. The essay is reprinted in *Kafka. A Collection of Critical Essays*, ed. Ronald Gray, Englewood Cliffs, N.J., 1962, pp. 133–46.

2. *Über Franz Kafka*, Frankfurt a.M., 1966, p. 83.

3. H. Uyttersprot, *Eine neue Ordnung der Werke Kafkas? Zur Struktur von 'Der Prozess' und 'Amerika'*, Antwerp, 1957, p. 76.

4. *The Diaries of Franz Kafka*, ed. Max Brod, Harmondsworth, 1972, p. 38. (All further page references are to this edition.)

5. Kafka criticizes the 'Kot des Endes' (messy ending) of *Schackale und Araber* (*Jackals and Arabs*), the 'Unlesbares Ende' (unreadable ending) of *Metamorphosis*, the 'Machwerk' (patchwork) of the final pages of *In the Penal Colony*, and there are various references in his *Letters to Felice* to the problem of ending *America*.

6. Ends of contemporary works by Oskar Baum and Ernst Weiss come in for critical comment, as do those of such classics as Franz Grillparzer's *Der arme Spielmann* and Heinrich von Kleist's *Michael Kohlhaas*.

7. Günther Anders, *Franz Kafka—pro und contra*, Munich, 1951, especially pp. 42, 55f; Martin Greenberg, *The Terror of Art. Kafka and Modern Literature*, London, 1968, p. 150.

8. *op. cit.*, pp. 62f.

9. *op. cit.*, p. 69.

10. See Friedrich Beissner, *Kafka der Dichter. Ein Vortrag*, Stuttgart, 1958, pp. 13f.

11. A succinct description of this view concerning an ending—where 'les dernières pages d'un livre sont déjà dans les premières'—can be found in Albert Camus's *Le Mythe de Sisyphe*, Paris, 1942, p. 26. On the other hand, the later Kafka reminds one more of André Gide's Edouard, who observes: 'X. soutient que le bon romancier doit, avant de commencer son livre, savoir comment ce livre finira. Pour moi, qui laisse aller le mien à l'aventure, je considère que la vie ne nous propose jamais rien . . . qui ne puisse être considéré comme un nouveau point de départ' (*Les Faux-monnayeurs*, Paris, 1925, p. 258).

12. See Gert Ueding's 'Fragment und Utopie. Zur Theorie des literarischen Bruchstücks', *Der Monat*, Vol. XX, 238 (1968), pp. 64–72, especially p. 71: 'Vollkommenheit wird antizipiert als Utopie, als ein nicht Erreichtes, als möglich oder unmöglich Fernes'. ('Completion is anticipated as a utopia, as something not attained, as something possibly or impossibly distant'.) Marianne Schuller makes the same point in *Romanschlüsse in der Romantik. Zum frühromantischen Problem von Universalität und Fragment*, München, 1974, p. 49.

13. See Joseph Gantner: 'Formen des Unvollendeten in der neueren Kunst', in *Das Unvollendete als künstlerische Form. Ein Symposon*, edited by J. A. Schmoll gen. Eisenwerth, Berne-Munich, 1959, pp. 47–82.

14. '*Das Urteil*: An Interpretation', *German Quarterly*, Vol. XLV, i (1972), p. 127.

15. Franz Kafka, *Sämtliche Erzählungen*, ed. Paul Raabe, Frankfurt a.M., 1970, p. 32. (My own translation.)

16. W. H. Sokel discerns a mood of dionysian tragedy to this end (in contrast to the *Novelle*'s apolline beginning), *Franz Kafka—Tragik und Ironie. Zur Struktur seiner Kunst*, Munich-Vienna, 1964, pp. 71ff. Franz Kuna, on the other hand, places it in a genetic framework: 'What Kafka sees through the window of his room enters the work as a piece of final and concrete evidence for the justness of his literary fantasy. The story ends where it began: conspicuously in the confines of an autobiographical situation'. (*Kafka. Literature as Corrective Punishment*, London, 1974, p. 42.)

17. It would make little difference to this interpretation whether one saw the final sentence as the narrator's distancing of himself from a previous congruence with Georg's perspective or as *style indirect libre*, with Georg at the moment of death achieving (like the man from the country in *The Trial*) a new sense of perspective.

18. *Briefe*, New York, 1958, p. 100.

19. *Motiv und Gestaltung bei Franz Kafka*, Bonn, 1966, pp. 258ff.

20. The formulation here is an implicit rebuttal of George Eliot's view that all endings are negative: 'a conclusion . . . is at best a negation' (Letter to John Blackwood, 1 May 1857, *The George Eliot Letters*, Gordon S. Haight, Vol. II *1852–1858*, London, 1954, p. 324).

21. *The Sense of an Ending. Studies in the Theory of Fiction*, New York and London, 1967, p. 175.

22. James Rolleston has argued, in his interpretation of *The Stoker*, that 'the use of antithesis is fundamental to Kafka's style', but that 'its quality of rigidity will only be exorcised when it becomes thematic . . .' (*Kafka's Narrative Theater*, University Park and London, 1974, p. 31).

23. Franz Kafka. *Parable and Paradox*, Ithaca, 1963, p. 212.

24. Viktor Shklovsky's distinction between the organic ending of the short story and the novel's epilogic ending (*O teorii prozy*, Moscow, 1929, pp. 68ff.) clearly breaks down when one considers Kafka's narrative structures.

25. John Fowles, *The French Lieutenant's Woman*, St Albans, 1970, p. 349.

26. *Buridans Esel*, Munich, 1971, p. 193.

27. *The George Eliot Letters*, Vol. 2, p. 324.

28. *Aspects of the Novel*, Harmondsworth, 1974, p. 102.

29. Preface to *Roderick Hudson*.

30. 'This is because the plot requires to be wound up . . . If it was not for death and marriage I do not know how the average novelist would conclude' (*op. cit.*, p. 102), a point also made by Mark Twain at the end of *The Adventures of Tom Sawyer*, London, 1970, p. 180: 'When one writes a novel about grown people, he knows exactly where to stop—that is, with a marriage.' The weakness of endings to the *Buildungsroman* is discussed by Roy Pascal (*The German Novel*, Manchester, 1956, pp. 28f) and Lothar Köhn (*Entwicklungs- und Bildungsroman. Ein Forschungsbericht*, Stuttgart, 1969, p. 35). See also: Alfred Döblin, 'Der Bau des epischen Werks' (*Aufsätze zur Literatur*, Olten u. Freiburg i.Br., 1963, p. 125), Charlotte Jolles, ' "Gideon ist besser als Botho". Zur Struktur des Erzählschlusses bei Fontane', in *Festschrift für Werner Neuse*, eds. H. Lederer and J. Seyppel, Berlin, 1967, pp. 76–93, Wolfgang Iser, 'Ist das Ende hintergehbar?' in *Der implizierte Leser. Kommunikatioñsformen des Romans von Bunyan bis Beckett*, Munich, 1972, pp. 391–413, Gerda Röder's *Glück und glückliches Ende im deutschen Bildungsroman*, Munich, 1974, and O. H. Richter: *Fable's End. Completeness and Closure in Rhetorical Fiction* Chicago, 1975.

31. Gustav Janouch, *Conversations with Kafka*, London, 1968, pp. 130f.

32. *Wedding Preparations in the Country and other Posthumous Prose Writings*, London, 1954, p. 42.

33. 'Kafka's Eternal Present: Narrative Tense in *Ein Landarzt* and Other First-Person Stories', *PMLA*, Vol. LXXXIII (1968), pp. 144–50. The quotation comes from p. 145.

34. See H. Henel, 'Das Ende von Kafkas *Der Bau*', *Germanisch-Romanische Monatsschrift*, Vol. XXII, 1972, pp. 4ff.; Binder, *op. cit.*, pp. 327, 339; and Klaus Ramm, *Reduktion als Erzählprinzip bei Kafka*, Frankfurt a.M., 1971, pp. 55ff. 35. *op. cit.*, p. 146.

36. n.b. the point at issue here is the nature of certain closed and open *endings* only. For a discussion of the separate issue of closed and open forms in Kafka's work, see James Rolleston's excellent treatment of the subject in *Kafka's Narrative Theatre*.

37. *Description of a Struggle and The Great Wall of China*, London, 1960, p. 52.

38. Kermode, *op. cit.*, p. 145. See also Philip Stevick, *The Chapter in Fiction. Theories of Narrative Division*, Syracuse, 1970.

39. 'Literaturny fakt', *Arkhaisty i novatory*, Leningrad, 1929, p. 8. 'Viele

Werke der Alten sind Fragment geworden', Friedrich Schlegel wrote, 'Viele Werke der Neuern sind es gleich bei der Entstehung' (*Prosaische Jugendschriften*, ed. J. Minor, Vol. 11, Vienna, 1882, p. 207).

40. See: Gert Ueding (*op. cit.*, pp. 64ff.), the title-essay in Walter Hilsbecher's *Das Zeitalter des Fragments* (pp. 229–45), G. Schmidt-Henkel, 'Anfang und Wiederkehr. Romananfänge und Romanschlüsse der deutschen Romantik', *Romananfänge. Versuch zu einer Poetik des Romans*, ed. N. Müller, Berlin, 1965, pp. 92ff., Manfred Diersch, *Empiriokritizismus und Impressionismus. Über Beziehungen zwischen Philosophie und Literatur um 1900 in Wien*, Berlin, 1973, especially pp. 124, 143, and Robert M. Adams, *Strains of Discord. Studies in Literary Openness*, Ithaca, New York, 1958.

41. *Letters to Felice*, ed. Erich Heller and Jürgen Born, tr. James Stern and Elisabeth Duckworth, London, 1974, p. 91.

42. *Ibid.*, p. 156.

43. *op. cit.*, p. 19.

44. *Short Works*, I, London, 1973, p. 39.

45. In this context cf. also the plot and ending of *A Message from the Emperor*.

46. 'See the Moon?' *Unspeakable Practices. Unnatural Acts*, London, 1969, p. 157.